Irish Women
&
Nationalism

Dr. Margaret Ward is Honorary Senior Lecturer in History at Queen's University, Belfast and former Director of the Women's Resource and Development Agency in Belfast.

Prof. Louise Ryan is Professor of Sociology at the University of Sheffield.

Both have published widely on Irish women and nationalism, and co-edited *Irish Women and the Vote: Becoming Citizens* (Irish Academic Press, revised edition 2018).

Irish Women
&
Nationalism

Soldiers, New Women and Wicked Hags

NEW EDITION

Editors

Louise Ryan and Margaret Ward

IRISH ACADEMIC PRESS

First published in 2004 by
Irish Academic Press
10 George's Street
Newbridge
Co. Kildare
Ireland
www.iap.ie

9781788550970 (Paper)
9781788551106 (Kindle)
9781788551113 (Epub)
9781788551120 (PDF)

British Library Cataloguing in Publication Data
An entry can be found on request

Library of Congress Cataloging in Publication Data
An entry can be found on request

Typeset in Garamond 11.5/13.5 pt

Cover: Women protest at Sinn Féin executions in 1921.
(Photo by © Hulton-Deutsch Collection/CORBIS/Corbis via Getty Images)

Contents

Foreword to the Original Edition

This book makes a valuable and timely contribution to the ongoing study of women and nationalism in Ireland. Its interdisciplinary approach provides us with a ground-breaking collection of new ideas and voices both historical and contemporary. Spanning over three centuries, the women's activism discussed in this collection clearly illustrates women's multifaceted participation in Irish nationalism. From the women of the 1641 uprising to women in contemporary Northern Ireland, the various chapters chart women's contribution to nationalist movements.

The stories of women imprisoned in the North bring to mind the accounts of women held in the South during the Civil War, in particular those in Kilmainham Gaol in 1923. These women's participation in Irish politics was not part of mainstream Irish history, which for far too long has trivialised women's participation in such historical events. In addition their involvement was hidden because the vast majority of those imprisoned moved away from active politics. Those who continued in activism, writing and politicising were too often seen as eccentrics and radical by their contemporaries and their participation was confined to the margins in the social and political life of the new state. Many have had their reputations restored in the past decades with biographies that show that they were individuals and independent thinkers who did not conform to the prescribed role for women in the Irish Free State.

The story of women revolutionaries and Kilmainham Gaol, *Guns and Chiffon*, was published in 1997. This and the accompanying travelling exhibition brought the stories of the female prisoners who had been incarcerated in Kilmainham Gaol during the Civil War to a wider audience. The material on Cumann na mBan that is now held in Kilmainham Gaol, the Military Archives and in University College Dublin Archive, much of it concealed within families for many years, was donated by the descendants of those women, who were pleased to acknowledge the role their female family members had played in militant nationalism.

However, to bring the scope of the research into the middle and late twentieth century, more primary source material has to be located in the public domain. In the early years of the revolution, given the sensitive nature of the subject matter, papers and documents were often deliberately not kept, or were destroyed by the women themselves. Others were lost during raids. The same has happened over the decades of 'Troubles' in the North. The use of oral sources, therefore, is central for any future study; their value is clearly seen in this publication where the voices of many activists tell us much about the role of women in fighting for the well-being of their families and communities. Just as new scholarship, particularly research into local history, is bringing fresh perspectives to bear on the role of the IRA and Cumann na mBan during the War of Independence, so too are oral history accounts of the Troubles in the North providing us with great insights into the everyday experiences of the people who lived through those times. By bringing together the scattered fragments of individual women's lives, ultimately the story of the collective will be told.

This collection draws on a range of disciplines – history, sociology, politics, literature and cultural studies – and brings together an impressive range of sources such as biography, novels, films, newpapers, oral narratives and archival materials. The result is analysis that offers new perspectives on Irish women's roles and representations in nationalism.

It is significant that so many of the authors in this book are up-and-coming scholars or researchers who work outside of academe, innovative in their approaches and open and honest in the issues they explore. It is publications like this that encourage new scholarship and inspire students to be proactive in sourcing material and conducting interviews themselves.

I would like to think that when I open my children's schoolbooks in ten years' time many more women will have found their rightful place in the history of revolutionary Ireland, North and South.

SINÉAD MCCOOLE
December 2002

Foreword to the New Edition

I welcome the re-issue of Dr Margaret Ward and Professor Louise Ryan's edited collection of inter-disciplinary essays on women and Irish nationalism, first published by Irish Academic Press in 2004. Published twenty-one years after the appearance of Ward's seminal work on the subject, *Unmanageable Revolutionaries*,[1] which traced the involvement of women in Irish nationalist politics from the Ladies Land League of the 1880s to Sinn Féin in the early years of Irish independence, the essays in the volume reflected the nature and extent of research and writing on Irish women's history more widely, and women and nationalism more specifically in the intervening period.

Leading up to the recent centenary of the granting of female suffrage, both editors have produced valuable works enhancing our understanding of the unique nature of the Irish suffrage movement. Ward's biographies of and commentaries on the writings of Hanna Sheehy Skeffington offer much more detailed insights into the political activism, and not just in regard to suffrage, of Ireland's most celebrated campaigner for women's enfranchisement.[2] The significance of publicity and propaganda to the success of the suffrage campaign is evaluated in Ryan's recent study of the *Irish Citizen*, the Irish suffrage newspaper.[3] Their successful collaboration as editors of *Irish Women and Nationalism* was followed up by a companion volume on *Irish Women and the Vote: Becoming Citizens*, first published in 2007 and re-issued last year for the suffrage centenary.[4]

Their valuable work on enhancing understanding of the uniquely Irish aspect of a larger transnational wave of feminism is only one aspect of their contribution to the study of women and gender in modern Irish history and society. As a sociologist, Ryan's extensive list of published work includes investigations of issues of contemporary relevance relating to families and migration in Britain and Ireland, effectively using a historical perspective to explore the evolution of public policy over a longer time period.[5]

Ward's historical explorations of the complicated relationship between gender and nationalism from the late nineteenth century mirrored similar explorations of contemporary Northern Irish society, undertaken as Assistant Director of the think tank Democratic Dialogue (a post she held at the time of the original volume's appearance), with particular emphasis on the role of women in politics in the north.[6] This combination of extensive research experience on issues relating to the experience of women in past and present Irish society brought to the editorship of the collection by both scholars is reflected in the range and coherence of the essays chosen.

While the majority of the essays in the book deal with the modern period, with specific focus on the Irish revolution (*c.*1916–23) and the later Northern Irish 'Troubles', the first two essays are fine examples of how landmark events in the traditional nationalist narrative of Irish history, the rebellions of 1641 and 1798, were open to new and more comprehensive analysis when examined from the perspective of contemporary female observers and protagonists. Both remind us that women's activism in Irish revolutionary movements long predates the modern period.

Andrea Knox's reassessment of women's involvement in the 1641 rising made effective use of the 1641 depositions, then only available for research purposes in original manuscript form in Trinity College Dublin. Her essay showed how these sources shed light on 'the involvement in rebellion of women from lower orders', the role of women in facilitating conflict by 'supplying munitions and weapons, as well as "she-soldiers"'.[7]

Since this was written, the 1641 depositions have now become freely and widely accessible having been digitised and made available online, with companion hardcopy volumes published by the Irish Manuscripts Commission.[8] This will enable a wider cohort of researchers, and especially those based outside Ireland, to conduct research on these sources, for which Knox's essay provides a useful basis from which to begin.

Jan Cannavan's essay was a timely reminder of women's involvement in iconic Irish nationalist uprisings in 1798 and 1848, well before either the Land League or revolutionary period: 'Women took an active part in both these struggles, working in military, propaganda and support roles', yet much of the literature was characterised by 'The erasure of militant women'.[9] In the intervening fifteen years, this theme has been expanded upon in a small number of articles but Cannavan's point about the under-exploitation of this research area remains the case and this is surely a fruitful area for further investigation.[10]

Sinead McCoole's foreword to the original edition identified the significance of recently available primary and oral history sources for developing our understanding of the role of women. In the intervening fifteen years, the availability and especially the accessibility of sources has enhanced even further the extent and nature of the raw materials available to historians seeking to construct a more comprehensive analysis of the activities of women in Irish history.

The digitisation of primary sources has been one of the biggest changes in the nature of Irish historical research since this book first appeared. As in the case of the 1641 depositions, research on the role of women in various aspects of the Irish revolution has been enabled by the release and digitisation of the Bureau of Military History and the ongoing release of the Military Service Pensions Collection.[11]

The book was published before the authors had a proper chance to examine the content of the Bureau of Military History, only released the previous year and then only in manuscript form in the National Archives and Military Archives. Louise Ryan's examination of the representation of women in the writings of republican men drew upon the published memoirs and autobiographical writings of male revolutionaries and found that 'the male narratives emphasised the essential masculinity of republican men', whereas the depiction of women was 'essentially feminine', emphasising the supporting roles of family members.[12] With over 1,700 narratives of the revolution now available in digitised format through the Bureau of Military History, this methodology can be extended to a far wider range of testaments to examine whether the same portrayal is to be found there.

This retrospective attitude of male revolutionaries, which tended towards diminishing the contribution of their erstwhile female comrades to the conflict-related aspects of the revolution, which Ryan identified in her essay, now emerges much more strongly from the Military Service Pensions Collection. The inclusion of women in pension eligibility appears to have been conceded reluctantly in 1934 by the then Fianna Fáil Minister for Defence, Frank Aiken, and even then women faced considerable obstacles in convincing pension assessors of the merits of their claims.[13]

The restriction of women to the two lowest grades for recognised service – 'D' and 'E' – was the same as that accorded to Fianna Éireann, effectively treating women's service as on a par with that of children.[14] Ryan's essay has laid the groundwork for subsequent studies of this perception which have appeared in the intervening period and will continue to do so as scholars exploit the richness of the material still coming available through the Military Service Pensions Collection.

Such representations of the role of women in the revolutionary movement as inferior or subservient to that of men were not unique to writings authored by men. Danae O'Regan's comparative analysis of the revolutionary era literature of Annie M.P. Smithson and Rosamund Jacob characterised the former as a 'traditionalist' who projected 'an image of republican women as subsidiary to male activists, always devoted and admiring'.[15]

This essay reflected and promoted a renewed interest during the first decade of the twenty-first century in a wider range of previously less well-known female republican activists. Along with Leeann Lane's subsequent biography of Jacob, published in 2011, it raised awareness of Jacob's significance, and also of the value of her writings, especially her diary, which has subsequently been selected for digitisation by the National Library of Ireland.[16]

While the collection drew greater attention to characters such as Jacob, it also shed new light on the better known protagonists of the period, as highlighted in Karen Steele's study of 'Constance Markievicz and the politics of memory'. While the recent centenaries of the Easter Rising and the enfranchisement of women in Britain and Ireland has produced an increased volume of writing on Markievicz,[17] the literature on her in 2004 was limited and dated; the last substantial biography by Diana Norman was published in 1991.[18]

Steele avoids the better known chronological landmarks of the rebel countess's career in order to evaluate the significance of her journalistic and dramatic writings during the 1920s, adding significantly to our understanding of her disillusionment with the Irish Free State and to propagating the memory of strong female republican activists through the medium of drama. As one of the few academic essays to deal with Markievicz between the early 1990s and the 2010s, Steele's is a significant work in the wider literature on the countess; as Professor Catherine Shannon noted, it was 'a succinct rebuttal to the characterization of Countess Constance Markievicz as a dilettante and poseur, incapable of intellectual rigor'.[19]

The essays by Regan and Steele are part of three literary-focused chapters located in the middle of the collection and acting as a bridge between the treatments of the earlier and later historical periods. The final essay in this triumvirate, Jayne Steele's exploration of how male writers portrayed Ireland as a matriarchal figure, has synergies with many other essays in the collection.[20] Her examination of how the feminine is portrayed in the writings of men resonates with Ryan's analysis of male-authored revolutionary memoirs. These essays exemplify one of the greatest strengths of the entire collection – its interdisciplinary approach.

Although the original collection was not subdivided into thematic sections, such a categorisation can be identified, as in the case of the three literary-focused essays described above. The final identifiable theme is that of the more recent northern Irish 'Troubles', which is the focus of four essays covering imprisonment, political activism and gender consciousness. The fact that all of these deal largely with the experience of women from republican communities is a reflection of the dearth of research at the time on how the political conflict impacted upon the lives of women from rival loyalist communities. In the intervening fifteen years, the situation has improved only slightly. Rachel Ward's *Women, Unionism and Loyalism: From 'Tea-Makers' to Political Actors* was published, also by Irish Academic Press, two years later in 2006. She concluded that unionist and loyalist women had been 'active at many different levels' that have not always been properly acknowledged.[21]

Recent studies of the political structures of the Democratic and Ulster Unionist Parties have explored the role of gender within modern unionist political culture; Connal Parr has explored the influence of Protestant backgrounds on the productions of the Charabanc Theatre Company in the 1980s; and Sandra McEvoy has sought to redress the imbalance of literature on female paramilitaries.[22] Nevertheless, the paucity of writing on the female experience of the Troubles from the loyalist and unionist perspective remains a substantial gap in an otherwise voluminous literature on the recent Irish conflict. What might a companion volume to *Irish Women and Nationalism*, focused on *Irish women and unionism*, look like if this potentially fertile area of inter-disciplinary research were to be developed further?

Many of the chronological periods covered in the volume have or are about to be the subject of significant commemorative anniversaries. This is especially the case regarding the essays on the revolutionary period. The original volume appeared prior to the onset of the 'Decade of Centenaries' and the way in which literature on these subjects has developed in the intervening fifteen years reflects a symbiotic relationship between public interest and academic research.

The Irish state's official commemoration of the centenary of the Easter Rising in 2016 was notable for the efforts to ensure that the involvement of women was a central part of the state ceremonial. For example, on 8 March 2016 a specific event was held at Richmond Barracks, the site of the incarceration of most female prisoners following Easter Week, to 'highlight the significant role played by women in the 1916 Rising'.[23] The substantial number of new works prompted by interest in the centenary included those with a focus on women but also embedded women more accurately within the wider narrative of the overall rebellion.[24]

Such work did not emerge in a vacuum and built upon the existing body of literature on women and nationalism that was developed in the preceding forty years, since *Unmanageable Revolutionaries*. In this regard the essays contained in the original edition of *Irish Women and Nationalism* were an important precursor to the commemorations of and publications on women in advance of the centenary events by raising awareness of their significance. The result was much greater focus on gender in 2016 than in any of the previous milestone commemorations, including 1966, 2006 and 1991.

In her foreward to the original edition, Sinéad McCoole hoped that 'when I open my children's school books in ten years' time many more women will have found their rightful place in the history of revolutionary Ireland, North and South'.[25] A glance at the 2017 Irish Leaving Certificate Higher Level exam paper suggests that the status accorded to women within the curriculum in the south has improved noticeably within the past decade. In that exam students were offered opportunities to write about Ellen Wilkinson's account of the 1936 Jarrow march, Asneath Nicolson's response to the Famine, the contribution of the Irish suffrage movement, the changing status of women in Ireland between 1949 and 1989, greater opportunities for women in the workforce during the First World War, Betty Friedan and Margaret Thatcher.[26] Thatcher had only recently been consigned to history when I sat my Leaving Certificate History paper back in June 1991, and apart from her I would not then have known who Friedan, Nicolson or Wilkinson were. The syllabus then in use, especially in the modern period, was limited to discussing the major themes of political and military history of Ireland and Europe since 1870.

The few women who made an appearance were the 'women wor-
thies'[27] such as Constance Markievicz, Maud Gonne and Rosa Luxem-
burg, whose inclusion was merited but which unfortunately also marked
the limits of women's representation within that syllabus which largely
reflected the dead white guy approach that many students find so off-
putting. The current Leaving Certificate syllabus is certainly a significant
improvement on its predecessor and has to some degree fulfilled Sineád
McCoole's hopes from a decade ago. The former paucity of women in
Leaving Certificate History was reflective of a gender gap throughout
many aspects of the curriculum. Recently I unearthed the iconic poetry
book *Soundings* used by generations of Leaving Certificate English students and was startled to recall that the only female poet we studied as
Emily Dickinson.[28] I was more startled to recall that I did not seem to
be aware of this imbalance, perhaps reflective of a general acceptance
of these things at the time.

Though that acceptance was starting to be challenged at precisely
that point in time: 1991 was not just the year of my largely female-free
Leaving Cert, but also marked the publication of the three volume *Field
Day Anthology of Irish Writing*, which was widely critiqued for its 'old-
fashioned' approach, one characteristic of which was the shortage of
women writers covered reflecting 'the lamentable dearth of scholarship
about women's writing in Ireland'.[29] The refusal of scholars to accept
this situation eventually led to the production of two additional volumes, focusing on Irish women's writing and traditions, in 2002.[30]

It was against this backdrop of a growing consciousness of the need
to put a greater emphasis on the contribution of women to Irish life, in
fields such as literature and history, that *Irish Women and Nationalism* was
published in 2004. Its appearance coincided with the introduction that
year of the new Leaving Certification History syllabus in the Republic
of Ireland which sought to broaden the chronological, geographical and
thematic focus of the course which had remained largely unaltered since
1969.[31] The objectives of the new syllabus specifically recognised the
need to examine the experience of women in order to achieve a fuller
appreciation of the past: 'In studying human activity in the past, attention should be given to the experiences of women'.[32] This was part of a
wider focus on social history more generally. The response of teachers
to this focus on women's history, as reflected in a survey of twenty
teachers conducted during the first year of teaching the new syllabus,
indicated that the majority were largely positive about the social and

women's history aspects, with a small number expressing concerns that compartmentalising it could be seen as tokenism. None disapproved but many were undecided, perhaps understandable in the context of such a major change to a long-established traditional curriculum.[33]

Of course this discussion relates only to those who actively opt to do History in the senior cycle, which usually accounts for about 20 per cent of those taking the Leaving Certificate annually.[34] Following on from the reform of the Leaving Certificate, a new Junior Certificate syllabus was introduced in 2018 and will be examined for the first time in 2020. As regards women's history, the new syllabus is certainly an improvement on the old one, which contained no specific references to women or gender, although specific concepts for individual study topics included 'Home and family'.[35]

By contrast, the new one will seek to show students 'How women's lives changed over time', 'explain how the experience of women in Irish society changed during the twentieth century' (the only two references to 'women' in the syllabus) and help 'Students develop their appreciation of diversity and difference (gender, culture etc.) through their encounters with different people, issues and events in the past.'[36] The most serious drawback with this is that History will no longer be a core subject at Junior Cycle, leading to the prospect that much of the progress hoped for by Sinéad McCoole back in 2004, and delivered through reform of curricula will be nullified by the downgrading of History as a subject in Irish post-primary schools.[37]

Looking to the future and hoping for positive change was also the tenor of the final essay in the collection, Margaret Ward's analysis of feminism and the participation of women in republican politics.[38] She posed an important question of whether the failure to elect any women to the Ard Comhairle of Sinn Féin was indicative of a backlash against feminism within republicanism. Had there been such it certainly appears to have ebbed now that the key leadership positions in the party are held at the present moment (June 2019) by Mary Lou McDonald and Michelle O'Neill, and in light of the party's liberalisation of its position on abortion.[39] Three of the party's seven abstentionist Westminster MPs, five of its twenty-two TDs, twelve of twenty-seven MLAs in the currently suspended Northern Ireland Executive, and one Member of the European Parliament are women.[40] The political representation of women in Ireland, north and south, has increased since 2004, though at a slow pace, and the Republic of Ireland at national parliament level lags behind the UK's national and regional parliaments for the proportion of elected representatives who are women. Less than one-quarter (22 per cent) of the TDs elected to Dáil Éireann in 1916 were women, which compares unfavourably to the current proportion of women in the House of Commons (32 per cent), the Welsh Assembly (42 per cent), the Scottish Parliament (35 per cent) and the currently dormant Northern Ireland Assembly (30 per cent).[41] One less positive development in Northern Ireland since Ward's essay was published in 2004 has been the disappearance of the Northern Ireland Women's Coalition (NIWC). Writing in the early party of the new century, Ward was reassured that 'the continued presence of the NIWC serves to ensure that no political party can ignore the potential threat to patriarchal practice posed by the existence of a woman's party at the heart of the political process.'[42]

The disbandment of the NIWC in 2006[43] leads to the inevitable question of whether there has been a reversion to such practices as a consequence of its disappearance. Perhaps the generally healthier, if still far from perfect, proportion of women in the other political parties is a symptom of the coalition's success in normalising the sight of women in northern Irish politics. Conversely, the continued failure to extend to Northern Ireland equal marriage and reproductive rights that exist elsewhere throughout the United Kingdom, and also now in the Republic of Ireland, is arguably a manifestation of the situation that Ward saw the NIWC as holding off. This chasm also reflects the fact that the sectarian divide remains paramount and all other issues, including those relating to gender, remain subsumed by it. The situation described by Ward in 2004 – 'The need to confront and resolve continued sectarian divisions existing in the North of Ireland has meant, and continues to mean, that gender equity sits far down the political agenda.'[44] Fifteen years on, the situation is no different, and possibly even worse since the suspension of the assembly and the all-consuming nature of the Brexit debate.

A series of essays on Irish women's history – *Women in Irish society: Historical Dimensions*, published in 1979 (edited by Margaret MacCurtain and Donnacha Ó Corráin and based a series of Thomas David lectures broadcast on RTÉ in November 1975) – is generally regarded as the first dedicated study of Irish women's history. *Irishwomen and Nationalism*, which appeared thirty-five years later, was a testament to the way in which the academic study of women's lives in Ireland's past had developed in the intervening period. Women were no longer to be excluded from the traditional periodisation and narrative of Irish history concerning events such as the uprisings of 1641, 1798, 1848 and 1916, and the recent 'Troubles'. The collection identified new areas of research and resurrected lesser known personalities. Many of these topics and characters have been developed further since, especially those relating to revolutionary subjects which have become more popular during the decade of centenaries, drawing upon the initial explorations of them contained in the volume. In this regard, it signposted many fruitful new avenues of research, some of which remain understudied at a remove of fifteen years. *Irishwomen and Nationalism* was a worthy descendant of *Women in Irish Society* and continues to be an antecedent of many explorations of the past experience of Irish women.

MARIE COLEMAN
June 2019

NOTES

1. Margaret Ward, *Unmanageable Revolutionaries: Women and Irish Nationalism* (Dingle, 1983).
2. Margaret Ward, *Hanna Sheehy Skeffington: A Life* (Cork, 1997), *Hanna Sheehy Skeffington: Suffragette and Sinn Féiner, her Memoirs and Political Writings* (Dublin, 2017), and *Fearless Woman: Hanna Sheehy Skeffington, Feminism and the Irish Revolution* (Dublin, 2019).
3. Louise Ryan, *Winning the Vote for Women: The 'Irish Citizen' Newspaper and the Suffrage Movement in Ireland* (Dublin, 2018).
4. Louise Ryan and Margaret Ward (eds), *Irish Women and the Vote: Becoming Citizens* (Dublin, 2007 and 2018).
5. For a full list of Professor Louise Ryan's publications see https://www.sheffield.ac.uk/socstudies/staff/staff-profiles/louise-ryan#tab03 (accessed 26 June 2019).
6. See for example, 'Women and the local government elections 2001' https://cain.ulster.ac.uk/dd/papers/women-local.htm (accessed 26 June 2019).
7. Andrea Knox, 'Testimonies to history: Reassessing women's involvement in the 1641 rising', in Ryan and Ward (eds), *Irishwomen and Nationalism*, pp. 22–4.
8. http://1641.tcd.ie/ (accessed 24 June 2019); see, for example, Aidan Clarke (ed.) *The 1641 Depositions, volume I: Armagh, Louth and Monaghan* (Dublin, 2014).
9. Jan Cannavan, 'Revolution in Ireland, Evolution in women's rights: Irish women in 1798 and 1848', in Ryan and Ward (eds), *Irishwomen and Nationalism*, pp. 43–4.
10. See for example Anna Clark, '1798 and the Defeat of Feminism: Women, Patriotism and Politics', in Terry Brotherstone, Anna Clarke and Kevin Whelan (eds), *Ireland, Scotland and the Making of Modern Britain, 1798–1848* (Edinburgh, 2006), pp. 85–104; Christine Kinealy, 'Invisible Nationalists: Women and the 1848 Rising in Ireland', in Kay Boarman and Christine Kinealy (eds), *1848: The Year the World Turned?* (Newcastle-upon-Tyne, 2007), pp. 130–45; Susan B. Egenolf, ' "Our

fellow creatures": Women Narrating Political Violence in the 1798 Irish Rebellion', in *Eighteenth Century Studies*, vol. 42, no. 2 (2009), pp. 217–34; Willemijn Ruberg, 'Cruelty and Sensibility: Emotions in Women's Narratives during the United Irish Rebellion of 1798', in *The Irish Review*, no. 42 (2010), pp. 1–14.

11. For the value of the Bureau of Military History as a source for women and the revolution see Eve Morrison, 'The Bureau of Military History and Female Republican Activism', in Maryann Gialanella Valiulis (ed.) *Gender and Power in Irish History* (Dublin, 2009), pp. 59–83.

12. Louise Ryan, '"In the line of fire: Representations of women and war (1919–1923) through the writings of republican men', in Ryan and Ward (eds), *Irishwomen and Nationalism*, p. 60.

13. See Marie Coleman, 'Military Service Pensions for Veterans of the Irish Revolution, 1916–1923', in *War in History*, vol. 20, no. 2 (2013) pp. 207 and 215, and Marie Coleman, 'Compensating Irish Female Revolutionaries, 1916–1923', in *Women's History Review*, vol. 27, no. 6 (2017), pp. 915–34.

14. Marnie Hay, *Na Fianna Éireann and the Irish Revolution, 1909–23: Scouting for Rebels* (Manchester, 2019), p. 215.

15. Danae O'Regan, 'Representations and attitudes of republican women in the novels of Annie M.P. Smithson (1873–1948) and Rosamund Jacob (1888–1960)', in Ryan and Ward (eds), *Irishwomen and Nationalism*, p. 94.

16. 'Minister Humphreys announces funding for National Library of Ireland project under new cultural Digitisation Scheme', 15 Nov. 2017 www.chg.gov.ie/minister-humphreys-announces-funding-for-national-library-of-ireland-project-under-new-cultural-digitisation-scheme/ (accessed 24 June 2019).

17. Lauren Arrington, *Revolutionary Lives: Constance and Casimir Markievicz* (Princeton, 2015). These were complemented by Lindie Naughton's, *Markievicz: A Most Outrageous Rebel* (Dublin, 2016) and companion edited collection of her writings *Markievicz: Prison Letters and Rebel Writings* (Dublin, 2018). Markievicz also figure prominently in Senia Pašeta, *Irish nationalist women, 1900–1918* (Cambridge, 2014).

18. Diana Norman, *Terrible Beauty: A Life of Constance Markievicz* (Dublin, 1991).

19. Catherine Shannon, 'Women in the Struggle', *Irish Literary Supplement* (Fall 2006), p. 6.

20. We were saddened to learn that Jayne died in October 2015.

21. Rachel Ward, *Women, Unionism and Loyalism in Northern Ireland: From 'Tea-Makers' to Political Actors* (Dublin, 2006).

22. Jonathan Tonge et al. (eds), *The Democratic Unionist Party: From Protest to Power* (Oxford, 2014), see especially Chapter 8: 'Women in the DUP: "The backbone of the Party"'; Thomas Hennessey et al. (eds), *The Ulster Unionist Party: Country before Party* (Oxford, 2019), see Chapter 9: 'Institutional Structures, Party Selection and Spotty Tights: Women and the UUP'; Connal Parr, *Inventing the Myth: Political Passions and the Ulster Protestant Imagination* (Oxford, 2017), Chapter 7: 'Loyal Women? Marie Jones and Christina Reid'; and Sandra McEvoy, 'Loyalist women paramilitaries in Northern Ireland: Beginning a feminist conversation about conflict resolution', in *Security Studies*, vol. 18, no. 2 (2009), pp. 262–86.

23. Government of Ireland, *1916–2016 clár comórtha céad bliain / centenary programme* (Dublin, 2015), p. 17.

24. Examples of works dedicated to women include Mary McAuliffe and Liz Gillis (eds), *Richmond Barracks, 1916: "We were there", 77 Women of the Easter Rising* (Dublin,

2016), while Fearghal McGarry's *Abbey Rebels of 1916: A Lost Revolution* (Dublin, 2015) gave equal regard to the role of the Abbey Theatre's male and female actors during the rebellion.

25. Sineád McCoole, 'Foreward', in Louise Ryan and Margaret Ward (eds), *Irish Women and Nationalism: Soldiers, New Women and Wicked Hags* (Dublin, 2004), p. viii.

26. State Examinations Commission, Leaving Certificate Examinations 2017, History Higher Level (Later Modern) https://lchis.files.wordpress.com/2010/12/2107-hl-paper.pdf

27. Gerda Lerner, *The Majority Finds its Past: Placing Women in History* (New York/ Oxford, 1979), p. 145.

28. Augustine Martin (ed.), *Soundings* (Dublin, 1969).

29. Kevin Barry, 'Anthology as History: The Field Day Anthology of Irish Literature', in *Irish Review*, 12 (1992), pp. 50–5.

30. Angela Bourke et al. (eds), *The Field Day Anthology of Irish Writing, Vols IV and V* (Cork, 2002).

31. John B. Dredge, 'The revised Leaving Certificate History syllabus, 2004: Teachers' perceptions and practices', M.Ed. thesis, NUI Maynooth (2005), p. 3.

32. Department of Education and Skills, *Leaving Certificate History Syllabus* (Dublin, 2003), p. 3.

33. Dredge, 'The revised Leaving Certificate History syllabus', pp. 93–4.

34. 'Leaving Cert: Record number taking higher-level subjects', *Irish Times*, 6 June 2017.

35. Department of Education and Science, *The Junior Certificate History Syllabus* (n/d).

36. Department of Education and Skills, *Junior Cycle History* (Dublin, 2017).

37. Gillian O'Brien, 'Draft report on Junior Cycle History' (18 April 2019) https:// gillianmobrien.wordpress.com/2019/04/18/draft-report-on-junior-cycle-history/ (accessed, 28 June 2019).

38. Margaret Ward, 'Times of transition: republican women, feminism and political representation', in Ryan and Ward (eds), *Irishwomen and Nationalism*, pp. 184–201.

39. *Irish News*, 18 June 2018.

40. The party's only sitting MEP following the 2019 European elections is Martina Anderson in Northern Ireland. Between 2014 and 2019 it had two more women MEPs sitting for Republic of Ireland constituencies, Liada Ní Riada and Lynn Boylan, both of whom lost their seats in a general swing against the party.

41. Yvonne Galligan and Marie Coleman, 'Hundred years of votes for women – but still they remain on the fringes of Irish politics', *The Conversation* (6 Feb. 2018) https://theconversation.com/hundred-years-of-votes-for-women-but-they-still-remain-on-the-fringes-of-irish-politics-91286 (accessed 28 June 2019).

42. Ward, 'Times of transition', p. 201.

43. Susan McKay, 'After 10 years, the party's over for Women's Coalition in North', *Irish Times*, 12 May 2006.

44. Ward, 'Times of transition', p. 201.

Chapter 1

Introduction

Louise Ryan and Margaret Ward

Theorising gender and nationalism

In the 1980s the pathbreaking book *Nationalism and Sexuality*, by George L. Mosse, offered one of the first theoretical analyses of nationalism as a gendered project. Writing primarily about Nazi Germany, Mosse showed that women were a crucial part of national-ism, both as symbols of the nation and guardians of national traditions. According to Mosse, the narrow domestic and traditional roles which nationalist movements have often ascribed to women have been underpinned by the need to preserve the virtue, uniqueness and authenticity of the nation. Mosse argues that nationalism not only idealises men but also represents women as the 'guardian[s] of the traditional order'.[1] He goes on to say that 'woman as a national symbol was the guardian of the continuity and immutability of the nation, the embodiment of its respectability'.[2] The portrayal of women as symbols of the nation defines women's role in nationalism as passive and secondary.

Since the 1990s a number of feminist scholars have contributed to the increasing theorisation of gender and nationalism. The work of Nira Yuval-Davis and Floya Anthias, Anne McClintock, Kumari Jayawardena and collections such as those by Andrew Parker et al., Tamar Mayer, Ruth Roach Pierson and Napur Chaundry,[3] to name just a few, have helped to broaden the analysis of nationalism beyond a narrow Western focus. Both Yuval-Davis[4] and McClintock[5] point out that it is necessary to go beyond narrow, Eurocentric models of nationalism. McClintock states that 'there is no single narrative of the nation … nationalisms are invented, performed and consumed in ways that do not follow a universal blueprint'.[6] Nevertheless, she claims that all nationalisms are gendered and contain women in subordinate and domestic roles.[7] Anti-colonial nationalist movements have frequently employed gendered ideologies that position women in 'traditional' roles within the domestic sphere.

Ailbhe Smyth suggests that Irish nationalist discourse uses woman as a sign 'in a discourse from which women, imaginatively, economically, politically disempowered, are in effect and effectively excluded'.[8] In this way, women become the bearers of the symbols of nation but their everyday experiences and agency are denied. They are 'excluded from direct action as national citizens, [and] … subsumed symbolically into the national body politic as its boundary and metaphoric limit'.[9]

The primary goal of anti-colonial nationalist movements is to eject the colonial authority and to establish, or re-establish, a sovereign nation-state. Therefore, the postcolonial period of nation-building is of crucial importance in terms of asserting the legitimacy of the nation and the authority of the State. The newly established nation-state has to act quickly to legitimise the cultural authenticity and uniqueness of the nation. The role of women is crucial to this process. As has been pointed out by numerous writers, nationalist movements have usually encouraged women to participate in particular ways.[10] However, once the goal of national independence is achieved the newly established state quickly reaffirms 'traditional' gender roles and excludes women from the sort of political activity they had experienced during the years of national conflict. As Kandiyoti argues, the association of women with the private domain 'reinforces the merging of the nation/community with the selfless mother/devout wife'.[11] The idealisation of the national mother in the home reinforces the limited role of women in the newly established nation-state. Whatever rights women may have won in the earlier part of the national conflict may be lost later on in the nation-building project.[12] Thus one could argue that while nationalist movements seek to mobilise women they do so in strictly limited ways and for strictly limited time periods.

However, as has recently been argued at length by Suruchi Thapar-Bjorkert and Louise Ryan,[13] it is important to distinguish between nationalist rhetoric and the more complex and diverse realities. As this book demonstrates, many women have shown a remarkable and long-lasting commitment to nationalism. The women who had actively participated in nationalist struggles were not always easily persuaded to return to the domestic sphere; they were not always dupes who could be mobilised in times of crisis and then sent back at the whim of the male leadership. Many of these women believed in the nationalist promises of freedom and justice and they were not about to let male leaders renege on these promises. The fascination of the peace process in Northern Ireland lies not only in attempts to reach an accommodation between the aspirations of nationalists and Unionists but also in the negotiation of gender politics that continues to take place in many different arenas.

As we shall see from what follows, it is necessary to distinguish between how women have been represented in national histories and cultural and symbolic repertoires on the one hand, and, on the other, how they have actually negotiated and challenged their roles and contributions to nationalism. This book shows how, at different times in history, women have engaged with nationalism in many varied and complex ways, and it uses a range of sources to reveal the extent of women's active participation in Irish nationalism. While nationalist symbols, images and texts have continued to depict women within a narrow range of cultural stereotypes, women's roles within nationalism have been, and continue to be, diverse, multifaceted and dynamic.

One of the enduring difficulties in analysing women's relationship to and role within nationalism is the fact that they are frequently located in the private sphere and thus are either invisible and outside the main focus of analysis, or are perceived as the victims of nationalist conflicts. A number of chapters in this book attempt to overcome this problem by using oral history interviews as a means of uncovering women's experiences of the conflict in Northern Ireland.

Looking beyond 1916–23

In a recent book Linda Connolly has argued that 'the relationship between anti-colonialism and feminism has received much attention in both historical and contemporary Irish studies'.[14] She is critical of the tendency to reduce the Irish experience of feminism to nationalism and colonial oppression. Connolly points out that feminism has in fact often had a somewhat problematic relationship to nationalism. While this is undoubtedly true it is also true to say that feminism in Ireland has always had to engage with nationalism and colonialism in particular ways, whether through the state nationalism of the Southern Irish state or the colonial authorities in Northern Ireland. In addition, as this book illustrates, Irish women have had a long, complex and dynamic relationship with nationalism which has often intersected with feminism in ways that have proved challenging and, at times, fruitful.

The relationship between nationalism and feminism is the subject of much theorising within feminist scholarship worldwide but, as Lois West has pointed out, much of this depends on how one defines feminism and what it means to be a feminist.[15] It is not the aim of this book to argue that nationalist women have always been feminist or that their nationalist activism has brought them to a feminist consciousness. Neither do we wish to suggest that nationalism was the only movement in Irish society to mobilise and politicise women. Nevertheless, unlike Connolly, we suggest that women's involvement in nationalism has not been over-studied and that there is still a great deal to be learned about this significant and influential movement in Irish society, North and South, and the women who actively participated in it.

Although it is almost a contradiction in terms to say that any aspect of Irish women's history has been over-researched, it is probably fair to suggest that the period between 1916 and 1923 has received more attention than many other periods. Women's involvement in the 1916 Easter Rising, and the role of Cumann na mBan in the War of Independence (1919–21) and the Civil War (1922–23), have been the subject of several books and a few dozen academic articles. This could hardly be considered overexposure. However, one of the difficulties involved in focusing on this particular period of nationalist militarism is that it tends to reinforce the notion that women were mobilised only as required, and were then disbanded and instructed to return to domesticity. While many of the male leaders of the movement attained positions of power in the newly established Southern Irish state, women were simply pushed out of public life. However, as many of the essays in this book make clear, women's relationship to nation-alism is far more complex and long lasting than this simple representation would suggest.

In this book we have deliberately chosen to focus on a long time frame, from the 1600s to the 1990s. This is not to suggest that we have no interest in nationalist women between 1916 and 1923. Indeed several essays in the book do engage with that period. Obviously it is important, not least because it witnessed the large-scale mobilisation and militarisation of nationalist women. However, we suggest that it is important also to look beyond it to examine the long-term role of women in Irish nationalism. The book shows that women have been a continual part of nationalism, not just occasional players who can be easily summoned and dismissed. In fact, nationalist women have often found themselves in disagreement with male leadership about what their roles and level of involvement should be. Such disputes and tensions indicate that nationalist men have not always understood or sympathised with the particular experiences and aspirations of women within the movement. The gender politics of nationalism is a theme running through many of the essays. It can be argued that current developments in Northern Ireland can only be fully appreci-ated by an understanding of the past, an observation which holds true equally for an appreciation of the efforts by women to remain actively involved within their communities and within the wider political landscape. Local studies of women's experiences in the North over the past thirty years have begun to be researched and published. The Dúchas oral history project in West Belfast, discussed here by Claire Hackett, is one such venture. Others, such as the Ardoyne Project, are also providing insights into the experiences of women in tightly knit, highly politicised, working-class communities.[16] Informed reassess-ment of women's contribution to the nationalist cause during the past thirty years of conflict will surely follow. Of equal importance is the opportunity provided for those within their communities to reflect on the vital roles performed by women – an essential part of the process of ensuring that women do not become marginalised in the years to come.

The peace process

The subject of women and nationalism has been of vital interest to feminist activists, particularly in Northern Ireland over the past three decades – where political pressures were often so acute that discussion on the issue quickly descended into acrimony. Those times, we hope, are over, never to return. There has been some rapprochement between different political tendencies within the women's movement at large, although this remains tentative, conditional on the overall political situation. We have not arrived at a position where feminist interests provide for cohesive unity. In some respects, the same trajectory of mutual hostilities later shading to some acceptance of mutual concern can be discerned within the works of feminist scholars, who have not been immune to the impact of revisionism on their work. The dominant view within the academy (influenced by the bitterly fought war between the Irish Republican Army (IRA) and the British state) has been that research that was not critical of republicanism was suspect, and the notion that feminist scholars could interrogate republican history and practice while retaining some sympathy with its political goals was inimical to the ethos of scholarship.

The contributors to this book are Irish, English, Welsh and American. Some work in universities, some are independent scholars. Although some originate from the Republic, it is significant that none of the contributors is from an educational establishment in the Republic. We believe that this says much about the nervousness with which Northern Ireland has been regarded, its potentially destabilising influence on a rampant Celtic Tiger an undoubted factor in this attitude. It is to be hoped that, with greater North–South engagement and with Sinn Féin now a significant all-Ireland political party, such attitudes will be replaced by a recognition on all sides that mature analysis and reflection are required before we can progress to a society based on equality. The editors of this book (as feminist scholars both critical of, and sympathetic to, Irish republicanism) have experienced the discomfort of the academic world. At the same time, they remain insistent that such research, reassessing the contribution made by countless nationalist women to the cause of Irish political independence, has not only brought women back into the history books and into the imaginations of many, but also has provided essential knowledge, without which there could be no realistic evaluation of the changing relationship women have had to Irish republicanism.

We believe that the continuing peace process in Northern Ireland, encapsulated by the Belfast/Good Friday Agreement of 1998, with its support for 'the right of women to full and equal political participation', provides us with space for reflection. Unionists and nationalists signed up to that Agreement, and while genuine support for women's political participation might be confined to a few, given the male-dominated nature of our political institutions, it has given us a valuable opportunity for retrospective appraisal of centuries of past endeavours by Irish women who asserted their right to have a voice in the affairs of the nation. While some of the essays provide assessments of revolutionary moments, others are concerned with appraising the cultural milieu in which nationalist women acted, wrote or reacted to what was written about them. Other chapters reflect on the activities of working-class women striving to defend their communities during the last decades of intense communal strife, and consider the strategies used by republican women prisoners to maintain and develop their sense of identity as women and as political prisoners. The range of disciplines, perspectives, political views and methodologies contained within this collection is great, providing us with a kaleidoscope of different insights and examples. Each contributor has used her particular discipline and expertise to reveal some part of the experience of women in Ireland who have worked over the centuries in many different ways for political autonomy.

Chapter summaries

The essays in this book are divided into three sections. The first section focuses on historical perspectives and brings together new archival research to reveal the complex and varied involvement of women activists in early phases of Irish anti-colonial conflicts. These chapters focus in particular on uprisings in 1641, 1798 and 1848. In 'Testimonies to history: reassessing women's involvement in the 1641 rising' Andrea Knox examines Irish female resistance to the growing English and Scottish colonial authority in Ireland during both the sixteenth and the seventeenth centuries, and in particular the period of the 1641 rising. Popular contemporary views portrayed the Irish as barbarous and violent, with women having a particular talent for aggression and rebellion. Indeed Irish women were viewed as barely within control. Irish court records and testimonies of women reveal the ways in which female rebellion, aggression and violence developed specific forms. Irish women were involved in rebel networks (including working with some Scottish women) and female regiments; they worked as fences in towns and as maverick individuals. This is an area of both Irish and women's history that has received little academic scrutiny. The essay focuses on the nature of women's involvement in rebel networks, gender identification and the developing sense of loyalty towards Ireland rather than local loyalty. Resistance was evidenced in the form of outright revolts, violence and aggression meted out to settler communities, but also towards colonial functionaries and army personnel. Women also organised trade in illegal armaments and used proceeds from urban prostitution to finance revolts. Knox, using a variety of sources, examines the actions of rebel women from all social strata.

In 'Revolution in Ireland, evolution in women's rights: Irish women in 1798 and 1848', Jan Cannavan examines the participation of women in two important nationalist movements. Women's agency is stressed in her analysis, which rejects accusations that such women colluded in a patriarchal agenda. Her argument is that women's active participation in these two major episodes of Irish anti-colonial struggle contributed to, rather than hindered, the evolution of Irish feminism. The writings of female participants in both 1798 and 1848, as well as contemporary men's accounts of their activities, show that many of them supported women's – as well as national – rights.

The second section of this book focuses on cultural representations of nationalist women and spans both historical and contemporary sources. The writers utilise a wide range of sources including autobiography, journalism, plays, novels and films to examine the multifaceted ways in which nationalist women have been portrayed and have portrayed themselves through cultural media.

Louise Ryan's '"In the Line of Fire": representations of women and war (1919–1923) through the writings of republican men' analyses the representations of women's involvement in the War of Independence and Civil War (1919–23). Her essay examines a set of popular and influential sources. The writings of republican men such as Barry, Breen, O'Donoghue, O'Malley and O'Connor have helped to shape the popular imagination of the war years. In addition, these sources have also informed historical studies and textbooks of the period. While these books offer very personal accounts of the military campaign, Ryan suggests that they also provide an invaluable and under-studied insight into the constructions of masculinity and femininity in militarised arenas. In the context of guerrilla warfare, the blurring of boundaries between home and battlefront repositioned women in war zones. The guerrilla fighters relied on women's help and support; indeed the men's autobiographies contain many allusions to the women who provided them with food, shelter and clean clothing and who nursed them when they were sick or wounded. However, Ryan's analysis also reveals the underlying tensions about women's roles and involvement in the conflict. As the fighting intensified and more women joined the republican movement there was growing unease about the transgression of gender roles.

In 'Constance Markievicz and the politics of memory', Karen Steele reclaims Constance Markievicz's intellectual merit by considering her nationalist writings of the 1920s. After her release from prison, Markievicz wrote for a range of publications including *Eire* and *An Phoblacht*. In addition, she also wrote several plays including *Blood Money* and *Broken Dreams*. Steele suggests that through her journalism and plays, Markievicz engaged with a politics of memory. Markievicz sought to repossess the memory of the 1916 Rising and, in particular, to recall feminist and socialist contributions to nationalism. In so doing she challenged the ways in which the newly established Irish Free State government was redefining nationalist icons and ethos. Markievicz asserted her position as a principal figure in the pre-Rising years. However, Steele argues that Markievicz was not only concerned with her own reputation. She also aimed to make visible the achievements of other nationalist activists who had become marginalised within the Free State. Steele suggests that this project of political and cultural memory enhanced Markievicz's standing as a republican socialist woman. Markievicz's writings provide critics today with a good deal of evidence to challenge literary, biographical and historical assessments of her as a poor thinker, bad writer and pretend player in key cultural and political debates about women and nationalism.

In 'Representations and attitudes of republican women in the novels of Annie M. P. Smithson (1873–1948) and Rosamond Jacob

(1888–1960)', Danae O'Regan examines the interplay between women's activism and women's writings. Annie M. P. Smithson and Rosamond Jacob were Irish novelists who, although from very different backgrounds, were both committed republicans and active members of Cumann na mBan and Sinn Féin. In their novels they both created strong women characters through whom they transmitted their own attitudes towards republican actions and ideals. Smithson, a convert to Catholicism and a traditionalist in outlook, projected an image of republican women as subsidiary to the male activists, happy to play a supportive role, and accepting without question the need for violent action in the republican cause. Jacob, an atheist, suffragist and pacifist, created free-thinking, liberal, analytical heroines who consider themselves fully equal to men and insist on their right to independent thought and action. Her women analyse both their own emotions and attitudes and those of their republican sons and lovers, and are not afraid to suggest that they may sometimes be flawed. A comparison of these two writers gives a valuable insight into attitudes in Ireland in the period following the 1916 uprising, as does the fact that Smithson's novels were hugely popular while Jacob's had little success.

Jayne Steel's chapter is entitled '"And behind him a wicked hag did stalk": From maiden to mother, Ireland as woman through the male psyche'. Historically, English, or British, and Irish iconographic images of Ireland as 'woman' have served different political purposes. This essay analyses the roots of these gendered symbols and examines the ways in which iconographic images of Irish nationalist women have been appropriated by British and Irish popular culture created by male authors and film-makers who in turn attempt to supply a 'realistic' narrative of the Troubles. Central to Steel's argument is the notion that, when it comes to portraying nationalist women qua Irishness, the British and Irish male unconscious has much in common. Steel supplies an in-depth discussion of Irish nationalist women portrayed within specific plays and films. Although there have been many films about 'the Troubles' in recent years, she begins her analysis with Carol Reed's classic film *Odd Man Out* (1947). Steel also traces the image of Mother Ireland and the imagining of a maternal other through a range of plays including *The Whore Mother*. She draws upon Lacanian psychoanalysis and considers the various ways that male representations of Ireland as woman illustrate a specific dilemma: the imagining of a desire that is ultimately maternal and demands devotion as well as self-sacrifice. Closely linked to questions about the male imagining of maternal desire are certain *repeated* images of the Irish nationalist female that are found in popular culture and reflect a universal scapegoating for the Irish as well as the British male psyche and for the citizens of every 'Ireland', be they nationalist or loyalist.

The third section of this book focuses on contemporary debates and in particular examines the experiences of women in Northern Ireland. Two of these essays focus on women's experiences as republican prisoners; two use interviews with local women's groups to highlight the varied ways in which women have participated in and been affected by the years of conflict Northern Ireland. The final essay in this section traces the changes and continuities of women's involvement in republican and feminist movements during the twentieth century.

In '"We had to be stronger": the political imprisonment of women in Northern Ireland, 1972–1999' Mary Corcoran uses oral narratives to examine the contemporary history of political women's imprisonment. Although one in twenty prisoners who were confined for politically related offences in Northern Ireland were women, their prison struggles tend to be viewed as having a comparatively marginal strategic place in the penal frontline, in comparison with those of the men in the Maze/H-Block. Corcoran's chapter seeks to redress this by tracing the culture of resistance developed by female republican prisoners in Armagh and Maghaberry women's prisons between 1972 and the 1990s. Discussion of women acting politically and collectively in prison confronts the critical gaps in criminological discourse, which usually conceives of women prisoners as being passive subjects of regulation and punishment rather than as exercising meaningful forms of agency. Corcoran explores the predicament of political agency and gendered subjectivity among women political prisoners. She traces the contradictory punitive drive in the women's prisons which fastened gendered forms of discipline that are common to the control of women in prison to modes of risk management and containment that are characteristic of political imprisonment. Using interview data from former prisoners, the chapter discusses how the prisoners made sense of their intersecting subject positions, out of which they developed complex and layered strategies of resistance.

Covering some of the same ground, but from a different perspective, Rhiannon Talbot in 'Female combatants, paramilitary prisoners and the development of feminism in the republican movement' analyses aspects of women's involvement in republicanism since the 1970s. In tracing women's involvement in the IRA and their growing politicisation, Talbot considers the extent to which women combatants and women involved in prison struggle contributed to the development of feminist understanding within the republican movement as a whole. While deliberately not taking a conclusive position on this issue, her essay provides useful reflections on the ways in which women's participation has changed over time, and how this has impacted upon republicanism.

In 'Narratives of political activism from women in West Belfast' Claire Hackett describes the experiences of eight women activists from West Belfast who have contributed interviews to the Falls Community Council's Dúchas oral history archive. The essay focuses on the range of ways in which women in nationalist West Belfast were politically active during the conflict in response to the British/Unionist military campaign in their communities. Various themes of activism are identified and illustrated with quotations from the oral history accounts. The oral histories come from women's experience as prisoners, prisoners' wives and relatives, feminists, political representatives, human rights campaigners and community activists. A very significant theme is the role of women in maintaining a social and community structure. The ways in which women directly opposed and confronted military occupation on the streets is outlined and the organised forms of activism developed by women to subvert and thwart military policies are described. Activism around imprisonment is a major theme; other themes that emerge strongly are isolation and hardship, friendship and comradeship. The emergence of a specifically feminist consciousness and activism are also discussed. Women's experience of empowerment through activism is discussed, as is their experience of being controlled within their own communities. Underpinning all the histories are stories of personal transformation of women's inner and outer lives.

Callie Persic takes up many of the themes identified by Hackett in 'The Emergence of a gender consciousness: women and community work in West Belfast'. In this essay, using the Greater Ballymurphy Women's Support Group as a case study, she examines community activism and considers the extent to which such activism led women to renegotiate gendered power relations. Persic suggests that community participation has encouraged a new gender consciousness among women. Whilst this new awareness may appear in line with feminist objectives, many women would not identify themselves as 'feminist'. This case study provides an opportunity to examine how the peace process has provided an opportunity for women to integrate a gender perspective on community development.

In the final essay, 'Times of transition: republican women, feminism and political representation', Margaret Ward offers a comparative analysis of two phases in the history of women's political activism in Ireland. In the periods of political transition in early twentieth-century Ireland and in the ongoing peace process in Northern Ireland, gender has proved an important factor in shaping the transition process. Both feminist activists and republican women organised to ensure representation of their specific interests, although their initial success in periods of political change has not been consolidated within the political structures that subsequently developed. In addition, the relationship between different groups of women has oscillated between cooperation and hostility, a consequence of the competing demands of feminism and nationalism.

Chapter 2

Testimonies to history: reassessing women's involvement in the 1641 rising

Andrea Knox

Introduction

One of the most successful and infamous female networks credited with playing a direct part in early sixteenth-century revolts against English colonisation was headed by Agnes Campbell and her daughter Finola. Lady Agnes was the sister of the Scottish Earl of Argyle, and went to Ireland in order to marry Turlough Luineach O'Neill in 1569, after the death of her first husband, James MacDonnell, Lord of the Isles of Scotland. When Agnes arrived in Ireland she brought with her a dowry of 1,200 Scottish mercenary troops. So did her daughter, who married the other Ulster chief, Hugh O'Donnell.[1] This act united two septs whose previous relationship had often been one of conflict over power. These factors were typical, if frightening, prospects for the colonial authorities. What was perhaps more significant was that Agnes was swiftly credited with ruling and directing her chieftain husband and 'making herself strong in Ireland'.[2] Agnes's role in the Desmond rebellion of 1579–83 was to make a new Scotland of Ulster.[3] It was she who was commissioned to raise munitions from the Scots.[4] Agnes was reported to be highly educated and intelligent, and it was she with whom the English negotiated in 1570 when she met with Sir Henry Sidney. They recorded that her husband, by contrast, was a 'rude, wild savage'.[5] It was also recorded that O'Neill 'accepts the lewd counsel of his wife'.[6] It was Agnes and Finola who united the O'Neills and the O'Donnells, who then banded together against the English in the north of Ireland. This was a result that the women facilitated, and it put an end to the feuding and conflict which had previously dominated the relationship between the O'Neills and the O'Donnells.

These networks between the Irish septs and Scottish clans were what the English colonisers feared most. It was clear to contemporaries that women in Ireland and to some extent in Scotland had control over their military dowries, and had considerable power in Irish politics. For Agnes and Finola loyalty to their sept meant loyalty to Ireland. For Finola hatred of the English triggered her outright loyalty and sense of belonging to an Irish sept and to a country she had not been born in. Finola's direction of her son had a crucial influence on future rebellions against the English. Agnes used her influence to pursue her own political agenda. The result of Agnes and Finola's work in bringing together the O'Neills and the O'Donnells was to unite most of the septs against the English colonisers during the 1590s. This would appear to reveal the development of a new loyalty and awareness in Irish septs and their Scottish wives. That sense of belonging and loyalty to Ireland which encompassed sept members born and raised in Scotland was becoming stronger than sept identity alone.

This essay deals with Irish women, rebellion, kinship and a sense of belonging to Ireland in the sixteenth and seventeenth centuries. During these centuries Ireland was experiencing a period of growing English colonial authority and settlement. The ideological views of the colonisers affected the personal lives of the Irish. Irish women, their families and networks became a particular focus of interest to authorities. Family and kinship in Gaelic Ireland was based upon sept or clan culture.[7] English colonial authorities viewed sept and Irish identity as subversive. What intensified this colonial concern was the fact that the Brehon legal system was unique to Ireland and had no basis in canon law. This legal system and its attending culture and customs threw the colonisers into a state of consternation.

Brehon law

Brehon law was the customary secular law of Gaelic Ireland. It had existed for centuries and was quite distinct from other European legal systems. The Brehon judges were the traditional lawyers of the Gaelic learned class. Lennon maintains that sixteenth-century colonial government recognised the use of Brehon law.[8] By the early sixteenth century a balance had been struck with even the colonial shire areas employing Brehon law, and the towns of Dublin, Drogheda, Cork, Galway, Limerick, Waterford and Wexford abiding by the English common law.[9] Brehon law operated for the benefit of both genders in early modern Ireland. Within this law women held property rights, were able to inherit money and land, could maintain their own property and land, and were able to divorce without the judgement of the Church. Brehon society was egalitarian rather than matriarchal. This was enough to distinguish it from many European societies which were patriarchal. There existed a number of matrilineal practices including the passing down from mother to daughter of the property of women, their titles and their mothers' family names.

Septs in sixteenth- and seventeenth-century Ireland

Central to the traditional culture of the Irish was the organisation of groups into septs. The term 'sept' was an indigenous term for a group of people bound by a common name. This did not mean that they were bound only by kinship or blood ties. They were made up by identification of a common ancestor, although this was often a person who was greatly admired rather than a biological ancestor. Septs were dynastic lineages, and until English colonisation in the sixteenth century, they were landowners. They were united by a common language, culture and legal system. Although nominally Catholic they had a complex religion wherein their priests endorsed the use of charms by women, and their sept leader would often employ a female prophet for the purposes of regular provision of supernatural and predictive knowledge.[10] Each sept had a chief, although this position was not always inherited, and could be nominated. The interaction between sept chiefs was not always harmonious, and the feuds between Irish sept leaders prompted the English to call the Irish 'savages' and 'barbarians'.[11] The dynamics of a sept covered ties of voluntary alliance as well as blood kin. The bonds of influence as well as the granting of lands or protection were exchanged for loyalty and armed service. During the period of early modern colonisation septs often came together to limit the influence of the colonisers.

One of the most distinctive ways of transmitting power within the septs was through the sept chieftains' wives. Sept chieftains' wives did not appear to follow the normal familial responsibilities and roles of the wives of higher strata English men. To the English sept wives appeared to be sexually promiscuous, they did not appear to control their children, they retained their maiden names whilst they were married and they did not reveal the paternity of their children until they were dying.[12] Documentary evidence suggests that Irish women had real influence over the dynastic affairs of the septs, and were a potential challenge to the control of parts of Ireland during early modern colonisation. The English colonisers prided themselves upon the impeccable behaviour of their high-born women; however, women of the septs did not appear to have been trained to display the breeding familiar to the status-conscious English.

Colonisation during the sixteenth and seventeenth centuries

Ireland in the sixteenth and seventeenth centuries was subject to major invasion and settlement. Tudor foreign policy towards Ireland attempted to introduce an English model of government, and during the reign of Elizabeth I attempts were made to introduce the Protestant religion. During the sixteenth century both England and Ireland were the focus of regular European Catholic plots. This led the Tudor monarchs to invade Ireland with a double agenda: to prevent European invasion and to subdue a country which had always appeared difficult to exercise any influence over. English officials in Ireland were quick to cite Irish women as rebellious and influential in opposition to English rule.[13]

Irish women were involved in diplomacy, spying and raising troops and munitions against the English, and therefore became the focus of criticism, blame and expulsion from Ireland when land was increasingly given over to English and Scottish settlers. Ireland was the only country in Europe successfully to reject a state-imposed religion in the sixteenth and seventeenth centuries.[14] Ireland did not undergo a reformation; instead, much of the country experienced a persistence of traditional culture which enabled Irish women and men to resist external pressures to reform.[15]

Marriage, kinship and women's legal agency

There exists considerable legal evidence relating to marriage and women's legal equality and agency afforded by Brehon law.[16] Early Irish laws recognised three major and five minor forms of marriage.[17] These ranged from an elite land contract through to a marriage based upon rape. Concubinage, prostitution and incest were legal. For the Irish, unlike the English during this period, it was not considered incestuous for an uncle or aunt to marry a niece or a nephew, nor was it incestuous for a godparent to marry a godson or goddaughter. Within the septs close kin often did marry for the purposes of dynasty, finance or land gain. This led the incoming colonisers to look on Irish marriages between close kin as incestuous unions.[18] Less regular unions were recognised by Brehon law. Both Cosgrove and Simms maintain that the broad principles concerning women's position with respect to marriage, property and legal guardianship remained constant between the thirteenth and sixteenth centuries.[19] Nicholls has noted that in the area of property Irish wives had, by European standards, considerable rights to acquire and hold property independently of their husbands.[20]

Irish women were accepted as independent witnesses in court, and sept women frequently acted as political agents for their families, as well as arbiters in disputes.[21] Irish women were also granted generous grounds for divorce. The legal texts relating to this were positive in their treatment of women.[22] Brehon law preserved partible inheritance rather than primogeniture, not only for sons but for daughters also. During the middle decades of the sixteenth century incoming English officials condemned Irish dynasties for the failure to regularise the transmission of lordship through primogeniture and bastardy rules.[23] However, the strong native traditions of partible inheritance continued. Haderman contends that even though the common law of England was imposed upon Ireland with the intended destruction of native Brehon law in 1603, the resulting legal anomalies meant that in practice many customs continued.[24] Throughout the sixteenth century a changing legal system flourished. MacCurtain has detailed the increasing interest the Tudor monarchy and government showed in Irish matrimony and the legal rights of women.[25] The broader context of the Reformation led to the reform of marriage into a formal ecclesiastical institution. MacCurtain maintains that this process was delayed in Ireland and enforcing the registration of marriages proved to be an extremely slow process.[26] Acts were passed in the Dublin parliament in 1537 and 1540 to prevent closely related family members marrying and solemnising marriage. In Gaelic society marriage among landholding families was often a political alliance and could be dissolved at any time. This presented a problem for the incoming English colonials in that it spawned a great number of politically powerful women who could act independently upon divorce and had powerful alliances within the septs. Unlike English elite wives who were put aside after divorce or annulment, Irish wives continued to exercise public power. O'Dowd has pointed to the use of multiple political alliances as a tactical political weapon both against other septs in Ireland and later as allied groups against the English.[27] In this way women were still connected to powerful septs, and were able to participate directly in resistance to English colonial rule. Kinship structures, the sept system and Brehon law worked to support Irish female resistance to early modern English colonial authority.

The 1641 rising

The events of the 1641 rising and the role of women within it form a crucial part of Irish history. Ohlmeyer maintains that the rebellion of 1641 ranks as one of the most successful revolts in early modern history.[28] A measure of this success was in evidence between 1642 and 1649 when the Irish experienced legislative and religious independence.[29] Barnard's work on the rising cites the deep tensions that existed.[30] A combination of constitutional opposition from Catholic lawyers and widespread regional revolts with a common purpose produced a campaign against Ireland's subordination to English interests, legislation and the erosion of Catholic political power in parliament.[31] The English colonisers' policy of plantation was intended as a means of governing the native Irish. Land confiscation with no compensation was used throughout Ireland.[32] Mitchison has noted how the policy of plantation and the later land sales destroyed traditional ownership and with it lordship.[33] Barnard maintains that dispossession in rural areas created a resentful Catholic population.[34] By 1641 various groups were united in opposition to the English. According to Barnard two crucial dynamics distinguish the 1641 rising from earlier risings. These are the greater political sophistication shown in the political debates of Catholic politicians and the fact that this coincided with a protracted political crisis in England.[35] The rising began in October 1641 and included the killing of Protestant settlers in large numbers. This in turn led to the retaliatory massacres of Catholics. Although the rising began in Ulster it then spread throughout Ireland during 1642. Initial success afforded Irish Catholics effective political and administrative control over most of Ireland from 1642 until 1647.

The 1641 depositions

The sources that relate to the 1641 rising include legal depositions. These are contained in thirty-two volumes of sworn statements from Protestant settlers who experienced the onslaught during autumn 1641. Canny has noted that despite the clear bias within the testimonies they are crucial sources.[36] Included in the depositions are details of the identities of attackers and the justifications given by the assailants for their actions. The deponents distinguish between political, economic and religious reasons for these actions. The depositions include details of all aspects of the risings, from robberies to murder and the trade in arms.[37] The depositions are drawn from a wide geographical scope which allows an examination of the rising in rural as well as urban areas. They range in time from autumn 1641 to autumn 1647. The form of the depositions are mostly standardised with personal details of the deponent and a description of the event. Some appear almost as inventories; others give much fuller details. Lengthy descriptions of atrocities also appear. Female involvement is sometimes glossed over, and at other times emphasised. The English legal commissioners who collected the depositions clearly had their own brief and biases. This is often identifiable in the appended additional information which often accompanied the sworn statements.

Recent studies that have revised scholarly work on the 1641 rising have utilised the experiences and perceptions of the Irish involved in rebellion. The work of Bennett and Canny brings to the fore the narratives of those who experienced rebellion in Ireland during the period of the 1641 rising.[38] Bennett's work reveals two very important factors: that women often took leading frontline roles, and that women swore depositions in their own right as well as on behalf of dead relatives. Overall he calculates that up to one third of depositions were made by women.[39] Canny's study of the process of plantation also utilises the 1641 depositions. Canny maintains that a high proportion of statements were sworn by women, either because they had engaged in military action or because a member of their sept had died during the rising.[40] However, Canny believes that the statements sworn by women concerned the exceptional or abnormal, rather than the mundane.[41] However, female involvement in the 1641 rising has been underestimated. The 1641 depositions need to be used alongside local legal records and the testimonies of women involved in a variety of activities associated with rebellion and resistance to colonisation.

The case of Agnes Campbell and Finola, as well as those of Irish women rebels, are contained in the Calendars of State Papers of Ireland and the Carew Manuscripts. These state papers were commissioned by the Tudor monarchs and I have found in them a wealth of detail relating to the rebellious activities of women throughout the sixteenth and seventeenth centuries.[42] The early colonisers' attempts to study and control Irish women led them to record the testimonies of these women. Yuval-Davis has promoted the need for a shifting definition of nation and the nationalist discourses of different groups.[43] Irish female discourses, however, have not been utilised. I have found that the use of depositions and testimonies of women themselves, though problematical, affords us a greater understanding of women's experiences.

I have also utilised the Gilbert Manuscripts, which detail the activities of female criminal networks including the links between urban prostitution and the raising of funds for purposes of rebellion.[44] These links have not previously been subjected to analysis. The opportunity for women to testify, offer mitigation and explanation of their crimes was often available, providing some indications of their motivation. The use of local records also avoids the complete dependence upon external English sources. Throughout the sixteenth and seventeenth centuries popular contemporary English views portrayed the Irish as barbarous and violent, with women having a particular talent for aggression and instigating rebellion. Irish court records and the testimonies of women reveal the ways in which rebellion and resistance developed specific forms. For the colonisers, women's activity in rebellion, whether they were directly or indirectly involved, was at the heart of colonial concerns over female behaviour.

Most of the surviving sources relate the activities of elite women, or women with some status. However, the 1641 depositions cite the involvement in rebellion of women from the lower orders. Women, and in particular wives, were considered to be suspicious. Agnes Campbell and Finola worked as negotiators, go-betweens, and raisers of finance and troops. This was appropriate behaviour for a chieftain's wife. However, when Agnes was perceived as the driving force behind her husband then real fears over female agency were expressed. Sources from the decades that preceded the 1641 rising clearly reveal the activities of Irish women involved in rebel networks. Many of these women dealt directly with major European powers.

In 1577 the wife of the Earl of Fitzmaurice is recorded as a go-between and negotiator between Fitzmaurice and the pope, who promised them eight galleys in support against the English.[45] Lady Fitzmaurice had also written to the French king for his support. She and her husband were the most conspicuous rebels in the early 1570s. Between 1574 and 1579 she visited France, Spain and Italy; however, her activities were closely monitored by the English authorities. In July 1577 the queen wrote to Sir Amyas Poulet that she had discovered many letters between the couple relating to European aid for the rebels in Ireland.[46] Monitoring the rebels became crucial to the English state and a whole industry of spying networks was built up in response to this problem.

The suspicions that surrounded women rebels are evident in the records of women suspected of spying. As early as 1581 the English were on alert over a Spanish woman who was also described as being Irish. She was travelling in the company of the Spanish ambassador, and used the codename Imperia Romana. What alerted Lord Burghley to her, in addition to the company she kept, was her ability to speak Spanish, Irish and English. Her activities included many secret talks, and she was termed 'a fit instrument for spying'.[47] Because she travelled with the Spanish ambassador she had a degree of diplomatic immunity and could only be followed at a distance. The records reveal a high degree of surveillance being operated by the English state by 1581.

Women's own testimonies appear to support female agency in revolt, and an increasing sense of belonging to Ireland. Finola O'Donnell stated in 1588 that she would hire the Spaniards to stir up wars against the English.[48] The Earl of Tyrone's wife announced publicly, in the presence of English officials, that 'she would to God that Essex would stir up trouble in England', in order that foreign powers would leave Ireland.[49] These women appear by their own words to have taken initiatives in acting and consolidating support for rebellion. Loyalty is expressed as being to Ireland first and foremost.

Women from across the social strata were directly involved in the military conflicts of the 1640s. Their activities included supplying munitions and weapons, as in the case of Mary Burke who was found to be carrying a coach full of gunpowder out of Dublin to the rebels in Westmeath.[50] Bridget Darcy was burned to death in Dublin in 1660 for admitting to murdering a number of English officers, and claiming to have made candles out of the fat sloughed from their cadavers.[51] Her testimony reveals that she targeted English officers in particular as enemies of Ireland. Lower strata women who were involved in murder and arson against the English include Jane McCraken, who was recorded to have, on 1 December 1613, gone to the mansion house of Dugald Craford of Kunningburne, an English gentleman, between the hours of eight and nine in the evening with a lighted torch, and with malice aforethought, and burned down the house with Craford in it. In her testimony McCraken said that she used a small pile of straw to make the fire, and explained that the reason for her action was the fact that she was Irish and he was English.[52] The assize court that tried Jane was made up of a jury which took the decision to acquit her. There is no more than a bald statement of acquittal, even though the circumstantial evidence and her testimony were enough to condemn her. The jury was made up of local English-born gentlemen. It is perhaps surprising that the culprit was acquitted of such a serious crime. McCraken's acquittal may be attributed to two reasons. The jury members and surrounding English landowners may have had something to gain, perhaps a land sale of the site of Craford's property, and they might have been reluctant to find a local woman guilty, risk the wrath of a supportive community, and perhaps trigger a local uprising. It would appear that in this instance confrontation was avoided. For women like McCraken without access to finance or military hardware the only way to express anger and aggression was through an arson attack on one of the English who had benefited from plantation policies.

Direct confrontation is evidenced in the actions of Irish women who embraced direct military conflict. It was not only women of high social status who expected to be involved in battles, or who were involved in providing mercenaries. Further down the social scale there are numerous accounts of 'she-soldiers', women who were part of troop activity. During one battle between the Irish and parliamentary troops at Connaught, amongst the dead on the Irish side was a young soldier who had his hat pulled off to reveal long tresses of flaxen hair, and on being further searched was found to be a woman.[53] Although both O'Dowd and Whelan discuss women's role in war during this period, it is Higgins who has produced evidence of the weaponry that women used, confounding the notion that women were unlikely to use muskets.[54] Higgins makes use of several records of Irish women fighters both in Ireland and in England who during the 1640s used weapons which they had fashioned into long knives.[55] This was in addition to muskets, which they had no problems carrying or firing. A number of contemporary records cite these long knives, which would indicate that these Irish female fighters had possibly designed and commissioned their own type of blade. Higgins was aware that external accounts of Irish women fighters could be hyperbolic; however, numerous contemporary sources repeatedly cite Irish women as cruel and aggressive, as well as being seriously well armed.[56]

Other lower strata women involved in wider criminal activities surrounding the 1641 risings and other rebellions were prostitutes and receivers. The Dublin corporation records covering the period from 1573 to 1637 detail women tavern keepers and prostitutes who worked as conduits, receiving stolen goods and trading them from taverns right under the noses of English officials and the army.[57] The number of indictments for trading for the rebellion increased steadily throughout the sixteenth and seventeenth centuries, alongside an increase in statutes attempting to prevent prostitution and suppress bawdyhouses. English soldiers were constantly warned to avoid these women lest they were tempted to confess information to them.[58] Selling stolen goods and operating prostitution to raise funds for rebellion was common. It was notoriously easy to raise money for the various rebellions, and in this way Irish women in Dublin were able to play a part in opposition to colonial rule.

The 1641 depositions also contain many accounts of women acting as receivers, sometimes with huge stores of hardware and ammunition, and the most improbable excuses for them. However, increasingly during the seventeenth century the intelligence service of the English government became more ruthless in their investigations and interrogation procedures. The English governors' suspicions were often borne out by the confessions which led them to discover urban links with the rebellions. The depositions also detail the desecration of English corpses by Irish women. Canny has cited the depositions covering Kilkenny and Queen's County where heads were severed from corpses: the English Protestant minister was beheaded and so were the town officials who were Protestant colonials.[59] Women were noted to have led this ritual humiliation. In addition the women refused to allow Christian burials, so intense was their hatred of the colonials. Rebellion was so consuming that women were involved at every level.

International links with the 1641 rising can also be observed in the work of women who dealt directly with major European powers. Rosa O'Dogherty was involved in several decades of work as a political intermediary, lobbyist and purchasing agent between Irish rebels and the monarchy and government of Spain.[60] Rosa spent almost forty years of her life carrying messages from Irish rebels to the Spanish government which was sympathetic to the Irish rebels.[61] Rosa dealt directly with the Spanish ambassador over issues such as finance for Irish women who had to flee Ireland for political purposes.[62] The responsibilities of negotiating with Spanish officials often fell to women, and this proved to be a task to which they were well suited. Spain may have considered invading Ireland, but the responsibilities given to women reveal the use of women as clandestine agents.[63] This clearly benefited both nations against the English.

Gender was an important dynamic in relation to rebellion and warfare. As far as the English were concerned, women, and wives specifically, incited their male kin to rebel. Sir Francis Rush, writing to Lord Justices Loftus and Carey in 1600, stated that the reason for male treason was having an Irish wife.[64] Irish wives were the prototypes of degeneracy. Not only did Irish wives spy, but they used their husbands. For Irish men, an Irish wife would corrupt, but for an English man, an Irish wife was simply beyond any kind of control. The political developments from the mid sixteenth century onwards put many Irish outside the law. The suspicions attaching to Irish women in the context of ethnic conflict are particularly interesting as intermarriage was seen as the key to degeneration. Intermarriage bred the problem of dubious loyalty. The state papers record numerous accounts of wives betraying secrets to the rebels and acting as duplicit interpreters and spies. An account of Captain Tom Lee's wife cites that she and Lee parted because he had used his wife as a translator and go-between. She then went over to the rebels' side after interpreting for them.[65] Andrew Trollope wrote to Lord Burghley asking for the removal from Ireland of all English soldiers and government officers who were married to Irish women, on the grounds that they would be compromised and corrupted. Conversely, English observers believed that an English wife would have a calming effect upon an Irish husband. In 1564 Sir Thomas Cusacke told Lord Cecil that after years of egregious rebellion, Shane O'Neill 'preserves good conformity', and this was due to his new English wife.[66] However, they were mistaken: a few months later O'Neill was rebelling and asking Mary Queen of Scots for financial assistance.

Whilst English government officials believed Irish women to be dangerous, barbarous and pestiferous, and all capable of turning men from reason, recorders such as Edmund Spenser, Fynes Moryson, Barnaby Rich and William Camden all concentrated upon savage aspects of Irish women. Not only were they politically subversive, but their behaviour was described as licentious boldness.[67] They were sexually promiscuous, and what most scandalised Fynes Moryson was the way Irish women of all strata did not name their children's father until their deathbed.[68] To Moryson this made women a dangerously subversive group, constantly influencing dynastic affairs. Whilst this was an external view of the English commentators, the traditions they referred to were an integral part of Irish legal culture. This tradition was intolerable to the English who maintained legitimacy and primogeniture as essential supports of patriarchy. The division illustrates the gulf between Irish and English legal culture.

The language used by these English writers is the language of hyperbole; for instance, in 1610 William Camden stated that once Irish women 'had given themselves over to lewdness they are more lewd than lewdness itself'.[69] The language used is often sexualised. Francis Rush described one Irish wife of an Englishman suspected of treason as being 'his whore wife', and having recourse to the rebels.[70] The constant use of 'whore wife', 'bitch wife', 'lewd woman' and 'amazon' in the cases of women cited in the 1641 depositions placed Irish women as the sexual as well as the rebellious subject. Their behaviour came under scrutiny increasingly during the seventeenth century when the colonial powers stepped up the level of violence used to obtain authority. Edmund Spenser's attack on the *mná siúl*, the wandering (masterless) women, illustrates how the cultural and the rebellious were often conflated. One of the overriding concerns of the English throughout the seventeenth century was the perceived numbers of masterless women and men who challenged English authority.[71] The language of women's testimonies is less hyperbolic, though still unrestrained. Both McCracken and Darcy spell out their intentions and actions. Both cite, within their testimonies, their purposeful selection of English officers as political targets.[72] Similarly O'Donnell and Tyrone did nothing to conceal their rebellious initiatives.

What emerges from a study of women and rebellion in this period is the evidence of a growing sense of belonging to Ireland in response to the excessive hostility of the colonial authorities towards Irish women and the development of early race policies. Ireland was England's first colonial possession, and to a large extent experimentation was taking place. Gender, kinship and sept played a very important part in early modern Ireland. Crucially, the construction and function of the septs worked to support women and their rebellious and subversive activities. The relative level of independence of Irish women in contrast to English women drew the suspicions of English colonial authorities. Whilst sixteenth- and seventeenth-century English men feared the power of women on many levels, their fear of Irish women appears to have been excessive. Scottish and Welsh women were not feared or demonised in the same way. The retribution meted out to Irish women rebels by the seventeenth century was not mirrored anywhere else in England. Apart from the few women Jansen has cited in her study of heretical women in the reign of Henry Tudor, there is no comparable display of brutality.[73] However, early racial views were contradictory; they included both prejudice and voyeuristic interest in Irish women as exotic, highly sexualised creatures. The sexualisation of Irish women was part of the colonial process. Mikalachki maintains that the English had a fear of 'savage femininity' which was a hangover from Boadicea and the ancient warrior queens who epitomised early modern beliefs in the inevitable excess and failure of female rule.[74] Powerful women loom large in early modern visions of native origins, and for colonisers the control of these unruly women who challenged the patriarchal order was doubly threatening because what they also challenged was growing colonial authority. The sept system did not accord with early modern English notions of family and kinship. It did not appear to overlap feudal models of relations. This remained a perplexing system for the colonials.

Conclusion

Central to the concerns of the colonisers was the very real fear of rebellious and violent women who appeared to act independently of their male kin, or who appeared to lead their male kin. Many Irish women, not just elite women, networked very effectively without the need or use of men. Armaments and munitions, as well as information, were passed through these groups of women. This was often done without the knowledge of their immediate family. Sometimes women did instigate rebellion and lead their male kin. Some women, tried for more covert activities, often worked without men. The perception of Irish women as violent in comparison to English women was a shared notion of the colonisers. Irish women had a longer traditional historical role in military activities than English women.

The question still remains concerning what the dynamics were within Irish society which, despite the continuing efforts of rebellious women, prevented the misogyny, torture and executions that existed during this period in England, lowland Scotland and much of Europe. Throughout the sixteenth and seventeenth centuries the English were attempting to destroy Irish culture; however, the west of Ireland and parts of the rural south outside of the colonised towns did not demonise or persecute their women. Supporting these women were communities that appear to show a greater cohesion than was found in English communities during this period. This cohesion appears to have had the effect of supporting rebellious and subversive women of all social strata. This minimised the colonisers' ability to deal with women who often put their loyalty to their country before any sense of safety. The perception that the whole Irish Catholic community had risen against them meant that colonial governors perceived the situation in Ireland to be different from that in England and Scotland in 1641. Elite Catholic landowners in all provinces of Ireland along with rebels at all social levels were united against the colonisers in a way that had not existed in previous insurrections.

Women appear increasingly to express their sense of belonging and identity as Irish rather than simply as a sept member. The external pressures of the colonising process produced cohesion between Irish women and men, fostering a sense of belonging and a shared identity which perhaps would not have continued to be so prevalent if colonisation had not occurred. This cohesion included Agnes Campbell and Finola O'Donnell, women born in Scotland but identifying with their Irish kin, united in their opposition to being colonised. There is a shift in women's sense of belonging. At the beginning of the sixteenth century, belonging, for the Catholic inhabitants of Ireland, tended to be expressed in terms of sept identity. By the end of the seventeenth century belonging was expressed in terms of being Irish. These were internal perceptions. English perceptions of the septs had always been surrounded by fear and cultural contempt. However, it would appear that English colonisation and rebellion against it produced such a strong sense of loyalty in the Irish that a new sense of Irish identity emerged which became stronger than sept identity.

Chapter 3

Revolution in Ireland, evolution in women's rights: Irish women in 1798 and 1848

Jan Cannavan

Introduction

The history of Irish republican/nationalist movements provides useful material for the study of women's attitudes about and participation in wars of national liberation. Were nationalist women simply following their men in a patriarchal agenda, as some feminist scholars argue, or did they discern benefits to themselves as women arising from their participation? In the different eras in which national struggles occurred, did women who took part succeed in placing specifically feminist demands on the agenda? In recent years feminist scholars and activists around the world have debated two questions regarding women's relationship to war, particularly wars of national liberation: are women naturally more nurturing and inclined to pacifism than men; and is women's sole – or at least primary – fate in wartime that of victim, or can they sometimes derive benefits from participation? The position of feminists on these questions tends to depend on where they situate themselves in relation to the dominant feminist paradigms of 'equality' and 'difference'.[1]

The equality paradigm, which builds on Mary Wollstonecraft's adaptation to women's needs of Paine's *The Rights of Man*, considers women and men to be primarily the same except for relatively minor physical dissimilarities.[2] Observed differences, such as women's tendencies to be more nurturing than men, are seen by equality feminists to be socially constructed and a factor of women's oppression.

Difference feminists, basing their views largely on the work of Carol Gilligan and Nancy Chodorow (as well as on a large body of nineteenth-century feminist thought) observe gender-based behavioural distinctions as well.[3] Most advocates of difference do not subscribe to the essentialist view that these distinctions are biologically innate but argue that they are psychologically reproduced in people from infancy and are nearly impossible to overcome. Difference feminists tend to find these gender disparities to be much less problematic than do those who follow the equality paradigm; in fact, they assert that women's nurturing qualities make them superior in important ways to men. Difference feminists argue that women's roles as mothers and caregivers lead them, far more than men, to abhor the tribulations of war, driving them to be strong peacemakers opposed to active participation in battle. This paradigm casts women solely as victims, during war, of men's deeply conditioned aggressive tendencies. Difference feminists rarely distinguish between wars of aggression and liberation (or 'just' and 'unjust' wars, to use the language of liberation theology) when discussing the impact of war on women. Equality feminists, on the other hand, are more likely to see women as individuals who, like men, decide whether or not to support a specific war based on a variety of considerations in their lives and beliefs. This paradigm allows for distinctions to be made between different wars and includes women's class, and ethnic and other identities. In the equality paradigm women – as well as men – can both gain and lose from participation in warfare.

The 1798 Irish rebellion and the 1848 Young Ireland rising are two intriguing case studies in which to explore the equality and difference paradigms. Women took an active part in both these struggles, working in military, propaganda and support roles. Primary source materials from these periods record a wealth of references to female activism, although historians have included little of this information. Apart from a few hagiographies of 'heroines', women had, until recently, been effectively erased from these stories. Recent research into the roles women played in 1798 would seem to challenge notions of women's lack of interest in war and their 'natural' pacifism.[4] In order to assess the feminist potential of women's participation in these two nationalist episodes it will be necessary to reinsert some female 'missing pieces' into the historical record. [5]

Women's activism in 1798

The United Irish Rising of 1798 was the outcome of cooperation between middle-class Presbyterians and a largely rural Catholic population, both of whom experienced political and economic discrimination by a British political and legal system that kept the Anglican aristocracy in the ascendancy. A system of penal laws enacted in the early eighteenth century restricted the rights of Catholics – and to a lesser extent Presbyterians – to own land and to follow certain professions, thereby assuring their second-class citizenship. The largely Presbyterian Irish business class chafed under a system of tariffs that protected English industry from the competition of Irish goods, while the Catholic peasantry experienced increasing financial hardship from rising rents and evictions.

Inspired by the examples of the American and French revolutions a group of Belfast reformers formed the Society of United Irishmen in 1791 to agitate for change to these laws and for equal political representation for Irish men of all denominations. Although the Presbyterian United Irish leaders felt that organised Catholicism was incompatible with their Enlightenment views, they realised that Presbyterians did not have enough strength alone to prevail against the ascendancy. They also saw that Catholics in France had adopted Enlightenment views and toppled their monarchy. They therefore united with the Defenders, a rural Catholic secret society that fought against landlord abuses, to work 'to substitute the common name of Irishman in place of the denominations of Protestant, Catholic and Dissenter', to quote Theobald Wolfe Tone, one of the founders of the Society of United Irishmen.[6] Until 1793 the Society worked within legal channels for reform but when the government – now at war with France – repressed the United Irish movement it went underground and began to consider the possibility of armed insurrection. Tone went to France as the movement's emissary to request military support for the planned popular uprising. Through a combination of factors, including the hesitancy of leaders, vacillation of the French government, arrests and terror tactics by the British government, divisions among the Irish population and poor weather, both French expeditions failed to connect with waiting rebels and the rebellion was repressed. The British government passed the Act of Union in 1801 which eliminated the Irish colonial parliament and gave Britain direct control over Ireland.

In the United Irish movement we have evidence, especially in memoirs by participants on both sides of the conflict, that women were more heavily involved with all aspects of the rebellion than had previously been noted by historians. Thankfully this subject has begun to attract more scholarly interest since the recent bicentenary of the rebellion. Female activism falls generally into three categories: material support, political organizing and military work.

Women provided much of the material support necessary to any guerrilla army. Some women's political activities were natural outgrowths of their domestic roles. For instance, women and children often accompanied male rebels to insurgent camps, such as the one at Vinegar Hill. While encamped, women cooked for the rebels and sewed their uniforms and ammunition pouches. Daniel Gahan, in his history of the Wexford rising, mentions that John Henry Colclough, one of the leaders, was joined by his wife and baby in the camp at Windmill Hill.[7] Many widows in that era supported themselves by continuing to run family businesses, often pubs, after their husbands' deaths. Several pubs owned by women served as United Irish meeting places, such as Molly Ward's the Belfast United Irish headquarters, which also served as the organisation's 'arsenal' where the local organisation secreted its supply of guns, ammunition and pikes.[8] A public house owned by Peggy Barclay was used as a meeting place for another Belfast United Irish group.[9] Women also transported arms for the rebels, as they were less likely than men were to be searched by British yeomen. Wicklow rebel General Joseph Holt warmly praised Susan O'Toole, his 'moving magazine', who transported most of his army's weapons in her skirts and baskets.[10]

Women's political activism took place within both the Society of United Irishmen and its sister organisation, the Society of United Irishwomen. R. R. Madden notes that a Miss Moore administered the United Irish oath to Dr James MacNeven, who later became a member of the Society's Directory.[11] This would indicate that Miss Moore herself (and, by extension, other women as well) must have been a trusted member. Madden also mentions a Mrs Risk of Sandymount, Dublin, a confidential United Irish emissary, who had much 'confidence placed in her intelligence and fidelity'.[12] The collected letters of William Drennan, a United Irish leader and poet, contain many that were written to him by his sister Martha McTier. McTier writes knowledgeably about the political issues of the day and as an insider about the work of the United Irish societies. In one letter, written as early as 1792, McTier states that 'our best writers, speakers, and actors are now those whom *nobody* knows. Of this number are two reading societies who for three years past have been collecting a number of the most valuable books …'[13] McTier's use of the adjective 'our' when speaking of Society members would seem to indicate that she considered herself to be a member of the organisation. Other contemporary sources also mention women being sworn into membership and present at meetings.[14]

The Society of United Irishwomen has been little studied, as yet. The few references I have found to this organisation note that members discussed political ideas, raised funds and carried secret messages and dispatches.[15] The United Irishwomen are also said to have held 'coming-out' parties at which young women were re-christened 'Miss Liberty', 'Miss Equality' and other such patriotic names. Samuel McSkimin, an anti-republican observer, opined that, 'judging from the violent language of these Amazons, they were anxious for an opportunity to rival, by deed of the dagger, the "Dames de la Halle" and the "Poissardes", those valuable allies of the French revolution.'[16]

Mary Ann McCracken, sister of the Belfast United Irish leader Henry Joy McCracken and an ardent republican herself, wrote to her brother when he was in jail in 1797, that 'the only real delight this world affords is to suffer in the cause of humanity and liberty – the cause of Ireland.'[17] In her letters to her brother she discussed the political direction of the movement and her assessment of the Belfast Society chapters that she visited.[18] John Gray believes that, although there is no hard evidence that McCracken was a member of the Society of United Irishwomen, the trenchant opinions about the organisation that she expressed in her letters would indicate a strong possibility of her involvement.[19] The sister of another northern leader, Henry Munro, was also an activist in her own right. Margaret (or Peggy) Munro was a member of the United Irishwomen who was arrested after the rebellion. She was never convicted because a yeoman who was to testify about her activities refused to do so, supposedly because he had fallen in love with her.[20] In the contemporary ballad 'Henry Munroe' a verse commemorates Margaret:

Then up came Munroe's sister, she was all dressed in green,
With a sword by her side that was well-sharped and keen,
Giving three hearty cheers, away she did go
Saying, 'I'll have revenge for my brother Munroe'.[21]

It would appear that the ballad writer saw Margaret as an activist and possibly as a combatant as well.

Women took part in much of the actual fighting in 1798. In some rebel encampments women and children accompanied their men. During lull periods the women cooked and performed housekeeping tasks but when the yeomen attacked, these women joined the men in battle. As Kavanagh stated in his account of the battle of Vinegar Hill, 'a great many women mingled with their relatives, and fought with fury; several were found dead amongst the men'.[22] Thomas Bartlett estimates the number of female combatants at Vinegar Hill to be around 200.[23] Revd Luke Cullen relates an incident in which a group of Protestant women in Newcastle freed a prisoner who was being dragged behind a horse by yeomen:

> When passing by Newcastle they were assailed by some Protestant women – none other dare interrupt the ovation. They intercepted their progress by standing in front of the rearguard with stones, and as this party advanced with Patrick they vigorously plied the missiles with all the insulting epithets to be found in indignant women's vocabulary. "Let go the young one, you villains; let him go" and Mrs. Jones and a few of her Amazonian neighbours plied the round shot of the road [paving stones] with such unerring effect that the no-quarter heroes gave the youth his liberty and life.[24]

Cullen and Samuel McSkimin both use the term 'Amazons' to describe female activists, which would seem to indicate that they considered political roles to be unusual or unsuitable for women. We also know of several individual women who fought. Betsy Gray, who fought and died at Ballynahinch, is undoubtedly the most widely known. She took part in the battle of Ballynahinch with her brother George and her lover William Boal. According to a contemporary ballad the three were fleeing the victorious yeomen cavalry after the battle when the men were surrounded by pursuing soldiers. Betsy rode back to try to rescue them and all three were killed.[25] In his historical novel *Betsy Gray or,*

Hearts of Down, originally a newspaper serial in the 1890s, W. G. Lyttle combined known facts with local legend to spread her story widely.[26]

Mary (or Molly) Doyle, called 'the point of war' by her comrades, is also mentioned in different accounts.[27] Doyle is said to have taken part in the battle of New Ross. When the rebels ran low on gunpowder, she turned the tide of battle by running under fire to cut the ammunition pouches from the bodies of enemy dead.[28] Insurgent Thomas Cloney in his memoir of the Wexford campaign reports another exploit of Doyle at New Ross. After the battle the weary rebels were preparing to withdraw from the battlefield, leaving behind a captured British cannon. Doyle allegedly sat on the cannon, refusing to move unless the men took it with them and, shamed, they complied.[29] A contemporary woodcut shows Doyle taking a turn at sentry duty.[30] Another Wexford woman, Anne Flood of Garrysackle, killed a Hessian captain with a mallet.[31] Madge Dixon was either a brave rebel or a bloodthirsty killer of Protestants, depending on the source consulted. She accompanied her husband, the Wexford sea captain (and United Irish captain) Thomas Dixon throughout the Wexford campaign. According to George Taylor in his 1800 history of the Wexford rebellion, Madge 'if possible, was more sanguinary' than her husband. She 'accompanied him on horseback with a sword and a case of pistols; clapped the rebels on the back and encouraged them, by saying, "we must conquer"'.[32] T. Crofton Croker, the editor of Joseph Holt's memoirs, includes Taylor's assessment of Dixon in a footnote to counter Holt's admiration of her bravery. Holt relates that after the battle of Vinegar Hill, 'Madge Dixon, a woman of great bravery, abused [Gen.] Roche to his face, called him a coward, and offered to lead a party against the enemy'.[33]

Rebel leader Joseph Holt's *Memoirs* mentions a woman with his army named Ann Byrne who was wounded by Yeomen in a skirmish at Greenane.[34] A later footnote by Croker quotes from the deposition of a young boy who had been in the rebel camp:

> At one time he [Holt] was constantly attended by a very handsome young woman dressed in a green habit, a kind of uniform with epaulets, her name was —, she was the daughter of a farmer, and was called 'the general's lady.' She was a determined rebel, and appeared highly gratified with her distinction. This lasted for some weeks, but at length Mrs. Holt joined the army, and from that time the heroine

in the green uniform disappeared, and we saw no more of her.[35]

Ruan O'Donnell speculates that this 'general's lady' was 'Croppy Biddy' Dolan, a notorious informer. However, Croker claims that she was almost certainly the Ann Byrne who had earlier been wounded,[36] a claim substantiated by the assertion in the deposition that the woman in question was a farmer's daughter. O'Donnell lists Dolan's father's occupation as thatcher. This confusion points up the lack of accurate materials recording the participation of women in United Irish activities.

Although many more women took part in all aspects of the 1798 rebellion than was earlier acknowledged, it is clear that they were not equal to their male comrades in political power. No women are known to have been in the military or political leadership and, although it appears that women probably took part in United Irish Society meetings, we have no evidence that they were instrumental in making policy decisions. At least one woman, Mary Ann McCracken, made it clear that she chafed under her perceived exclusion from decision-making. However, it is important to remember that most men, especially 'the men of no property', involved in the movement had little or no leadership role either, and probably had similar experiences to the women in respect of their lack of influence.

As the examples above testify, not all women involved in the United Irish movement were content with the usual role of 'heroic subordinate',[37] working quietly in the private sphere to support their men's public participation in revolution. Some women chose to take more public roles, thereby opening up these possibilities for future generations. And even women like Matilda Tone, the wife of United Irish leader Theobald Wolfe Tone and a prime example of heroic subordination, is credited by Nancy Curtin with contributing – perhaps unintentionally – to the opening of public space for women.[38]

Women's activism in 1848

The year 1848, a year of revolutionary activity throughout Europe, did not leave Ireland untouched. Continuing agitation to increase political rights for Catholics, and increasing economic hardship for the peasantry – culminating in severe famine in 1845, had kept political

activism at a high level. This activism was influenced by the examples
of democratic and/or nationalist struggles in France, Germany, Italy,
Hungary and other nations. The most radical Irish political activists
became known as 'Young Ireland', following the examples of 'Young
Germany' and 'Young Italy'. The revolutionary French government
even designed the Irish tricolor flag, which is still used today, model-
ling it on the French tricolor.[39]

Young Ireland stressed economic matters more than the more
abstract political rights that had been demanded in 1798.[40] Its founders
had been members of Daniel O'Connell's Repeal Association, a
narrowly focused organisation which sought to sever Ireland's constitutional union with Britain. They became impatient with O'Connell's
conflation of Irishness with Roman Catholicism, as well as with his
lack of economic demands and his insistence on pacifist tactics. In
1842 these dissidents began a repeal newspaper, the *Nation*, which
gradually over the next three years adopted far more radical and
militant positions than those of the main body of the Repeal
Association. In 1846 the *Nation* group was ejected from the Repeal
Association, which left them freer to pursue openly revolutionary
aims. Young Ireland used discourses of both the Enlighten- ment and
Romanticism to argue for national rights. Enlightenment ideas, inherited from the United Irishmen, included the desire for a democratic
state with strong individual liberties and complete secularism.
Romanticism, mainly expressed through poetry and art, stressed the
primacy of emotion over rationality.[41] Romantic nationalists attached
symbolic importance to ties of blood and land and they created
mythic histories with their use of folklore. Young Ireland combined
these discourses in order to appeal both to rational political and
economic interests and to emotional ties to Ireland's lost pre-colonial
past.

Women involved with the Young Ireland movement of 1848 have
come down to us as a more visible presence than those of 1798.
Women's most important contribution to the Young Ireland
movement was as writers – both of prose and poetry – for the *Nation*.
Several of the most prolific (and militant) correspondents in the
1847–48 period were female. Since political journalism carried with it
the danger of prosecution for sedition, most of the *Nation*'s writers
used pseudonyms. Three of their best-known female writers were
'Eva', 'Speranza' and 'Mary'. 'Eva' was Mary Anne Kelly, who came

from a family with strong republican sympathies – a grand-uncle had been a United Irishman and her closest uncle supported Young Ireland. As she wrote in her journal, 'By ancestry, I came of rebel stock, and I early developed the traits of my ancestors, not long after having learned to read. No one, it appears to me, could be other than an Irish rebel, who had a heart to feel or a brain to think.'[42] Kelly moved alone from Galway to Dublin in 1848 (an unusual step at that time for a young single woman) because she was 'imbued with a burning desire to be at the centre of the campaign against the British domination of [her] country'.[43] In contrast to Kelly's republican background, 'Speranza', or Jane Francesca Elgee (later Lady Wilde and the mother of Oscar Wilde), came from an upper-middle-class Anglican family that strongly disapproved of her nationalist activities.[44] Elgee and other women activists who defied family expectations in order to join the movement refute the charge of some historians that women only joined republican organisations because of family ties. 'Mary', or Ellen Mary Patrick Downing, was the most militant of the three, leaving the *Nation* for the *United Irishman* when it broke away in 1848 to pursue a more military strategy. As she wrote to Kelly in 1848: 'I think in treason … It tortures me to think of this pen work when we have so much need of swords.'[45]

Although a combination of ineptitude and repression prevented Young Ireland from carrying out a large-scale insurrection, women took part in the one skirmish that did occur, in July of 1848, in Ballingarry, Co. Tipperary. William Smith O'Brien, trying to rouse the countryside before arrests of the organisation's leadership made resistance impossible, gathered local people into an untrained, poorly armed force. According to Reverend P. Fitzgerald, a hostile witness to the skirmish, Smith O'Brien arrived at the village of Ballingarry, 'attended indeed by a considerable multitude, but consisting chiefly of women and children, and not having in the entire procession more than fifty men capable of carrying arms'.[46] One of the Young Ireland leaders who was present at Ballingarry, Terence B. McManus, gave a similar account of the rebel forces. He said that the crowd consisted 'of all ages and both sexes', but with women 'more numerous than the men'.[47] When the insurgents were eventually routed by a numerically superior British militia, at least one woman was listed in the record of those arrested.[48]

Women are also reported to have staged the only demonstration to protest Young Ireland leader John Mitchel's sentence of transportation to Van Diemen's Land (now Tasmania). Mitchel had been arrested and convicted of treason in May of 1848 when the government, growing uneasy about the possibility of Irish rebellion in the wake of the overthrow of the French monarchy, moved to suppress Young Ireland. Mitchel's wife Jenny, an activist who wrote several of the most militant articles in the *Nation* and was called its 'war correspondent',[49] urged the Young Irelanders to mount a rescue attempt:

> But let me tell the Confederates of Dublin that I firmly believe that to allow any Confederate, no matter how insignificant the part he may have taken in their cause, to leave Ireland in a felon's fetters for his advocacy of that cause, would be the most fatal madness, and would but rivet the chains more closely than ever, so that they would be unable to regain the noble position they now held, by all that they might say or do for half a century to come.[50]

Hesitant leaders like Charles Gavan Duffy vetoed her request. On the day of Mitchel's transportation the only disturbance came from 'a group of women on a prominence [who] threw stones and sticks at the sabred dragoons. They were directed by a leader of Amazon stature'.[51] We have no evidence regarding the identity of these women or whether Jenny Mitchel took part in organising them.

Women had much more influence over the political direction of Young Ireland than they had had in the United Irish movement. One reason for this difference is that Young Ireland did most of its organising through its newspaper, writing for which was a socially acceptable female activity. Both male and female correspondents used the pages of the *Nation* to debate women's proper roles in the national movement.[52] From an 1843 article in which women were urged to work in the domestic 'private sphere' to educate their children in nationalist principles, through 1848 when, following the arrest of male leaders, 'Speranza' and Margaret Callen edited the final two issues before the paper's suppression, these discussions continued. Female correspondents argued for their right to work for the cause in the public sphere, by joining nationalist clubs like the Irish Confederation[53] and they argued that militancy and political polemic should not be seen as gendered. 'Eva' urged readers to realize that 'what is virtue in man is virtue also in woman. Virtue is of no sex. A coward woman is as base as a coward man. It is not unfeminine to take sword or gun, if sword and gun are required.'[54] Another reason for women's stronger influence in 1848 is that some Young Ireland leaders encouraged women to be militant participants. John Mitchel urged them to learn to make bullets and cartridges, while Thomas Devin Reilly included women in his plans for insurrection, throwing boiling water and heavy objects onto attacking troops.[55]

Demands for women's rights

The above examples show that some women at least in 1798 and 1848 undertook the same types of revolutionary activities as did men. But what about women's rights? Did any of the militant women in the republican arena raise feminist concerns? We have little evidence that the majority of female participants in either struggle put forward gender-specific demands, yet some germs of feminist arguments are evident. The writings of female participants in both 1798 and 1848, as well as contemporary accounts of their activities, reveal that some argued for women's – as well as national – rights.

Mary Ann McCracken, who was an admirer of Mary Wollstonecraft's work, adapted Enlightenment ideas to women's emancipation when she wrote in 1797 to her imprisoned brother Henry Joy that she would prefer to have the Society of United Irishwomen merge with the male organisation because:

> There can be no other reason for having them separate but keeping the women in the dark and certainly it is equally ungenerous and uncandid to make tools of them without confiding in them. I wish to know if they have any rational ideas of liberty and equality for themselves or whether they are contented with their present abject and dependent situation, degraded by custom and education beneath the rank in society in which they were originally placed ... there can be no argument produced in favour of the slavery of woman that has not been used in favour of general slavery ...[56]

Another woman who worked with the United Irish movement, at least until 1796 when the movement began to espouse armed revolution, was Quaker writer Mary Shackleton Leadbeater of Ballitore, who mentioned in her diary that she was influenced by Wollstonecraft's and Godwin's ideas on women's rights.[57] It is likely, if these two women were reading Wollstonecraft and assimilating her ideas, that other United Irishwomen and their supporters were doing so as well. This supposition is bolstered by the fact, mentioned by John Gray, that the publisher of the Belfast United Irish newspaper, the *Northern Star*, published his own edition of the 'justly celebrated' *Vindication of the Rights of Women* in 1792.[58] And, as Nancy Curtin comments, even though the United Irish movement failed to specifically address feminist concerns, 'in the long run, the universalism which underscored this republicanism, and of the Enlightenment and the radical dissent tradition which reaffirmed it, contained the seeds for women's political liberation'.[59]

The women writers for the *Nation* combined these Enlightenment ideas with those of the Romantic movement to argue for women's rights. Sometimes female correspondents used the Romantic 'ethic of care'[60] to stress that they had a maternal duty in the public sphere to care for the nation; at other times they used the language of the Enlightenment to demand 'rights'. In 1847, 'an Irish Mother' expressed frustration in a letter to the editor about 'our sex, or rather its shackled condition ... where women rarely speak on politics, however much they may think on the subject'.[61] In an article in 1848 'Eva' wrote rather sarcastically that, 'every citizen should have a voice; and, I trust, I shall be excused for this exercise of my right'.[62] Over time, women's political experience empowered them to raise demands for equal education, employment opportunities and citizenship rights. 'Speranza', probably the *Nation*'s most consistent demander of women's rights, railed against the enforced idleness of upper- and middle-class women in an article written in 1850:

> Out of the four million of women at present in Ireland, how few there are in whose lives can be discovered any beauty of utility! ... At present myriads of eternal souls come on earth as 'ladies', and, in right of the title live a life of vacuity, inanity, vanity, absurdity and idleness ... This idle life of ladyhood is indeed the most deplorable thing in the universe.[63]

In the same year she noted in her journal that married women should not only have the right to employment and economic independence, but that they, like men, should prioritise career over family.[64]

Conclusion

Reasons for the lack of progression in Irish women's rights, despite evidence that some women in both the United Irish and Young Ireland movements broached the subject, remains a subject of debate by historians. Although this is a complex issue composed of many factors, one important point has been made by Margaret Ward: both of these – as well as all subsequent – Irish national movements lost their battles, and their most progressive leaders were jailed, exiled or killed. It is therefore a dubious proposition to infer that the suppression of feminist demands would still have been inevitable had the progressives won.[65] I would argue that the tentative steps taken by women involved in these two movements towards demands for a change in women's position helped to set the stage for later Irish republican feminists to make further demands. Most, if not all, movements for women's rights throughout the world have begun when women who are participating in another cause begin to see that they are not treated equally within their organisations. For instance, 'first wave' feminism in the United States grew out of women's role in the Abolitionist movement against slavery, while the second wave in the 1960s came primarily from women of the civil rights and anti Vietnam war movements. Their work in political movements both allows women to recognise their oppression as women and empowers them to struggle against it. Therefore, women's work in national liberation struggles, far from being a diversion from women's issues as some feminists argue, is often a necessary precursor to women's liberation. As Anne McClintock points out in her study of South African women's involvement in the fight against apartheid, 'refusal to participate in a nationalist revolution contributes to powerlessness in the post-revolutionary era'.[66]

As can be seen from this outline – necessarily sketchy and rudimentary – of women's activities in 1798 and 1848, many women remain to be excavated from the places where they have been 'hidden from history'.[67] The erasure of militant women from many episodes of Irish history has made it difficult to test the relevance to Irish women of theories about women and war being developed by feminist theorists and historians. These women must be recovered, not only because this is an interesting project in its own right, but also because discussions about women's relationship to war will be inherently flawed without them. Hypotheses of strong female tendencies toward pacifism, largely based on secondary historical works which have excluded women's activism, may have to be rethought as more revolutionary women are rediscovered.

Chapter 4

'In the line of fire': representations of women and war (1919–1923) through the writings of republican men

Louise Ryan

At intervals, those two gentle ladies, no longer young, came in to ply us with tea, food and cigarettes. I marvelled at their calmness and courage. Looking only to our comfort, those two did not seem a whit concerned that at any moment they might be in the line of fire and their home and business a shambles.[1]

Introduction

The War of Independence (1919–21) and Civil War (1922–23) form a defining period in Irish history. During these turbulent years the foundations of the Irish Republic were laid by a guerrilla warfare which at first united the majority of the Irish people against British forces but later split them apart in a bitter civil war. This chapter forms part of an ongoing project in which I am attempting to understand various aspects of women's participation and experiences in the campaign for Irish self-determination. In the early decades of the twentieth century the nationalist movement successfully mobilised thousands of women from diverse social backgrounds and geographical regions. In fact, one could argue that because so many women participated in the movement, the male leadership was unsure how to control them or contain their involvement. Although militant republicanism led to the formation of what was in many senses an army and hence a male-dominated hierarchy, the guerrilla nature of the conflict and the reliance on civilian support fractured the usual boundaries between male and female roles. As republican men went into hiding or were arrested and imprisoned, the visible face of republicanism was often female. But women were more than grieving widows and wives and daughters holding vigils outside prison gates. The uniformed women of Cumann na mBan regularly occupied public spaces, held noisy rallies, disrupted meetings and heckled politicians. These women were capable of being both public representatives of the militant movement and secret participants in military activities.

The secret, invisible nature of their participation has made it difficult to uncover and locate these women within nationalist histories. My research has drawn on a variety of sources ranging from the national and provincial press to underground republican news- sheets, women's autobiographical writing and other scattered fragments. In this chapter I take a different approach and turn to some well-known and widely read sources that have helped to shape the public imagination of those war years. The memoirs of IRA men have been instrumental in shaping the ways in which republicans have been historicised. However, in using these sources I go beyond the stories of war to analyse the gender dynamics that lie beneath. From as early as 1924, men such as Dan Breen began to publish their personal accounts of the war years. These books have not only influenced historians of Ireland but have been read in many countries, in some cases almost as textbooks of guerrilla warfare. For example, Dan Breen's book was being read by nationalists in India in the 1920s and 1930s.[2] Despite his difficulty in getting a publisher, Ernie O'Malley's first book, *On Another Man's Wound*, was eventually published in 1936 to critical acclaim and was described by the *New York Times* as 'a stirring and beautiful book'.[3] It quickly became a 'classic of Revolutionary literature'.[4]

In this chapter I will draw on the autobiographical writings of a selection of republican men: Barry, Breen, Brennan, Deasy, O'Donoghue and O'Malley, and the 'fictional' wartime stories of Frank O'Connor. These sources are useful for many reasons, not simply as personal memories of war but also as insights into the strategies of the IRA. The books offer vivid accounts of the relationship between the guerrillas and the local people who provided them with information, food and shelter. Although these books reveal a very masculine world of warfare, brotherly camaraderie, courage, self-denial, torture and brutality, they also provide fascinating images of femininity, home, motherhood and the role of women in a guerrilla war. What do these books tell us about women's participation in the war and what do portrayals of these women reveal about republican men?

The opening quote is taken from Tom Barry's account of the War of Independence in West Cork. His description encapsulates many of the characteristics common to representations of women in the writings of republican men. Although the women are clearly depicted as brave and calm, they are contained within the parameters of narrowly defined gender specific roles; situated in the domestic sphere, they have a motherly relationship with the young IRA men. In the context of guerrilla war, the blurring of boundaries between home and battlefront re-positioned women in militarised arenas. However, these books reveal many of the underlying tensions around women's involvement in military conflict.

Stories of the War of Independence emphasise the heroic deeds of brave young men.[5] An underdog, guerrilla army of courageous amateurs taking on the might of the British army carries all the hallmarks of heroism and martyrdom. Representations of women are usually contained within the conventional narratives of grieving mothers or passive, nameless victims. There is no doubt that women did suffer greatly from the effects of war and the restrictions imposed under martial law. Several commissions and reports at the time emphasised the particular experiences of women.[6] While the predominant image of republicanism is that it is both male-dominated and male-defined, there is evidence that women were actively involved in many areas of the conflict.[7]

The republican women's group Cumann na mBan (Women's Council), founded in 1914, had established over 800 branches by 1921[8] and is estimated to have had in excess of 3,000 members.[9] During the War of Independence, Cumann na mBan branches became affiliated to units of the IRA and became 'an army of women'.[10] These women carried out a range of diverse tasks as despatch couriers, gun-runners, cooks and nurses. As well as the young women of Cumann na mBan, many hundreds of women throughout the country played active and essential roles in the guerrilla war.[11] These women took enormous risks for the republican cause. Hundreds were arrested and imprisoned.[12] Thousands had their homes raided and searched.[13] Many were interrogated, intimidated and threatened.[14] In addition, large numbers of women were shot at, many were injured and several were killed.[15] There is also growing evidence to suggest that sexual violence was used as a weapon of war.[16] However, the presence and obvious importance of such large numbers of women raised several complex issues for the male-dominated republican army.[17]

As the fighting intensified and more women joined the movement there was growing concern about the transgression of gender roles.[18] During the Civil War, in particular, the national press frequently highlighted the extent of women's involvement in the fighting. On 16 October 1922, the *Cork Examiner* alleged that 'young girls' had thrown bombs at a lorry of national troops. This allegation was strenuously denied by republican sources.[19] The Catholic Church vehemently condemned women's participation in the conflict.[20] Opposition politicians such as William Cosgrave called republican women 'die-hards' who were hysterical and irrational.[21] P. S. O'Hegarty, who was a vocal critic of the IRA during the Civil War, called the women 'furies' who were helping to perpetuate violence and unrest.[22] But it was not just their opponents who criticised women's involvement in militarism. Ernie O'Malley wrote that 'the girls and women glorified the fighting', adding that they were 'more bitter than the men'.[23]

The active participation of women in the republican movement and the widespread condemnation that they attracted proved a dilemma for many men. On the one hand, they needed the women's help and support, but on the other, their reliance on women could be seen as a sign of weakness. In my view, these tensions underpin the particular ways in which women's involvement was either marginalised or sanitised in the writings of republican men.

'Cumann na mBan girls': representations of militant women

> The women rendered heroic service. Even outside the ranks of the young and active girls organised in Cumann na mBan, who carried despatches, nursed the sick and wounded, providing clothing, first-aid equipment, funds, and risked their lives as freely as the men, there

were women and girls who kept many a long vigil, who cooked and washed and provided shelter, and who were, when the tests came splendidly silent, immune alike to threats and blandishments.[24]

In his biography of IRA leader Liam Lynch, Florence O'Donoghue provides some fascinating snippets of information about the role of republican women in both the War of Independence and the Civil War. O'Donoghue acknowledges the courage and determination of women and the risks they took to support the republican cause. However, he does not explicitly address the various contributions of women but rather mentions them in passing. The following examples provide glimpses into women's experiences but these stories are never followed up or elaborated on by O'Donoghue; the women appear as shadowy figures in the background not central characters in their own right. O'Donoghue remarks that information 'received from Judy O'Riordan in Buttevant post office, indicated the probability of large scale raiding in the Banteer direction'.[25] There is no further mention of Judy O'Riordan, who certainly must have taken a great risk in passing on secrets about troop movements to the IRA. He also mentions other similar women: 'At Mallow Post Office, Siobhan Creedon had been active on behalf of the Cork Brigade as early as 1917, and she continued to work for Cork No. 2 Brigade with great efficiency and success during the whole period of the struggle'.[26] O'Donoghue presents a brief but fascinating account of Siobhan Creedon cycling past a convoy of British troops as she went into the countryside to warn the IRA. The role of post mistresses in rural districts who secretly worked for the IRA throughout the campaign for independence is a story still waiting to be told. When caught these women were severely punished. Lil Conlon records that a Limerick postmistress, May Burke, was sentenced to two years imprisonment for passing on information to the IRA.[27]

O'Donoghue also mentions the work of women couriers who, at a time of curfews and martial law – when thousands of British troops occupied Ireland, managed to travel undetected across large areas of countryside. Although Liam Lynch spent months on the run in remote mountainous landscapes, 'a line of communication to him from Dublin had been organised and maintained by Kathleen Barry, who had done and continued to do very valuable work as a courier'.[28] The contribution of women like Barry, O'Riordan and Creedon is usually a footnote, a brief sentence, in the biographies of male leaders and hero/soldiers. This representation of republican women is typical of many biographies from the period. For example, Dan Breen, in a brief aside, mentions the value of one woman's contribution to the war effort: 'Maggie Frewin's newspaper and magazine stand at Limerick Junction became a clearing house for all our despatches'.[29] Breen also mentions the courageous work of two sisters, Brighid and Aine Malone, 'active members of Cumann na mBan'. He describes how they 'carried our despatches and even helped in the removal of munitions to Kingsbridge Station'.[30]

NiraYuval-Davis writes that women who actively participate in military conflict have usually been perceived as threatening to gender hierarchies 'unless controlled and distinguished from male soldiers by emphasizing their femininity'.[31] In the autobiographies of republican men it is obvious that Cumann na mBan women are repeatedly portrayed in gender-specific ways.[32] Even though the women are often depicted as active and courageous, they are also clearly distinguished from republican men by their feminine qualities. Describing an IRA training camp in 1921, Ernie O'Malley emphasises the particular role of republican women:

> The Cumann na mBan girls in their turns came to cook and wash. Fresh flowers in empty tin cans would appear on tables; sweet pea, wild roses, bunches of heather, and carnations. The girls came on foot, on bicycles, in ponies and traps, some of them in uniform. They always brought presents: honey, homemade jam, freshly churned butter ... packages of cigarettes.[33]

Thus even independent, confident young women cycling around the countryside wearing military uniform were safely contained within the parameters of femininity. I suggest that their participation in warfare was mediated through their femininity. For example, although republican women were expected to shun British soldiers and police, on some occasions it seems that these women used their femininity to entertain or charm British forces, usually in an attempt to collect information or to act as a decoy while IRA men escaped. In his autobiographical account of the War of Independence, *The War in Clare*, Michael Brennan, Commandant of the East Clare Brigade, relates one such story. While on the run, Brennan and three of his colleagues sought shelter in the home of the Punch family. Exhausted, the men fell asleep in an upstairs bedroom. Later they were awoken by the sound of music and singing. Deciding to remain hidden in the bedroom the men wondered why the family was suddenly hosting a party. Hours later they discovered that while they had slept several military lorries had arrived in the district to carry out a house-to-house search. The young women of the family casually wandered down the road and engaged the officers in conversation. They invited the officers inside for tea and began playing the piano and singing. Thus the Punches' home was used as the base of operations for the entire raiding party and so was never actually searched. The young women took a grave risk in deceiving these British officers while they concealed four wanted IRA men upstairs. Had they been discovered the women would have faced long prison sentences.[34]

Florence O'Donoghue has described republican women as not only courageous but 'splendidly silent'.[35] Their loyalty was demonstrated by their ability to keep their mouths shut. Their silence and invisibility enabled them to be effective couriers and trustworthy secretaries. In contrast to the newspaper images of bomb-throwing 'furies' and hysterical 'diehards', the ideal republican woman was silent, calm and dutiful. O'Donoghue divided the women into two camps: the first were predominantly young women who, as members of Cumann na mBan, were organised and trained; they carried despatches and generally played an active role in the guerilla warfare. The other women, while remaining within the domestic sphere and keeping long vigils for their menfolk, also played dangerous roles in providing food and shelter for wanted men. This categorisation of women is very revealing and suggests some of the ways in which women's activism may have been negotiated, accommodated and contained. Firstly, there are the 'girls' of Cumann na mBan: young and active, risking their lives for the cause. This is a recurring image in the autobiographies of male republicans.[36] While acknowledging the bravery of these women, this image reduces them to a homogeneous group of nameless 'girls'. Secondly, O'Donoghue refers to civilian women and girls who provided food and shelter. Although these women were of crucial importance to a guerrilla army and are acknowledged by all the republican autobiographies, they are narrowly contained within the domestic sphere doing traditional 'womanly' tasks.

According to Cynthia Enloe, nationalist warfare frequently

involves a split between older, married women who 'perform support or homefront roles, while unmarried women are channelled into more military roles'.[37] While there was an obvious tendency to represent Irish republican women in this way, I believe that this is an unhelpful dichotomy which underestimates the blurring of boundaries between 'homefront' and 'battlefront'. Such a dichotomy also simplifies the complex constructions around militarism and domesticity. In my view, the writings of IRA men such as Breen, O'Donoghue and O'Malley, as well as the many other similar autobiographical accounts of the war years, indicate attempts to negotiate gender roles. Women's roles are represented as militarised and simultaneously feminised. The emphasis on clear-cut gender roles and hierarchies attempts to frame the relationship between republican men and women.

Courageous, chivalrous and clean heroes

In their memoirs and autobiographical accounts of the war, IRA men construct themselves as chivalrous, clean, sober, well-disciplined and pious. Dan Breen says that 'discipline in the matter of personal cleanliness was very strict. A columnman with a dirty or unshaven face was unheard of'.[38] Razors and toothbrushes were carried in the breast pocket 'after the manner of a fountain pen'.[39] There are no mentions of sexual encounters with women. Instead these accounts emphasise brotherhood, comraderie, discipline and chivalry towards women. The few who do hint at romance describe it in purely innocent terms.[40] Even in the case of IRA men who later married their female colleagues there is little or no mention of any physical contact between them.[41] Ernie O'Malley, for example, perhaps one of the least conservative of the IRA commanders, does not refer to any sexual liaisons in his two lengthy accounts of the War of Independence and the Civil War.

Florence O'Donoghue paints the following picture of the 25-year-old Commandant Liam Lynch, his friend and leader:

> Most strongly marked of his characteristics were those two so consistently representative of the best of his race – soldierly spirit and missionary zeal … He had been little troubled by the unrest of adolescence. Thoughts of love and marriage he put aside so that

nothing might stand between him and complete dedication in service to the duty he envisaged.[42]

In contrast to the righteousness, honesty and morality of the IRA men, British forces were represented very differently. They engaged in such 'contemptible outrages' as 'the execution by shooting or hanging of prisoners of war taken in honourable combat, the torture of prisoners, the reign of terror, the burnings and lootings'.[43] Lynch had 'a high nobility of character', believing that 'the service of freedom only stood below the service of God'. 'He would not deviate from honourable methods of warfare, no matter to what depths of depravity his opponents descended'.[44]

O'Donoghue is not the only biographer to comment on Lynch's absolute dedication to the republican cause. In another biography, *The Real Chief: The Story of Liam Lynch*, it is claimed that Lynch met a young woman 'to whom he was particularly attracted'.[45] However, he ruled out pursuing the relationship because 'my whole time is required by old Ireland'.[46] This young woman 'was never to know the fulfilment of her dream of happiness, but was to take her place … with the generation of Irish women who stood aside for the cause of Roisin Dubh'.[47] The fact that women were expected to take second place behind the cause of Irish freedom, symbolised by the beautiful young woman Roisin Dubh, suggests something of the gendered nature of the republican campaign. It also underlines the desexualised image of republicanism and the ideal of celibate devotion not to real women but to a mythical, virginal woman. The potential overlap between love of Ireland and devotion to Mary, virgin mother of God, is apparent. Such characteristics played an important role in creating the divergent images of IRA men and British soldiers.[48] The slippage between real women and allegorical woman is particularly apparent in a passage from Ernie O'Malley's first book, *On Another Man's Wound*:

> Sometimes an old woman as I left a house would say: 'Goodbye, God save you … may you have the strength to fight well', and press a strong, firm kiss on my mouth. For the moment I was her son whom she loved and was proud of. I could see the peaceful, quiet strength of her worn, serene face when I was on the road. It was as if Ireland herself, An Shan Van Vocht, had saluted one who was fighting for her.[49]

C. L. Innes has argued that the simultaneous representation of Ireland as both the young, beautiful maiden (Roisin Dubh) and the motherly old woman (Shan Van Vocht) enabled nationalists to enact a range of masculine roles from devoted son to chivalrous hero.[50] Such images also helped to construct appropriate roles for women: caring mothers and selfless assistants. Sobriety, youth, courage and chivalry towards women were the characteristics self-ascribed to Irish republican masculinity. Representations of Irish femininity were frequently circumscribed within these masculine discourses. The potential slippage between images of Irish women and female allegories of the Irish nation further served to define Irish womanhood.

However, in his book on the War on Independence, *From Public Defiance to Guerrilla Warfare*, the historian Joost Augusteijn claims that many IRA volunteers were 'diverted from their tasks by a strong interest in socialising, which included meeting the opposite sex'.[51] He argues that there were 'numerous examples of courting taking precedence over Volunteer activities. In attempts to impress the ladies Volunteers sometimes jeopardised their own safety'.[52] Augusteijn claims that 'members of the opposite sex did not shy away from the attentions of the Volunteers either. Young men in uniform with zeal, determination and authority attracted young females, who often were already involved in the national struggle themselves'.[53]

Dan Breen's memoirs give two examples which perfectly illustrate this point. In the first incident he and a group of comrades, although 'on the run' from the authorities, decided to attend a local dance. As a result of staying too long at the dance, one of Breen's friends, 18-year-old Sean Hogan, was arrested. In a later incident in Dublin, Breen, despite having a 'price on his head', went to the cinema with two female friends. He was observed and followed by a British agent, only narrowly avoiding arrest.[54] Augusteijn suggests that liaisons between young IRA men and their female friends did not only involve pursuits like dancing and going to the cinema. Although he only cites vague sources he claims that there are 'some unconfirmed reports of illegitimate children springing from these liaisons'.[55]

Accusations of sexual 'impropriety' between republican men and women formed part of British anti-republican propaganda during the War of Independence. For example, on 1 July 1921 the republican underground newspaper, the *Irish Bulletin*, reported that propaganda leaflets had been distributed by the British authorities which contained

'Filthy Libels on Irish soldiers'.[56] The leaflets claimed that republican men were 'safely hidden in the bedrooms of their female admirers in Dublin'. 'Many of our once pure Irish girls have lost their virtue in the abnormal lives they are leading. Many have been contaminated by the women sent down from Dublin by loose living Headquarter staff.' The *Bulletin* was outraged and claimed that this was a slur not only on the honour of the IRA but also on the virtue of Irish women. The existence of such rumours and allegations probably influenced IRA men to distance themselves from any hints of sexual liaisons. The extraordinary conditions of guerrilla warfare meant that hundreds of young men were moving around the countryside sleeping in different houses every night. These men were cut off from their families and leading very secretive lives. They relied heavily on local, civilian populations, particularly women. In addition, they worked closely with an army of women who provided essential information and kept lines of communication open in very hazardous conditions. One of the ways in which republican men asserted their masculinity against the backdrop of these extraordinary circumstances was to present the women within family narratives. The women in the safe houses are clearly defined as mothers and thus their relationship to the young men is both sanitised and naturalised.

Guest (houses) of the nation: The feminisation of hearth and home

> Molly was like a mother to us … It was her kindness and good cooking that really revived us. She was good humoured and cheerful. It was a tonic just to hear her merry laugh, her banter and her bright homely talk … She was unshaken in her conviction that no harm would come to us; that God would save us from our enemies. She kept a lamp constantly burning before the image of the Sacred Heart in intercession for our welfare.[57]

At the age of 23 with a price of £1,000 on his head, Dan Breen was permanently on the run. Molly was one of many women who offered him a night's shelter, food and respite from the hardships of life on the run. His description of her as 'motherly' is typical of the way in which republican men depict their relationship with the women who provided them with refuge. Of course these men were very young, most were in their early twenties and the women in the safe houses were usually many years older than them. Several of these women were the mothers of IRA men and Cumann na mBan women.[58] In addition to providing food and a night's shelter some women also washed and ironed the men's clothes.[59] The women also nursed men who were injured or suffering from the ill effects of weeks spent in the open countryside. As Liam Deasy recalled, 'I can never forget the kindness of the lady of the house who cared for me with all the skill of a trained nurse'.[60] Similarly, Dan Breen described how his life was saved by a woman who took him in after he had been shot. While soldiers patrolled the streets, the woman of the house risked her life by setting out in the early hours of the morning to get help for Breen.[61]

The descriptions of these women as 'motherly' and 'homely' naturalises their relationship to the men. Their devotion is that of a mother rather than an activist or a political actor. The image of mother sanitises what was an intensely political act. As Breen reminds us, the crime of harbouring a rebel was punishable by death.[62] Mrs Tobin provided a safe house at Tincurry, Co. Tipperary, and was so important to the men on the run that she features in the memoirs of Deasy, O'Malley and Breen. 'Her home was ever open to "the boys" until it was burned to the ground as an official reprisal'.[63] Men on the run had effectively abandoned their own homes and families, often with severe consequences for those left behind. Breen recalls that his own home was repeatedly raided by police and soldiers. While expressing sympathy for his mother, he also suggests her steely resolve: 'The dear old soul had suffered much … Her house was looted and set on fire over her head … Through all her trials she never lost heart and would always have her jibe at the enemy'.[64]

If the military raids and attacks on women and homes were intended to weaken IRA morale then they were, on occasion, quite successful. Following an IRA attack on Mallow military barracks, Ernie O'Malley recounts the feelings of his men as they withdrew into the countryside and realised that the British forces, the infamous Black and Tans, were carrying out reprisals on the town. 'There was silence for a time as we watched, helpless'.[65] One man remarked: 'Damn it, its terrible, to think of the women and children in there and the Tans and soldiers sprawling around drunk setting fire to the houses.' O'Malley says that although the IRA men had successfully accomplished their mission, they felt 'cowardly and miserable' as they left the towns people to cope with the reprisals.[66]

While the home was a feminised space associated with comfort, food and warmth, the outside spaces of city streets or open country-side were masculinised spaces of war. But the contradictions underpinning this dichotomy were barely concealed beneath the surface. The safe house was not always safe. Unlike the wide open spaces, the small country cottage was often a very dangerous place and an ideal location for a military ambush. Breen, Deasy and O'Malley, who had all evaded capture for many months while they travelled huge distances across the open countryside, were each trapped and ambushed as they rested in safe houses. While Breen managed to shoot his way out, though receiving life threatening injuries, both O'Malley and Deasy were arrested and imprisoned. Such incidents not only indicate the dangers of the safe house but also the blurring of boundaries between the homefront and the battlefront. Although the men were often aware of the dangers faced by the occupants of the safe houses, they frequently took the hospitality of these people for granted. As Liam Deasy wrote, 'they had continued to provide us with food and shelter without any material compensa-tion … No people could have been so brave and so generous. It may be that we had come to take all this for granted and too many of us were inclined to bask in the sunshine of hero-worship'.[67] Deasy describes how the numbers of available safe houses began to decline rapidly with the onset of the Civil War. Most of the people were war weary and did not support the IRA campaign.[68] With a shrinking number of safe houses, the demands on loyal supporters became even more draining on their meagre resources.

In his collection of short stories, *Guests of the Nation*, Frank O'Connor draws on his own experiences as a member of the IRA and a soldier in the War of Independence and Civil War. This collection of wartime stories provides an important insight into the feelings, fears and frustrations of life on the run. Most of the stories in the collec-tion centre around earnest, strong and somewhat reckless young men. Although many of them begin in the field of battle, the stories usually unfold when the men go into hiding in isolated farmhouses, barns or sheds. The women they meet there are usually old and motherly, and are frequently portrayed sitting by the hearth. Such domestic images

are common in nationalist iconography of the home as a 'warm nest'
into which one can withdraw from the chaos of the outside world,
and the woman as 'the guardian of national tradition', the keeper of
the flame.[69] In his stories, O'Connor reproduces many of the stock
nationalist images of women and home. The older women provide
food and shelter, they represent cosy warmth, home comforts, they
treat the men like their own sons. The women also provide not merely
a shelter from the enemy but also a refuge from the relentless brutality of war. The home is a highly feminised space.

> They sat down to tea in the kitchen, a long white-washed room with
> an open hearth, where a kettle swung from a chain over the fire.
> Everything in the house was simple and old-fashioned ... but
> comfortable, with a peculiar warmth when she drew the shutters to
> and lit the lamp.[70]

While this image is typical of male republican writings and
contains the woman within the enclosed domestic space, O'Connor
uses his position as a storyteller to introduce a more complex dimension. In another story, 'Machine Gun Corps in Action', a group of
republican men arrive at a remote cottage, opening the door to find 'a
young woman sitting by an open hearth in the twilight'.[71] This young
widow is described as 'motherly', but she is also highly sexualised 'she
was tall, limber and rough, with a lazy, swinging, impudent stride'.[72] By
the end of the story there is a strong hint of romance between her
and one of the men, who cleverly contrives to remain behind when
the rest of the column moves on. Unlike those in the autobiographical writings, the men in O'Connor's stories frequently discuss women
and romance; he describes intimacy between the men and the women
in the safe houses. His characters indulge in passionate embraces,
kisses and a hint of something more. This chimes with the sugges-
tions put forward by Joost Augusteijn (page 54 above) that, despite
their claims to piety, republican men did engage in romantic relationships with young women.

Because O'Connor's accounts are clearly presented as fiction, the
author is able to relate events and engage with topics in a way that
would not be possible within the genre of republican autobiography.
To my mind one of the most interesting stories in the collection is the
story entitled 'Laughter'. This begins with a group of young men

waiting for hours in the pouring rain to ambush a lorry of British soldiers. Numb with the cold and drenched to the skin, the men seek shelter in a safe house, the home of an elderly woman and her two daughters. The house also serves as a hiding place for IRA guns and bombs. Although this elderly mother at first seems to conform to the stereotypical 'motherly' figure, O'Connor presents a more complex picture. The women had endured numerous raids but were defiant. 'Every other day her house was raided, but crippled as she was with rheumatism, and with two sons in prison, it brought no diminution of her spirits'.[73] The mother described how she stood up to the soldiers and called 'the jackeen of a lieutenant' a rat and threatened to 'give him me boot'.[74] The older daughter, Norah, then helped the IRA men to escape from a military patrol. She concealed two revolvers under her coat and calmly left the house walking passed the military patrol. The two young men followed her at a distance and later, when it was safe, she handed the revolvers back to them and went on her way. This story is significant because it presents republican women in a fairly typical light but also goes further and complicates the image by emphasising, not only the courage, but also the steely resolve of mother and daughters alike. The mother is described as 'cool',[75] while the eldest daughter is 'cold'.[76] Their fervent republicanism plus the brutalising effect of war and the repeated military raids may well have hardened these women. O'Connor also complicates the usual image of the safe house. There is nothing particularly 'homely' about their home. Despite the presence of three women, this is not the usual warm, peaceful, feminine domestic space. It is clearly a military arena where guns and bombs are hidden, while soldiers, from both sides of the conflict, are a constant presence. The boundaries between homefront and battlefront are clearly ruptured, not only by the intrusion of military personnel into the home but also by the activities of the women themselves. Norah leaves the house and calmly transports weapons through heavily militarised streets.

Although O'Connor's women are fictional characters, they are the creations of a republican man and bare similar characteristics to the women who feature in the more explicitly autobiographical writing of Barry, Breen, O'Donoghue or O'Malley. However, I suggest that O'Connor uses his licence as a writer of fiction to offer a more multi-dimensional and perhaps an unsettling image of the women and the home in the context of guerrilla warfare.

Conclusion

Nationalism, armed conflict, activism and the construction of masculinity and femininity are all closely connected and interlocking issues.[77] Guerrilla warfare ruptures the boundaries of home-front/battlefront and so challenges the duality of masculinity and femininity. The militarisation of the domestic space took place on several levels: it was a refuge for guerrilla fighters, a hiding place for guns and bombs, a place where information was exchanged and transmitted, and it was frequently invaded and attacked by enemy forces. Thus 'the home' is vulnerable to attack, it is a place of danger; however, it can simultaneously be seen as a site of resistance.

Women are potentially empowered as activists and important players in guerrilla warfare.[78] The militarisation of the domestic sphere can also mean that gender roles are challenged as men leave their homes and families, while women become defenders of the domestic space and the mainstay of the guerrilla army. However, as we have seen in the Irish context, the increasing involvement of women in militarism caused widespread criticism which ridiculed republican women as hysterical 'furies'. There had also been some allegations that young republican men and women were indulging in sexual 'impropriety'. Both of these accusations sought to undermine the discipline, legitimacy and essential masculinity of the republican army. How then did male republican narratives seek to reinforce gender roles and hierarchies? In this chapter I have argued that the male narratives emphasised the essential masculinity of republican men. They are portrayed as pious, sober, honourable, noble, clean, respectful, they bond with each other and display courage and camaraderie. The open countryside and the city streets are their domain; these are masculine spaces. The women are essentially feminine, their relationship to the men is familial, usually motherly and occasionally sisterly, but rarely comradely. The women are contained within the domestic space, closely associated with soft, warm interiors, the hearth, food and a resting place. Mothers in particular are contained on the inside, younger women are depicted outside, but even then their femininity is established.

The women in the homes were usually depicted as old enough to be the mothers of the republican men. Mothering rebels could be seen as a highly dangerous and subversive role that required great courage and resourcefulness. However, mothering was usually portrayed as natural. Writing about Palestine, Peteet says, 'maternal sacrifice was categorized as belonging to the realm of the natural'.[79] It was therefore denied a political dimension and active agency. It also masked the great effort required on the part of poor women to provide endless mothering to the countless young men who turned up on their doorsteps in the middle of the night. Mothers were a national icon in nationalist rhetoric and symbolism. Mothering meant not only giving birth but, in times of war, it also involved sacrifical mothering, mothering of martyrs, mourning of the dead. Peteet argues that mothers are constructed 'as repositories of a nationalist reproductive potential and as sacrificial icons'.[80]

What then do these narratives tell us about republican women? Are these sources of any use in furthering our understanding of women's role in the Irish republican movement of the period? The memoirs of all the men I have read share many common features and portray republican women in very similar ways. These representations are very different from the accounts of republican women that appear in the national press of the period[81] and the self-representations in women's autobiographical writings.[82] Based on the hard work of feminist historians we know that many hundreds, perhaps thousands, of women actively participated in the War of Independ-ence and Civil War. However, in the classic texts of republican men the best we can hope to gain are fleeting glances of these shadowy female characters. Nevertheless, this is not to suggest that these texts are invalid as tools in feminist historical research. Although they are of limited use in providing detailed information about women's actual involvement in the war, they provide a fascinating insight into the complex gender dynamics of guerrilla warfare. The attempts to contain, sanitise and depoliticise women's involvement in the war can be read as a strategy for reasserting the gender hierarchy. The absence of any explicit reflection upon gender politics within these texts underlines the marginalisation of gender discourses within the republican movement of the period. These sources reveal far more about the blurring of gendered boundaries and the tensions around gender roles than may be apparent on first reading. Hence, when taken in combination with other documentary sources, such as newspapers and women's autobiographical writing, these classic republican texts form a valuable and revealing insight into the complex gendering of war, nationalism and identity.

Chapter 5

Constance Markievicz and the politics of memory

Karen Steele

Introduction

Constance Markievicz, née Gore-Booth (1868–1927), enjoys a well-thumbed page in the annals of Irish history for her autonomous achievements: as the founder of Fianna Éireann (the Irish nationalist boy scouts), as a female warrior in 1916, as the only woman sentenced to death for her leadership in the Rising (a sentence later commuted to life imprisonment), as the first woman elected to the British Parliament in 1918, and as the only female cabinet member in the first Dáil Éireann. Markievicz is remembered not only because of her militant political activism, however. A statuesque Ascendancy beauty who married a Polish count, she dazzled Dublin Castle society (in her youth) and relished the life of an artist, painting in Paris, co-founding a dramatic company in Dublin, and befriending many of the leading artists, playwrights and poets of the Irish literary revival. A habitual joiner of causes living in a city erupting with competing political clubs, Markievicz soon relinquished her society friends to become a member or officer in many of the leading revolutionary organisations of the day: Inghinidhe na hÉireann, the Irish Citizen Army, the Irish Volunteers, Cumann na mBan, and Sinn Féin. During Dublin's great labour crisis, the Lockout of 1913, Markievicz helped to run the soup kitchen in Liberty Hall, cementing her commitment to James

Connolly and his vision of an independent socialist republic. After the execution of Connolly in 1916 and her release from prison during the general amnesty of 1917, Markievicz spent the final decade of her life alternating as soldier, statesman, dissident and inmate, fighting with words or with guns to keep Connolly's ideals alive.

Nevertheless, Constance Markievicz continues to suffer from a terrible reputation. W. B. Yeats deemed her final decade, in particular, wasted and hollow: 'lonely years/conspiring among the ignorant'.[1] Sean O'Casey, more severely, judged her a dilettante and poseur, someone who could not even be pronounced a flop, 'for she hadn't the constitution to keep long enough at anything in which, at the end, she could see a success or a failure facing her'.[2] Even her most sympathetic biographers, as Amanda Sebestyen remarks, have seriously underestimated her intelligence, as well as her continued commitments to what she called 'the three great movements': socialism, feminism and nationalism.[3] Sean O'Faolain, for example, austerely remarked, 'one baulks just a little at the phrase "intellectual honesty"' to describe Markievicz 'not because one questions for a second the honesty of it but the quality of it'.[4] Although historians and biographers have since expanded our appraisal of Markievicz's socialist, feminist and nationalist achievements,[5] such evaluations as O'Faolain's have typified the assessment of Constance Markievicz for approximately seventy-five years.

So too has Irish nationalism suffered ill renown, and not only due to revisionist historiography. Feminist critics, in particular, have been too quick to dismiss Irish nationalism as a movement of failed potential.[6] Whereas Eavan Boland, Edna Longley and Ailbhe Smyth have lamented the limitations of Irish nationalism for women activists and artists, the cultural work of Constance Markievicz provides a telling example of how Irish nationalism has always accommodated, if sometimes resisted, the contributions of and criticisms from women and workers. This essay proposes to reclaim Constance Markievicz's intellectual merit through a consideration of her nationalist writings of the 1920s. Markievicz's body of copious journalism and slender plays is most significant for its investment in the politics of memory, notably recalling feminist and socialist contributions to nationalism. By repossessing the memory of the Rising, wresting republican icons and ethos from the Free State, and revising many of the gendered imperatives of the literary revival, Markievicz sought to reposition herself as a principal figure in the pre-Rising years; she also aimed to make visible the enduring, often overlooked achievements of other activists marginalised in the process of nation-building. Such a project of political and cultural memory enhanced her standing as a republican socialist woman; at the same time, her challenges to the Free State – which were premised on her revolutionary, egalitarian and militant principles – sought to dismantle the edifice and, more fundamentally, to reform the building blocks of the nation. Significantly, Markievicz's memories – as well as her faith in keeping accurate records – provide critics today with ample evidence to challenge literary, biographical and historical assessments of her as a poor thinker, bad writer and pretend player in key cultural and political debates about women and nationalism.

Constance Markievicz and the nationalist press

Markievicz frequently professed that reading nationalist newspapers awakened her to the growing movements of feminism, socialism and nationalism in *fin de siècle* Ireland.[7] Irish radical newspapers, in fact, recorded and shaped her own legacy as a rebel within and outside of each of the three great movements of the day. Within months of joining her first overt nationalist organisation, Inghinidhe na hÉireann, in 1908, she embarked upon her recurrent calling as a journalist, writing a monthly feature ('Woman with a Garden') in *Bean na hÉireann* that generated a devoted following at the time and has continued to beguile historians and cultural critics to this day.[8] Over the next two decades of her life, Markievicz contributed editorials and poems, letters and speeches to pre-eminent socialist, feminist and nationalist papers, such as the *Workers' Republic, Irish Worker, Bean na hÉireann, Irish Citizen, Sinn Féin, Poblacht na hEireann, Éire, An Phoblacht,* and the *Nation*.[9] Her output is surprising given the demands on her time during the War of Independence (1919–21) and Civil War (1922–23), when she often found herself alternating between war, underground governmental operations, imprisonment and hiding.

R. F. Foster has remarked that the Irish Civil War 'looms larger in Irish history than the "Anglo-Irish" war, because it was both more traumatic and more influential … It created a caesura across Irish history, separating parties, interests, and even families, and creating the rationale for political divisions that endured.'[10] If Markievicz's journalism of the 1920s amply illustrates Foster's reading of Irish history, her poetics were more characteristic of the enjambed line: spilling over the fixed boundaries of constituencies and party politics, rushing beyond the protocol of tight-lipped diplomacy, she nudged and pushed women and workers to maintain pressure on the Free State. On the dais, she appealed to Cumann na mBan members to keep both physically and intellectually fit for a future in Irish politics.[11] Indeed, when civil war ensued, Markievicz fought briefly, but she also produced her own paper, writing many of the articles and drawing cartoons; when the duplicator was seized in a raid, she moved to Glasgow, where she helped to edit and write for a new republican paper, *Éire*, as well as give speeches galvanizing support for the anti-Treaty side.[12]

Despite her own well-established, if anomalous, role as a New Woman with a gun, Markievicz was deeply aware of the problems with her position in Ireland, forever an outsider by class, gender and disposition. Æ (George Russell) hinted that it was her impulsive, industrious nature that made her a stranger when he suggested that 'she should have been born in America',[13] but her Polish surname, her aristocratic title and her high-pitched English accent also imposed cultural and rhetorical limitations for Markievicz in advancing the cause of workers and women. By the 1920s, defeated in the Treaty debates and in the Civil War, Markievicz had ample cause to worry about her political credentials as the new Irish State was emerging. Politically mobilised women were sidelined, in particular, because so many of them were opposed to the Treaty. Indeed, the Irish Free State often framed republican women as 'outsiders' in order to silence their dissident voices.[14] One classic example of the Free State effacement of republican women can be heard in the paternalistic tone of the pro-Treaty side when it appealed to women during the Treaty debates. In seeking to canvass its female constituency, the pre-eminent pro-Treaty newspaper *An Saorstát* ('the Free State') appealed to this putatively innocent and inexperienced class of citizens by speaking slowly with simple words since women were 'still in the babyhood of their political training' and 'spoke as one entirely unknowing the active side of the struggle'.[15] In rebuke of such mainstream misogyny among Free State writers, Markievicz composed editorials and plays that emphasised Irish women's political agency, which in turn legitimated her role as a Free State critic.

Markievicz's dissident journalism of the 1920s

Some of her contemporaries, such as Sean O'Casey, dismissed Markievicz's mind because she was an indefatigable woman of action; in fact, her journalism demonstrates her stalwart valuation of the pen as well. In a devastating critique of Eoin MacNeill, Chief of Staff of the Irish Volunteers in 1916, for example, Markievicz reminded her readers that 'with the stroke of a pen' his countermand on Easter Sunday doomed the Rising before it could begin.[16] His written words, she suggests, left a greater imprint than the military action that was to ensue. With such imprimatur came weighty responsibility. In the same column, Markievicz recalled that even after MacNeill had 'cut the ground from under their feet by dispersing their army', the leaders of the Rising considered the impact of MacNeill's signature on the Proclamation of the Republic; worried for his fate, the leaders 'reprinted [the Proclamation] without Professor Eoin MacNeill's signature to safeguard him so that he should be spared the fate the signatories knew would probably be theirs'.[17] Like MacNeill's black countermand and the signatories' printed words, Markievicz's pen left an indelible mark on many of the key cultural and political battles concerning women and nationalism during the 1920s. While she never relinquished militant means to solve political troubles, her journalism also shows us that Markievicz refused to serve as a palimpsest of male nationalism ever again.

Markievicz opted to publish her oppositions to the Free State in several of Ireland's more prominent anti-Treaty publications: *Poblacht na hÉireann* ('the Republic of Ireland'), *Éire: The Irish Nation* and the *Nation*. These papers were often edited by the same cadre of anti-Treaty activists – Liam Mellows, Erskine Childers and Frank Gallagher – who changed the papers' names repeatedly to evade censorship. During the 1920s, when these papers were in circulation, overt challenges to the Free State government and its leadership often had to be smuggled in from abroad, but the message of repudiation was hardly covert. For Markievicz – as well as for many writers of the advanced-nationalist press – armed struggle and biting rhetoric were less divergent roads than different vehicles to the same destination. In fact, her rhetorical style and her recurrent arguments indicate that Markievicz viewed journalism as another form of battle. Her defiance of the Free State sometimes brings to mind a bruiser itching for a fight. In an open challenge to Kevin O'Higgins, TD and Minister for Justice and External Affairs from 1922–27, Markievicz characteristically pledged, 'I am ready to meet him on any platform, anywhere, or to meet him in his own Press with my pen. Let us see if he has the courage to take up my glove'.[18]

In contrast with Arthur Griffith, who agitated against keeping signed minutes during the first Dáil Éireann in order to protect the Cabinet and to safeguard the intents of the illegal government, Markievicz proclaimed, 'I would have preferred to take the risk and keep accurate records'.[19] Although her journalism of the 1920s is suffused with this persistent, subterranean theme, her writing betrays an even more eager interest in reclaiming and reinscribing popular memory. In a ten-part series in *Éire*, entitled 'Memories', Markievicz concentrated on revisiting the memory and the meaning of venerable, dead or exiled leaders. Like W. B. Yeats in 'Easter 1916', who authorised his own ambivalence ('a terrible beauty is born') by enumerating his old acquaintanceship with MacDonagh, MacBride, Connolly and Pearse, Markievicz invoked the popular memory of key figures such as Tom Clarke, Frank Sheehy Skeffington, Jim Larkin and James Connolly in order to castigate the values and the achievements of the Free State. Published over a four-month period immediately following the Civil War (23 May to 1 September 1923), these articles also allowed Markievicz to recall and to keep alive her own contributions, an apt foil to what she considered the equivocating, craven men who were now in charge.

Markievicz's biographical sketches and anecdotes of national history afforded her instrumental occasions for creating an alternative vision of citizenship, one that vividly contrasted with the law-and-order imperatives and conservative family-values rhetoric of the new Irish Free State; these memories inevitably alluded to her own example as a brash, militant egalitarian. Thus, in Markievicz's memory, Tom Clarke was best remembered in the context of a family committed to republican principles: 'Both he and Mrs Clarke found the highest expression of their great love for each other in the absolute oneness of their love for Ireland, and their ambition to devote their lives to her cause; their desire, too, to train up their boys in the Fenian faith, and worthy to be the nephews of that great Fenian, John Daly, Mrs Clarke's uncle, who, boy and man, had worked and suffered and lain half a lifetime in an English jail.'[20] This short introduction, then, quietly reminded readers of another woman's involvement in the struggle, the venerable republican Kathleen Daly Clarke. Although Markievicz describes Kathleen Clarke's political involvement in domestic terms – connubial and maternal love – Markievicz emphasises that republican principles and conduct, not wifely devotion or maternal duty, signalled her commitment to Ireland. In recalling the male martyr in the context of his still active wife, a woman who maintained a vital link between republican families and the IRA in the wake of the Rising and who steadfastly opposed the conditions of the Treaty, Markievicz thus pronounced that active commitment, not marriage or motherhood, constituted national citizenship.

The relationship of family to citizenship would preoccupy her to the end of her journalistic career. In her final editorial, published just a month after her death in 1927 and originally written for the Fianna boys by their 'Chief Scout', Markievicz explicitly sought to discredit the family as the moral foundation of the Free State and, instead, to reform with building blocks made from youthful, socialist militancy. As the research of Mary Clancy, Breda Gray and Louise Ryan has demonstrated, women in the Dáil and Seanad debates loudly protested the Free State's attempts to exclude women from public life.[21] In response, the Free State employed rhetoric and enacted legislation that repeatedly 'placed the family at the center of Irish culture'.[22] Rebuking the conservative tactic of asserting the nuclear family as the founding unit of the nation, Markievicz insisted that the socialist republican militancy of the Fianna constituted 'the first real step in citizenship',[23] a topic she also thematised in her play *Broken Dreams* (discussed below). Drawing a parallel between the family as a social collective and the Fianna as a republican socialist collective, Markievicz explained that citizenship must be based on free will, active service and a civic conscience, not membership in a certain kind of family:

> We begin life then as citizens of our family, but the first real step in citizenship that we take is when we join the Fianna. We can be good or bad members of the Fianna, just as we can be good or bad members of our family or of our nation. It is that our brotherhood is growing with our growth. We have already found new brethren in our schoolmates, girls as well as boys, and now we find ourselves in a still closer and deeper brotherhood within our nation. It is of

deeper significance for us, because we were not born into it as we were into our family, nor were we sent there, as we were sent to school. We joined the Fianna because we chose to of our own free will. We made this choice because we wanted to work for Ireland, and we wanted to take up the task of training ourselves.[24]

With these words Markievicz plainly repudiated the notion that involuntary aspects of identity – race, class, gender, religion – should determine Irish citizenship, championing instead tireless devotion to a cause that one is 'not born into'. Rejecting, as well, the Free State's bourgeois Catholicism, Markievicz adapted the Christian golden rule to pose another republican, socialist command:

No men who loved their neighbour as themselves could conspire together to conquer in their own greedy interests a weaker neighbour and oppress them, as England conquered and oppressed Ireland for centuries. No one who loved his neighbour as himself could bear to see people living in squalor and misery, overworked and underfed, while others are idle and have more money than they know how to spend.[25]

As the above remarks make clear, Markievicz's idea of citizenship implicitly included women, though she rarely spoke with the explicit vocabulary of a feminist like Hanna Sheehy Skeffington. In fact, while Markievicz's Easter memories interposed the example of republican women such as Kathleen Clarke, Helena Molony, and Nora and Ina Connolly, she introduced republican and labour men with descriptions that could, as easily, portray herself. Thus, the taciturn, middle-aged IRB man Tom Clarke was 'an impulsive and steadfast lad', adjectives that were often used of Markievicz, especially when she was leading her Fianna troops.[26] Frank Sheehy Skeffington was similarly praised for the combative qualities she most valued in herself, a 'champion of the rights of women, of the workers, and of the nation ... utterly incapable of compromise, though he could be kindly tolerant of those who [did]'.[27] Jim Larkin, Markievicz emphasised, possessed not merely socialist credentials but also nationalist character, for 'he always talked about the "principles of Tone and Emmett"'.[28] Even further, the egalitarian ideals of James Connolly, in Markievicz's memory, influenced republicanism into a socialist as well as feminist movement. In her profile of Connolly, Markievicz noted that it was Connolly's daughters Nora and Ina — 'pioneer' members of a girls' Fianna in Belfast — who introduced Markievicz to their father. In a sentence, then, Markievicz underscored the activism of other women, as well as her own supporting role as the founder of the first Fianna in Dublin. Connolly's open-minded, fatherly support for his daughters' activism, Markievicz stressed, set a pattern for his treatment of women in the nationalist and socialist movements overall: 'We were never in his mind classed for work as a sex but taken individually and considered just as every man considers men and then allotted any work we could do'.[29] Such a spirit of inclusion inevitably contrasted with the Free State's official attitudes toward women, as exemplified in the editorials addressed to women in *An Saorstát*.

If Constance Markievicz evoked the memory of venerable leaders to authorise her critique of the Free State and its conservative values, she also reclaimed icons of the nation as 'public property' that superseded Free State possession. As Ben Novick and John Ellis have shown, Irish nationalism during the First World War was marked by a caustic quarrel over competing ideas of Irishness.[30] The advanced-nationalist press, as well as less traceable ephemera such as posters and handbills, sought every opportunity to challenge and to condemn Irish participation in England's war effort, and these battles over which war to fight – Great Britain's present conflict or Ireland's future bid for independence – invariably contested, as well, differing attitudes of Irish nationality. Markievicz resurrected this contest in the Free State years, attacking what she considered England's proxy – the Free State – not only for its ideological and strategic failures but also for its 'theft' of 'the most valued insignia of the Republic'.[31] Naming the present government the 'Fraud State', Markievicz drew up a list of its purloined possessions, from the titles of the Republic (Saor Stat), and its parliament (Dáil Éireann), to the tricolour and the green uniform of the Irish Volunteers.[32] In later articles for *An Phoblacht*, Markievicz extended her catalogue to include martyrs as 'public property' as well. In recalling the contributions of Liam Mellows, whose execution by the Free State remained one of the most galling examples of Free State treachery, Markievicz insisted that all of his activism – from his fighting in Galway in 1916 to his repudiation of the Treaty in Dáil Éireann to his insurgency in the Four Courts in 1922 – constituted 'public property, they belong to Ireland and to all patriots the world over'.[33] Not satisfied to reclaim the political and historical meaning of anti-Treaty leaders, Markievicz reached back to 1798 to establish the 'true' foundation for revolutionary socialist republicanism. Revisiting addresses and manifestos written by Wolfe Tone and other leaders of the United Irishmen, Markievicz reimagined the blue-blooded Tone as an egalitarian proto-socialist, with views that were 'as revolutionary as Bolshevism would be today'.[34] Taking a sideswipe at the 'monarchist, capitalist' Griffith, Markievicz maintained, 'No one can fail to see that Wolfe Tone gave his life for the freedom of Ireland from not only foreign political and military control, but from the more subtle and cruel oppression and enslavement that resulted from the Establishment of the English social system and the English economic class.'[35]

Markievicz's nationalist drama

Constance Markievicz has often been derided for her irrepressible 'craving for the dramatic' and her 'talent for scene-stealing'.[36] A recurrent literary representation of her, from Lennox Robinson's 1917 *roman-à-clef*, *A Young Man from the South*, to D. J. Smith's 1983 biographical essay, insists that she was 'caught in the grip of forces over which she has no control' – that is, a bit player in a grander dramatic production.[37] Such descriptions have served to deny Markievicz her own political agency, but the historical record, as well as Markievicz's own literary efforts, show us that drama afforded Irish women a tantalising opportunity to seize political power.[38] The Irish National Theatre provided Markievicz with a route from the Dublin Castle circle to Connolly's Liberty Hall crowd. When Markievicz first attended Yeats and Augusta Gregory's 1902 play *Cathleen ni Houlihan*, she remarked that it became 'a kind of gospel' to her.[39] Inspired by the Abbey Players, she and her husband Casimir joined Æ's Dublin United Arts Club in 1906. Soon after, the Markieviczs were performing in small theatricals; Con's first public performance was as Druidess Lavarcam in the Theatre of Ireland's production of *Deirdre*, by Æ. In 1908, she and Casimir became founding members of the Independent Dramatic Company, performing plays by Casimir and other amateur writers in the group. By that autumn, she had joined Inghinidhe na hÉireann, launched her career as a columnist, and, the following year, she established the Fianna.

In the years leading up to the Rising, her interest in drama for entertainment's sake waned, but she never relinquished the wigs, capes, playbills and scripts. Indeed, her well-documented tableau as Joan of Arc for the Irish Women's Franchise League Daffodil Fête in 1914 indicated the militant potential for her later public performances. As in her gardening columns, where she sublimated her tactile pleasures in working a little sod of earth for the higher calling of her nation's independence, Markievicz found that her delight in 'dress up' could also be put to Ireland's service. Her theatrical gifts turned out to have practical applications in conflicts that centred on identity boundaries, such as class and nationality: during the Lock-out, she dusted off these relics of a bygone era to disguise trade union leader Jim Larkin, who had been prohibited from speaking to the Dublin crowd. Later, while on the run during the War of Independence and the Civil War, she donned other treasures in her trunks to evade G-men, Black and Tans, and Free State soldiers who viewed her as a threat to the state.

After the Civil War, Markievicz roused her old curiosity in the theatre, establishing, in September 1925, the Republican Players Dramatic Society, which put on dozens of plays in its first year of operation, including two of Markievicz's one-act plays, *Blood Money* and *The Invincible Mother*. In a letter to her sister Eva, the poet, Markievicz apologised that these plays lacked belletristic merit: 'Of course it is not literary, only just a thrilling story.'[40] Indeed, every critic who has glanced at her plays is eager to emphasise this point.[41] Her writing certainly betrays a stronger investment in propaganda than in artistry: uncomplicated characters, gauche dialogue and dubious plot resolutions frequently remind readers of Markievicz's amateur talents. Yet, her 'second-rate' drama offers far more than a biographical gloss on this singular woman. Markievicz's drama, as we will see, has both historical and cultural implications for how we view these crucial years of identity formation and national awakening. We can witness how women refused to be silenced by the ideology of the Free State. Moreover, the plays reveal how some of the most venerated, iconic images in the literary revival – feminine emblems of Ireland – were being rewritten and revalued even as Yeats, Gregory, and O'Casey were circulating and promulgating the images in their plays and poems.

As a one-act play set in 1798, *Blood Money* inevitably evokes *Cathleen ni Houlihan* (1902), Yeats and Gregory's iconic opening show for the

Irish National Theatre. Like the Ascendancy authors Yeats and Gregory, who empowered their cultural nationalism by lionising Protestant republicanism, Markievicz selected a setting that also obliquely authorised her own participation in nationalist theatre, as well as theatrical nationalism. The domestic drama of Yeats and Gregory challenged a bourgeois male audience – Michael Gillane, though implicitly all strapping young men of Ireland – to sacrifice lucrative dowries and charming colleens for the promise of Cathleen's kiss of immortality: 'They shall be remembered for ever …/The people shall say their names for ever', Cathleen sings.[42] *Blood Money* instead imagines what Cathleen – and Ireland – would have been like if she had had the courage to act on her own behalf. Befitting the vision of a socialist republican, *Broken Dreams* also thematises the economic dimension of betrayal, a recurring topic in Markievicz's editorials excoriating the Free State, as we have seen, but also a common motif in nationalist drama, from Padraig Colum's patriotic play *The Saxon Shillin'* (1902) to Sean O'Casey's tragi-comedy *Juno and the Paycock* (1924).

Blood Money opens, then, not in a comfortable home but on the outskirts of a wood, where three members of the British army bicker and fret over the corpse of a tortured United Irishman, Donal McCarthy. The soldiers' disagreements stem from the cultural divisions of the British occupying forces; the brutally efficient British officer Sergeant Ames and his mercenary native-born troops Dan Mullen and Andy MacGuinness distrust one another because of historic enmity. In tracking the native characters' reasoning in joining the British army and justifying the dictates of law and order, these early lines also betray Mullen and MacGuinness's uncommon resemblance to the green-suited soldiers of the new Irish Free State. Savouring the promise of fifty pounds while mollifying his surging guilt, MacGuinness brazenly insists to Mullen, 'What's a corps [*sic*] at all but a dead rebel? And what's our trade at all but making corpses of them'?[43] Mullen, however, can only parrot a tentative response: 'Sure wasn't I only obeying orders? And didn't Sergeant Ames say that the man was a danger to king and country?' They are hardly rewarded for their moral questionings, for Ames displays open contempt towards both in his response, 'You dirty Irish savages. Sticking pigs is what you're paid for, not jawing to your superiors, and by God, it makes an educated man sick to listen to you.'

With the entrance of Peggy O'Byrne, a slim girl whose dark hair, pale skin, and outer garments suggest her affinity with the Dark Rosaleen, the dramatic action begins. Quiet and demure, bearing poteen and a basket brimming with fine cakes and fowl, Peggy arouses in the men visions of domestic pleasures or forbidden sexual promise; as an audience well-schooled in nationalism would know, however, this Dark Rosaleen will demand physical potency far beyond consummation or a kiss. Although each man preens and struts in an effort to capture her attention, only the Sergeant is flattered with her proud notice and her stern tongue. She berates him – and his men – for her people's suffering: burning roofs and dead sons are hardly evidence of British civility in her mind. As Ames mutters, 'They are a strangely ungrateful people these Irish', Peggy asserts the colonised perspective: 'It's a poor thing when the best that's left to a people is a corpse and a decent burial.'

Befitting a play about betrayal, Peggy's purpose is not to chide her conquerors or claim the body of the dead United Irishman. It is only when she disparages Mullen's betrayal, however, that Ames recognises her Irish gift of deception. In contrast to *Cathleen ni Houlihan* or 1798 fiction, such as Alice Milligan's romances-across-the-border published in the *Shan Van Vocht*, feminine political agency is never fully transferred to the men at this moment of dramatic tension.[44] Peggy, like Markievicz, proves handy with a gun. Although she uses her feminine charms to placate and beguile Ames, she resorts to militant, masculine means to achieve her ends. Soothing Ames and pleading for privacy to explain herself, she entreats, 'Come here till I give you what you've earned. You've earned it well.' Pulling out a gun that she has hidden under her mourning shawl, she shoots him while offering a motherly prayer, 'God rest his soul. He was a dirty villain but maybe there's some poor soul praying that he may return to her safe.'

The play closes, as tragedies do, with punishment for the mercenary men, but not before reversing some of the most gendered imperatives in the nationalist canon. Turning on its head the notion of 1916 as a staged performance, the final scene reveals that our 'dead rebel' is no corpse but an uncommonly capable actor, feigning death and biding his time until his comrades could attack the British forces and release him. As Peggy modestly unties his ropes and Donal struggles to his now liberated feet, we witness another astonishing reversal, this time the characteristic overtures of the *aisling* poems: instead of a gallant hero liberating the captive woman, we witness Dark Rosaleen taking care of business herself. We also learn that rebels in the woods have ambushed the turncoats, killing MacGuinness and capturing Mullen. Granting Mullen rebel due process – the opportunity to explain his actions – Donal ultimately issues unsparing judgement, placing Mullen among the progeny of Judas. Donal's description of Mullen's perfidious betrayal, a comparison that depends upon an audience's deep-seated Christianity, as well as its understanding of the symbolism of the Easter Rising, thus closes with another oblique commentary on the moral values of the Free State: read against Markievicz's 'memories' of 'traitors' such as MacNeill and Griffith, Donal's dismissal of Mullen suggests the retributive fate of Free State leaders as well.

If *Blood Money* challenged the Free State ideal of passive femininity, Markievicz's three-act drama *Broken Dreams*, which was first produced posthumously in December 1927, more broadly repudiated the moral foundations of this 'Fraud State' by challenging the centrality of the family.[45] As we have seen in her editorial on citizenship, Markievicz sometimes channelled her resistance to the Free State by eroding the State's conservative emphasis on clan and kin. No less caustic about the prim ideology of the time, poets and playwrights of the literary revival, such as Yeats and O'Casey, articulated their disappointments by dreaming up coarse, bawdy women such as Crazy Jane or Bessie Burgess. Similarly disillusioned about the Free State's 'fatal addiction to respectability',[46] Markievicz nonetheless imagined another scenario that would challenge the centrality of family while validating feminine militancy too.

In the play bill for the Republican Players' production, *Broken Dreams* was described as 'an incident in the Black and Tan war', though, as Van Voris notes, its tone and argument clearly stem from the 'discontent, pain, and loss during civil war'.[47] In its narrative structure and theatrical tension, *Broken Dreams* recalls the informer plot of O'Casey's *Juno and the Paycock*, as well as his scathing indictment of 'respectable' nationalism, in dramatising a female activist wounded by the treachery of false republicanism. In keeping with O'Casey's realistic drama, which could never quite repress the Victorian melodramas of his youth,[48] Markievicz composed a play bent on exposing fraudulent political posturing while suffused with histrionic poses of another kind, from the Victorian mama as overstuffed as the settee in her parlour to her Cumann na mBan daughter who falls for the wrong sort of man. Where O'Casey stages vacuous and hollow Diehards whose commitment to Mother Ireland supplants a responsibility to Irish mothers, Markievicz redirects the spotlight on an amiable female Volunteer, Eileen O'Rourke, a New Woman with gun whose modernity in dress and action challenges the pieties of traditional nationalism far more than O'Casey's characters ever did.

Broken Dreams is nevertheless hampered by an irreconcilable will to dramatise Markievicz's 'three great movements' in one modest piece. A New Woman play, it features the plight of a female officer who resists marriage for the right reasons (republican values), marries for the wrong ones (mistaken notion in her husband's shared commitment), is charged with the murder of her turncoat spouse and, finally, is acquitted of the crime when a member of the IRA reveals that Seamas was executed because he was a spy and an informer. A materialist critique of the middle-class values of Eileen's mother and aunt, women who cluck over Eileen's 'disgraceful' activism and whose comfortable homes vividly contrast with the impoverished hovels that Eileen and her comrades must endure, *Broken Dreams* exposes the grim existence of the West in a style sympathetic to the people. A republican tragedy containing a republican romantic sub-plot, it offers a parallel commentary on women's domestic and political choices. As Eileen disastrously chooses the 'sensuous', 'suspicious' Seamas and consequently suffers from his traitorous, self-interested behaviour, her comrade Bride falls in love with the serious, self-controlled Eamon while composing and typing spy reports. The play, though imperfectly realised, nevertheless offers a powerful corrective to O'Casey's representation of women and republicanism. As Declan Kiberd points out, O'Casey's plays cynically indict republicanism for victimising the poor in order to justify his absence from the revolution.[49] Conversely, Markievicz's play censures cynics like Seamas in an effort to legitimate the anomaly of feminine participation at all. Hence, for Markievicz, the theme of duty allows her to enliven the robotic voices of republicanism in O'Casey plays.

Markievicz's 1925 play *The Invincible Mother* recalls another classic of the early Irish National Theatre, Augusta Gregory's *The Gaol Gate* (1906), a one-act tragedy that, as Mary FitzGerald has remarked, derives a 'reversal of expectation' from the nationalist perspectives in the play.[50] In Gregory's dramaticisation, two illiterate country women

– a mother- and daughter-in-law – endure a day of vacillating emotions as they seek to discover what has become of Denis Cahel, their son and husband. Fearing the worst – betrayal – they return home from the gaol gate in Galway triumphant over his death: 'Tell it out in the streets for the people to hear, Denis Cahel from Slieve Echtge is dead ... Denis would not speak, he shut his mouth, he would never be an informer.'[51] In Markievicz's rewriting of the informer plot, we meet a mother, Mrs Fagan, who has trudged to Mountjoy Jail in Dublin to learn the fate of her Fenian son. The British police officers hope to extract information from her or encourage her son to betray his comrades. This 'old schemer', however, has other plans; like the women in *The Gaol Gate,* the invincible mother reverses the detectives' (and the audience's) expectation about maternal love, for it turns out her son's life is less important than his pursed lips.

If Markievicz's characters in *Broken Dreams* invigorate O'Casey's hollow republicans, her indomitable Mrs Fagan in *The Invincible Mother* poses a feminist challenge to Gregory's politically passive women. In *The Invincible Mother*, for example, Markievicz erases the feminine weakness and conflict evident in Gregory's play. Whereas Mary Cahel and Mary Cushin cannot read and consequently differ over the meaning of the letter in the long blue envelope nestled under Mary Cahel's cloak, Mrs Fagan, the invincible mother, proves a worthy opponent to British spies. Even Detective Smith recognises this when he tells his superior, Commissioner Mallon, 'She has more Irish than English but she is no fool.'[52] Although the detectives hope to use her maternal appeal to elicit her son's confession, Mrs Fagan outmanoeuvres and outsmarts both men in getting precisely what she came for: the promise of her son's silence. Unnerving the men with her elliptical answers to their leading questions about Jim's past ('He was always a good son and attended to his duties regular', she quietly tells them),[53] she quashes their hopes when they discover, to their horror, her own political agency. Thinking a mother would fight for the life of her son and perhaps the promise of a young grandchild to nurse on her lap, Smith and Mallon are surprised to learn she is after one thing: 'the kiss of a hero', the assurance that her son has refused to be 'a stag and an informer'.[54] This final scene, with Mrs Fagan's Electra kiss, inevitably revives the incestuous maternal appeal of Cathleen ni Houlihan. Her final words, as well, evoke the unseen 'girl with the walk of a queen':

'Now I'll walk the long road to Mullingar, my old feet dancing to the tune of my light heart, and tell the neighbours before I die that my son stood true.'[55]

Bonnie Kime Scott has suggested that this dramatic close brings to mind not only Cathleen, but Con herself: in calling for youthful male sacrifice, the Invincible Mother has adopted 'a role that Constance Markievicz actually assumed with her Fianna boys and with the troops on St. Stephen's Green'.[56] Such a reading implies that Markievicz functioned more as muse than militant in the wartime years. Markievicz's journalism, in fact, poses challenges to reading this Invincible Mother as Cathleen. As Markievicz drew on her two personae – the Ascendancy Countess and the Red Revolutionary – to mask the subversive content of her gardening columns in *Bean na hÉireann*, so too the very potency of the Invincible Mother depends upon her ability to use – and undercut – traditional expectations about her gender, class and age. Markievicz's dramaturgy, more tellingly, contests Scott's reading of *The Invincible Mother* as a poor imitation of Yeats and Gregory's play. In transforming the passive icons of nationalist drama into robust republican women, Markievicz enhanced both cultural and political nationalism: improving upon the hasty, sometimes lazy characterisations of better-known playwrights, she also corrected and cursed Free State nationalism by staging women's roles in the earlier revolution.

Conclusions

In the spring of 1922, during a tour of the United States, Markievicz delivered a speech that sought to remind foreign allies of the sacrifices of Ireland's recent war; it was a lecture suffused with memories of women:

> The work of the girls of Cumann na mBan was fine. It was they who carried messages backward and forward from the different communities; it was they who supplied the troops with the necessaries of life, and who sought information for them and brought it to them. It says a great deal for their cleverness that so few of them were ever caught, and many of the best girls were never even suspected.[57]

As Markievicz makes clear in these remarks, the very success of political women involved in guerrilla conflicts made their achievements that much more vulnerable to historical amnesia. It is no wonder her nationalist writings of the 1920s were suffused with the imperative of remembrance. Despite her insistence that 'Easter Week comrades don't fall out: they laugh and chaff and disagree',[58] Constance Markievicz's journalism and drama of the 1920s indicate that memory could serve as a trenchant theatre of battle to ensure that Irish nationalism would not become a 'solid, cast-iron thing' but rather an arena where 'a jumble of people of all classes, creeds, and opinions'[59] could debate the future of the Irish state.

Chapter 6

Representations and attitudes of republican women in the novels of Annie M. P. Smithson (1873–1948) and Rosamond Jacob (1888–1960)

Danae O'Regan

Introduction

Both Annie M. P. Smithson and Rosamond Jacob, Irish novelists of the first half of the twentieth century, were nationalists, committed republicans, and active members of Cumann na mBan and of Sinn Féin. Both felt the need to transmit their belief in Ireland's republican future to a wider public, and both chose the novel form in which to do it. Both were devoted to the ideals of the Gaelic League,[1] were thoroughly anti-English and were ardent admirers of the heroism of the young men and women of the Easter Rising of 1916. They wrote on similar nationalist themes, reflecting contemporary events and attitudes through the eyes of their female protagonists. Here, however, the similarities end, and a glance at some of their most nationalist novels reveals strong differences of approach. This is not surprising. In social background, religious beliefs and attitudes towards feminism they were worlds apart. Jacob was prosperous, agnostic, feminist and suffragist. Smithson, an adult convert to Catholicism, was a traditionalist, concerned with women's situation in Irish society, but no suffragist. A comparison of their backgrounds and of their novels can therefore give an interesting insight into the diversity of attitudes among republican women of their time, while the popular success of Smithson's novels and the relative failure of Jacob's allow further conclusions to be drawn about the attitudes and expectations of the general reading public. Both writers throw considerable light on the social, political and religious attitudes of Irish middle-class society from 1916 through what has come to be known as 'de Valera's Ireland'.

Rosamond Jacob was from an unusual family. Her parents came from a Waterford Quaker background, but were openly agnostic and nationalist and practised the Quaker belief in the equality of the sexes.[2] From an early age she was familiar with Irish history, literature, myth and folklore. She and her brother joined the Gaelic League in 1906, where they began to learn Irish. In 1911 she was already active in the republican movement, in Inghinidhe na hÉireann, collecting the signatures of 'Irish Marys' in protest against the official tribute for the Dublin visit of Queen Mary,[3] and she organised the earliest branches of Cumann na mBan in Waterford. By 1914 she was a strong suffragist, sufficiently important to be forcibly removed from a meeting of John Redmond's supporters.[4] At the Sinn Féin Convention of 1917 she intervened successfully to ensure the inclusion of women in all future discussions of the constitution of a free Ireland.[5] Her political activities continued through the War of Independence, and in 1921 she was briefly imprisoned for allowing typists from the republican publicity department to use the house of Hanna Sheehy Skeffington,[6] where she was staying. Her pacifist convictions, however, prevented her taking part in armed action. Instead, she joined the White Cross,[7] investigated and reported on British atrocities, served on numerous committees, and was an indefatigable writer of letters and articles in the Dublin and Waterford press. She had difficulty, nevertheless, in finding publishers for her longer works.

Annie Smithson was born in Dublin into a relatively prosperous Unionist family. Her father, a barrister, died young, and the family was plunged into 'genteel poverty'.[8] Her schooling was patchy, with no exposure to Irish history or culture. When she was 21 she trained as a nurse in England, and then returned to work in Ireland. She says in her autobiography, *Myself – and Others*, published in 1944, 'I do not know when I became an Irish Irelander, it seemed to have just come naturally to me',[9] but by 1913 she was a convinced republican. In 1916 she was disappointed to be far from the centre of action, nursing in

Ballina, a remote market town in Co. Mayo, where she 'did not know one real Republican',[10] but by 1918, back in Dublin, she canvassed for Sinn Féin, 'talking over doubtful voters, and doing any odd job which was useful to help on the Cause'.[11] In 1920, when a Health Visitor in Waterford, she joined Cumann na mBan, and gave lectures on first aid and bandaging. When the Civil War came she was back in Dublin as a Red Cross nurse with the republican side, finding herself at one stage in the thick of the fighting in Moran's Hotel. Imprisoned after an attempted expedition to bring 'surgical dressings and the help of nurses and doctors'[12] to republicans in the west of Ireland, she was released only after she threatened to go on hunger strike. Her career as a novelist started in 1917 and was to continue, with a considerable number of published works and huge success, until 1946.[13] Jacob's publications, however, were few: two novels for adults, one for teenagers, a biography of Matilda Tone, written in the style of a novel, and a historical work, *The Rise of the United Irishmen*.[14]

Given their nationalist affiliations and their personal commitment to republican activity, it is not surprising that the first novels of both authors, Smithson's *Her Irish Heritage* (1917) and Jacob's *Callaghan* (1920), should have been based on recent political events, namely the run up to the Easter Rising. Irish nationalism continued to be one of the major subjects in all of Jacob's and most of Smithson's later works – there are, in fact, very few of Smithson's novels where there is not some element of nationalism, if only a brief patriotic outburst from one of the characters faced with English incomprehension of the Irish situation, or a strongly expressed interest in the Irish language.[15]

Her Irish Heritage

Smithson's *Her Irish Heritage* can be seen as providing a template for the treatment of nationalism in all her later writing. Dedicated 'to the Memory of the Men who Died. Easter, 1916', the emotions it expresses were in tune with contemporary post-Rising outrage – the novel is a hymn to the republican dead, their politics and their religion, and to the glory of the 'blood sacrifice'. Her enthusiastic insistence on the need to be an 'Irish Irelander', speaking, dressing and buying Irish, had been typical of popular nationalism since the nineteenth century, and by this stage the suggestion that to be genuinely Irish one should also be Catholic had gained ground.[16] Both elements form an integral part of all Smithson's patriotic novels, as does a strong anti-English prejudice. Where Jacob accepted, but also attempted to analyse these aspects of republicanism, Smithson's talent was to integrate them into a romantic novel in a way which carried contemporary readers along on a wave of emotional enthusiasm.

The plot of *Her Irish Heritage* is simple. It tells the story of Clare Castlemaine, the orphaned daughter of a Catholic Irish mother and an English father who was technically Protestant, but in fact an atheist. Clare has been brought up an English agnostic. After her father's death she leaves England to live with Irish Catholic cousins and discovers her double heritage of Catholicism and republicanism. Her love for and marriage to a friend of her cousins, one of the few young men in the novel who survive the Rising, provide, in theory, a romantic interest, but are very briefly sketched. A secondary plot deals with the spiritual suffering of a more experienced woman, a recent convert to Catholicism, who is betrayed by the man she is to marry and almost loses her faith; this affair, too, is linked to the republican theme.

Smithson's dislike of all things English is clear from the start. Although Jacob's diaries show similar anti-English prejudice, even down to the same dislike of English accents, criticism is muted in her novels. In *Callaghan*, for instance, the hero's anti-English obsession is shown to be excessive, if understandable, and the ridiculous, but 'really good-hearted',[17] pious Englishwoman, Angela French in *The Troubled House*, is treated gently. However, in Smithson's novels, from *Her Irish Heritage* on, even the best representatives of the English are invariably cold, reserved and unable to express their emotions. Their ignorance about Ireland and indifference to the disastrous role they played in its history are frequently stressed. Working-class characters are depicted as vulgar, loud, crude, ignorant, incapable of under-standing any form of spirituality, and always possessing the ugliest of local accents. The anti-English prejudice is made even more clear by the fact that representatives of the Irish working class tend to be portrayed as naturally more refined, more open to spirituality, never vulgar, speaking in beautiful, soft, Irish voices. Even the slum dwellers of Dublin, who are shown as living at the lowest possible level, are treated with sympathy. *Her Irish Heritage* sets this pattern of criticism, and it is frequently repeated. Although later novels present Smithson's criticisms more subtly, the same prejudices remain throughout her work, and, judging by the success of her writing career, were perfectly acceptable to large numbers of readers in the Ireland of the first half of the twentieth century.

As a contrast to the hated English, both Jacob and Smithson tend to provide a lovable Irish family. In *Her Irish Heritage* we meet Clare's cousins, the Blakes, a family of 'Irish Irelanders', through whom Clare will finally come to her 'Heritage'. They are warm, lively, idealistic, tolerant, devoutly Catholic republicans, and it is clear that they are intended to represent all that is best in the nationalist tradition. Through them Smithson introduces her readers to the Gaelic League. Shamus, a 25-year-old solicitor's apprentice is, according to his brother's joking introduction, 'the new spirit of the age – the reincarnation of the Celt – the great revival of the Gael! ... He would not condescend to speak your Saxon tongue – the very accents would choke him!'[18] His Gaelic League friends are described. Norah Donovan is a school teacher. 'After her day at school she devotes most of her evenings to the study of Irish, attending Irish Classes and lectures, and giving a helping hand to others ... a great dancer, – Irish dances of course! – sings very well.'[19] She is dressed in 'a plain, "tailor-made" coat of Donegal tweed',[20] and is obviously a supporter of Irish home industries. Another friend is Eithne Malone. 'Music is her speciality, particularly the old Irish music ... She is a hot Sinn Féiner.'[21] The presentation of Gaelic League ideas is unsophisticated, but a love of Irish culture and, above all, an interest in the Irish language will remain an indication of the 'Irishness' of Smithson's favourite characters throughout her work.

Callaghan

There is a similar pattern in Jacob's novels. In *Callaghan*, for example, Jacob presents Callaghan's cousins, the Quinlans, as a contrast to the more formal and snobbish Protestants – in her later works 'Irishness' tends to be taken for granted in the main protagonists, and, although extremely important, is only one aspect of a relatively complex personality. The contrast between Jacob's portrayal of the Cullen family in *The Troubled House* and that of the Blakes in *Her Irish Heritage* is striking. The Cullens are, like the Blakes, Catholic and strongly republican. They are open, warm and outgoing. But Jacob also insists on the complexity of their characters, revealing possible flaws, while Smithson's Blakes are without blemish. The two authors were obviously writing for very different audiences. It is interesting that with *Her Irish Heritage* Smithson immediately became a best-selling author, while Jacob, after *Callaghan*, took ten years to find a publisher who would risk publishing *The Troubled House*, and then it had to be an English publisher.

Despite the greater complexity of her characters, however, Jacob's protagonists do have the same preoccupations as Smithson's. All her main characters are republicans, most are anti-English. In *Callaghan*, for instance, the eponymous hero is a returned Irish-American, intensely anti-British, who returns to his village in 1913 to work for the republican cause. The plot is exciting, and reflects elements of Jacob's own experience,[22] but what is especially interesting is that, intermingled with the lively, patriot plot, an almost documentary portrayal of pre-1916 attitudes, and much entertaining social comment, there is a strong thread of perceptive and very modern analysis of the growth of republican violence and of the character of one of the many men who experienced no doubts about the right to kill in a just cause.

The background to *Callaghan* is a country area with the social/political/religious divide that was typical of the period. Jacob, like Smithson, interprets it as a divide between warm, spontaneous, lower-middle-class, republican Catholics and snobbish, upper-middle-class or aristocratic Unionist Protestants. Although the novel is told in the third person, and recounts the story of Callaghan's life in the republican movement, much of the interest centres on Frances Morrin, and characters, events and environment are seen almost entirely through her eyes. She is very much like Jacob herself, from a prosperous, liberal family, and not obliged to work for a living. She is nevertheless progressive and independent in her ideas, and takes equality with men for granted. When *Callaghan* opens she is living with her married brother, a doctor, and his wife, supported, presumably, either by him or by inherited money. When she later moves to Dublin to work for the suffrage movement she moves in with an elder sister. The framework within which she lives and functions is therefore traditional. However, her psychological independence from the norms of her society is established in the first chapter. She is shown travelling in the same railway carriage as Callaghan, and spending time admiring his good looks, assessing his less attractive points, and analysing her own reactions to him with a dispassionate coolness that would have been inconceivable in one of Smithson's romantic young ladies. When a bigoted Northern Protestant and an equally anti-Catholic Southern clergyman start up a dialogue about 'southern laziness', 'the shiftlessness of the Celtic nature', and 'the paralyzing influence of the Romish priesthood',[23] she goes so far as to wink at Callaghan and initiate a lively conversation in which they turn the tables on their fellow travellers with tales of the iniquities of Northern Protestantism and the Orange Order. A sizeable section of *Callaghan* is devoted to Frances' involvement with the suffragist movement. She is easily persuaded to join, finding that she had, in fact, 'been a suffragist ever since she was old enough to know what a vote was'.[24] She becomes 'assistant secretary to a suffrage society and unofficial helper to other revolutionary organisations'.[25] Her work for the movement reflects Jacob's experience – she learns:

> to mind offices, to organise poster parades, to sell at jumble sales, to help in getting up dances, to sell flowers and vegetables at Aonach na Nodlag, and keep the accounts of the stall straight, to cook soup by the gallon for locked-out workers and their children, to distribute leaflets, to ignore the attentions of little boys in the street, to do propaganda work among poor women without losing her temper, to heckle speakers at public meetings, and to make speeches herself.[26]

The suffragist life ends with Frances' marriage to Callaghan, but the reader assumes from the fact that she is married in a registry office and insists on paying half the cost of the wedding celebrations that her character remains unchanged. It is through the character of Callaghan, not Frances, that the growth of militant republicanism is mainly illustrated, but her reactions inevitably have an influence on the reader's reactions to events. Callaghan is both republican and socialist, and these ideals are shared by Frances. He is, however, unlike her, convinced that violence is the only way forward. He is happy, without regret, and possesses a 'matter-of-fact manner'.[27] She analyses her feelings, and decides that she will have to accept these facets of Callaghan's character (and, by implication, of republicanism in general). His deadly hatred of the English and ruthless cruelty in the cause of nationalism are a result of years of brutal repression – and he will never change. Although *Callaghan* is obviously a highly patriotic novel, and a sympathetic portrayal of the attitudes, aspirations and suffering of ordinary people in the years running up to 1916, Jacob also highlights the less attractive characteristics of the republican ethos, and she does not hesitate to reflect them in her hero. Callaghan's excessive hatred of the English, his longing for a fight, no matter what the outcome, and his unrepentant cruel streak are depicted, not as noble patriotism, but as possible weaknesses in his character. This results in a complex and rounded hero, but in 1920 it must have disturbed the ordinary reader, who was used to a more romantic and unquestioning approach to the patriotic theme, and this may well have contributed to the novel's lack of popular success.

Portraying women and nationalism

One of the most noticeable differences between Jacob's and Smithson's portrayal of the nationalist world is that whereas the religion of Jacob's characters is not relevant to their politics it is hard not to assume from Smithson's novels that republicanism and Catholicism are inseparable concepts. Smithson was, however, extremely proud of her father, who, although a Protestant, and a graduate of Trinity College (the traditionally Protestant university of Dublin), had played an active part in the 1867 Fenian uprising, and in *Her Irish Heritage*, as in many later novels, she reminds the reader of Protestant participation in the nationalist movement. One of the Gaelic League group at the Blakes' gathering is Robert Hewson, 'a North of Ireland Presbyterian – and an out-and-out Home Ruler. His ancestors fought with Henry Joy McCracken "in the days of yore", and the family have always been good Irishmen down to the present time'.[28] The religious situation in Ireland is explained to Clare by the man who will later become her husband: 'As far as religion goes it just happens that Catholicity is the religion of the majority in this country in spite of every possible effort on England's part to make it otherwise … and so most Irishmen are Catholic – but many a Protestant has been a better Irishman than his Catholic fellow countryman'.[29]

Once again, this is a fairly crude history lesson, but the theme that Protestants, and Trinity students in particular, can be republicans does recur in other novels, most strongly in *The Marriage of Nurse Harding* (1935). In Jacob's work, although most Protestants are Unionist, there is no suggestion that Catholicism and republicanism are necessarily linked. Indeed Callaghan, reflecting Jacob's personal views, claims that 'England could never have held us for the last three centuries without the church's help.'[30]

Active participation in the republican movement was, as can be seen from her memoirs, an important element of Smithson's nationalism. In *Her Irish Heritage* the events of the 1916 Rising are evoked briefly and from a distance – just as Smithson herself was in Ballina at the time of the Rising, the two heroines of the novel are isolated in Co. Clare, and news takes time to filter through. The deaths of two of the Blake young men are, however, significant. Shamus, the out-and-out IRA militant, like Callaghan, is, in true 1916 tradition, eager to die for his country: 'Do you think I would grudge the last drop of blood in my body if it was for Ireland! ... I often and often think what an honour – what a joy unspeakable it would be for me, if I could only say when Death called me – "This is for Ireland."'[31] And his death is exemplary, 'He lifted his hand to the salute and saying quite loudly and clearly – "For Ireland!" he fell back – dead!'[32] His brother, Tom, a medical student, and a moderate and caring young man, is shot while trying to save the life of an English soldier, and buried 'with the Flag of the Irish Republic wrapped round him'.[33] In some of her later novels Smithson tends to suggest that the stirring events of 1867, 1916 and the Civil War have been largely forgotten in a more materialistic Ireland, but, as in Jacob's works, such events continue to be remembered by true nationalists with nostalgic pride.

Jacob's second novel, *The Troubled House*, written by 1928 but published in 1938 after much difficulty in finding a publisher, also deals with the question of active participation. It is to a large extent a novel of ideas, and its ambiguous attitude towards the use of violence, even in the republican cause, as well as its unconventional ideas on women, sexuality and art, provide a marked contrast to Smithson's more simplistic views. It is, at first glance, another patriotic romantic adventure story. The plot, set this time in 1920, concerns the members of the Cullen family and their attitudes towards republican activity during the War of Independence. Again, the situation is seen through a woman's eyes. Maggie Cullen, the narrator and heroine, is older than Frances Morrin, and married with three sons. Like Frances, she is from a prosperous professional background – her husband is a solicitor – but has unconventionally progressive ideas and attitudes. As in *Callaghan*, the first chapter of *The Troubled House* stresses modernity and independence. Maggie is introduced as a woman returning from a three-year-long stay in Australia, having left her husband and family to take care of themselves while she went to look after a seriously ill sister and allow her niece to finish her studies at college. Again as in *Callaghan*, the reader is given the impression of a remarkably clear-sighted and intelligent woman, but one wonders what the reaction of the traditional Irish reader of the period may have been towards this decidedly liberated wife and mother.

Maggie is a firm republican, but has always avoided discussing politics with her husband, a Catholic Home-Ruler. When she returns to Dublin she finds her three sons deeply involved, each in his own way, with the republican movement. Theo, the eldest, named, 'in a fit of enthusiasm,'[34] after Theobald Wolfe Tone, is secretary of a Sinn Féin club, but, like Jacob herself, a convinced pacifist. Liam, the second son, has been thrown out of the house by his father because of his active participation in the IRA. Roddy, the youngest, is still at school, but this does not prevent him carrying messages and ammunition for Liam's company. The story follows Liam's activities with the IRA, leading up to involvement in the 'Bloody Sunday' murders,[35] after which he falls ill and has to go into hiding. Theo, a committed republican despite his pacifism, carries a message for Liam which leads to involvement in an armed attack, and eventual arrest, torture and condemnation. He will die unless Liam hands himself over in his place. Theo is eventually saved by a daring IRA raid on Kilmainham Jail, but the family's problems are not over – Liam, now active again, accidentally kills his father in an ambush. The novel ends with the mother accepting Liam back into the family and the truce with England bringing about the end of political hostilities. It seems clear that the Cullen family is intended, at least in part, to represent Ireland itself, but this point is not laboured.

Although the novel tells an exciting, not to say melodramatic, story of disguise, safe houses, ambushes, Black and Tan raids and IRA assassinations, its nub is, however, not the dramatic action, but a study of the moral questions involved, the motivation of the various participants in the drama, and, above all, the continuing theme, stronger in this novel than in _Callaghan_, of whether violence is ever justified. Jacob, having suffered raids herself, such as the one on Hanna Sheehy Skeffington's house which led to her imprisonment, and having worked for the White Cross, was writing again from experience, and the plot, which starts on 'one of the last days of October when ... the newspapers were still full of the death of Terence MacSwiney',[36] is, as in _Callaghan_, largely documentary. The actions she describes reflect the reality of life in Dublin at the time, and her readers would have recognised the truth of her accounts of curfews, raids and ambushes, and of the public reaction to 'Bloody Sunday' and the massacre at Croke Park.[37] They would also have recognised and been able to identify with the problems of a family divided between Home-Rulers and Republicans.[38] What the ordinary reader might well have found less immediately accessible, and thus less attractive, would have been the lengthy passages of discussion and analysis, much longer than in _Callaghan_, in which Maggie questions her own, her husband's and her sons' motives, beliefs and behaviour. As in _Callaghan_, Jacob's characters, although representative of contemporary attitudes, are not oversimplified. Maggie realises that her husband's anti-republican, pro-British prejudice is not simply a result of his class and background, but that he is also jealous of her love for their IRA son. Theo, the admirable, calmly strong, pacifist son, who echoes Jacob's own beliefs about war, is described by his mother as also being at times 'terribly dogmatic'.[39] In spite of his convictions, he cannot prevent himself longing for action and enjoys his participation in the IRA attack. Liam, the active IRA soldier, is an equally ambiguous character, and it is never entirely clear to what extent he is motivated by patriotism or, as his father claims, by 'a blend of obstinacy, gang-feeling, and love of excitement'.[40] He is also not as tough as he suggests. Where his pacifist brother discovers an unwelcome pleasure in violent action, Liam, the committed soldier, suffers a breakdown after murdering an English officer in front of his wife. He has none of Callaghan's 'matter-of-fact' approach. Even Maggie, tolerant and non-violent as she is, finds herself, when watching the funeral procession of the assassinated British officers, experiencing unaccustomed emotions: 'All the evil in my heart woke at the sight of it. I felt a thrill of exultation at the sight of the long line of coffins';[41] and after Theo's arrest and torture 'hatred, like a fever, burned through [her], and it seemed a perfectly righteous passion'.[42] Maggie knows that her own feelings are as complex as those of her sons, and Jacob uses this character to transmit a sympathetic analysis of three current attitudes to Irish politics: her husband's Home Rule convictions, Liam's IRA militancy, and Theo's non-violent but equally courageous republicanism. Although the rightness of commitment to the republican cause is never questioned, and the novel is an exciting and emotional patriotic adventure story, long passages of reflective analysis of this commitment, and Jacob's refusal to offer easy answers to the moral dilemmas of the time, may have helped to delay its publication and prevent it, too, achieving any extensive popular success.[43]

A comparison between *The Troubled House* and another of Smithson's most nationalist novels, *The Walk of a Queen*, may also help to explain why Smithson experienced such huge popular success, whereas Jacob's writing remained comparatively unknown. Both novels are set at more or less the same period, Terence MacSwiney's death occurring towards the end of *The Walk of a Queen*, and at the beginning of *The Troubled House*. They have the same Dublin background, realistically portrayed, and the same theme of British and IRA military action in the city and around. Both use the dramatic background of a divided family, men on the run, safe houses, false names and disguises, all recognisably real elements of the contemporary scene, and at the same time, of course, invaluable ingredients in an adventure story. Smithson, however, while giving graphic descriptions of Black and Tan and Auxiliary raids, plays down IRA violence, mentioning 'the Croke Park shootings',[44] but avoiding any reference to the IRA action that preceded them, while Liam's horror at his part in the 'Bloody Sunday' assassinations is an integral part of Jacob's more objective approach. The backgrounds may be realistic, but Jacob's plot can at times seem far-fetched, and Smithson's is truly melodramatic. Both novels are concerned with two devoted brothers who are working for the IRA. One brother falls in love with an artist. But where Jacob's Nix is an example of a 'new woman', the 'artist' Smithson's Desmond falls in love with is the traditional Mata Hari-type femme fatale of fiction, who ensnares her lover and persuades him to betray his colleagues. Again in both novels, the 'good' brother ends up in jail, and can only be saved by the other taking his place. In

Jacob this gives rise to discussion of whether it is Liam's moral duty to give himself up in exchange for his brother, and the dilemma is resolved by an IRA-organised escape. In Smithson the brothers are identical twins, and the traitorous Desmond saves virtuous Anthony by a Sydney Carton-like last minute substitution.[45]

Another element that is common to both novels is a woman character who plays an active role in the republican cause. As mentioned above, both Smithson and Jacob were members of Cumann na mBan. Smithson was happy to serve in the traditional and subordinate role of a nurse, albeit a highly courageous one who, during the Civil War action in Dublin, was extremely angry to be sent away to safety before the soldiers she was nursing.[46] Geraldine Moore in *The Walk of a Queen*, described as 'a very modern young person with an intensely independent mind',[47] performs gratefully the equally traditional role of transmitting messages. '"I was wishing", she says, "that I could do something – no matter how small it was – for Ireland"',[48] and she takes an office job which allows her to act as messenger and go-between. There is obviously a potential for drama in this dangerous occupation, but Smithson chooses not to exploit it. She gives the dramatic action to the male protagonists, and Geraldine ends up married to, rather than the active militant partner of, a Callaghan-type leader. In *The Troubled House* Jacob reintroduces both Callaghan and Frances. He is still a strong IRA leader, she still a supportive, but non-participating wife. Jacob does create a new, more modern, woman militant, Kate Ryan, who is an active and authoritative IRA leader but she appears only briefly, to organise Theo's escape from Kilmainham Jail. Callaghan treats her as an equal, and leaves the organisation of the jailbreak entirely to her, pointing out that 'Kate's got out of the Joy (Mountjoy Prison) herself before now',[49] but, unexpectedly, Jacob, like Smithson, does not choose to develop this character further.

Finally, in both novels there is a woman character who has an affair with a British officer. In Smithson, this woman marries her handsome British officer, is miserably unhappy with him, sees the error of her ways and redeems herself by conversion to republicanism and risking death in the IRA cause – truly the stuff of romantic fiction. Jacob's Nix, the unconventional artist, has a casual affair with her officer simply to shock her friends, and characteristically refuses to feel any guilt.[50] It is easy to see which author is more in tune with the Catholic, republican morality of Ireland in the 1920s.

The very different approach of the two authors to the question of Irish republicanism is clear. Smithson's remains emotional and uncritical throughout all her work. It is also hard to imagine that Jacob, if she had written more novels, would have changed her attitude of objectivity and analysis. Her biography of Matilda Tone, *The Rebel's Wife*, continues the pattern. Matilda is portrayed sympathetically. Jacob had studied closely Tone's diaries and letters to Matilda, and found there a strong woman who was loved and respected as an equal, and to whom she could in all honesty attribute the qualities of mind of an intelligent modern woman. History also showed her to have been a devoted, traditional wife and mother, who supported her husband in every way, held the family together during the long periods when they were apart, and kept his memory alive after his death. She is, in Jacob's interpretation, fully willing to sacrifice her own happiness for the good of the nationalist cause, and sends Tone off to France saying 'It would break my heart if I felt that I stood in the way of you keeping your promises to your friends and to Ireland.'[51] However, as in both *Callaghan* and *The Troubled House,* Jacob is not uncritical of the nationalist heroes – Tone's selfishness in deserting his family to lead his patriot life is seen as a fault, albeit an understandable one, and Matilda receives little support from the United Irishmen after his death. In this novel, however, the women seldom voice criticism, and Jacob's comments on the evils of war, and in particular on the suffering it causes to women, are given to male characters. There is nevertheless an interestingly feminist dialogue between Matilda and Mary, Tone's sister, when they are waiting for news of Tone and the French invasion:

> At intervals Matilda told herself that her situation, unbearable though it might seem, was nothing out of the way, women had endured it constantly since the beginning of time. One day when they sat sewing together, she said this to Mary, and Mary's reply was prompt. 'More shame for the men. Oh, not The (Theobald Wolfe Tone) – The is only doing his duty – I mean the lords and conquerors who force honest men to be rebels … Women will suffer like you as long as they can make us, 'tis time women took some of the power themselves, and stopped them.' 'Oh! I wish they would!' said Matilda. 'There should be women in parliaments.'[52]

These words, which echo Jacob's feelings exactly, were doubtless less unacceptable to an Irish audience in 1957 than they would have been in the 1920s, when she was looking for publishers for her earlier novels. There is also an inevitable sense of nostalgia about *The Rebel's Wife* which makes it easier reading than *Callaghan* or *The Troubled House*, with their emphasis on contemporary problems. It had a certain amount of critical success, and won a Women Writers' Award, but Jacob had still not managed to please the general public, and, to her disappointment, its commercial success was limited.[53]

Conclusion

A comparison between Jacob and Smithson, strange as it may initially seem, does provide the modern reader with an interesting insight into the Ireland of the first half of the twentieth century. Both authors look at republicanism first and foremost from the woman's point of view. Smithson is a traditionalist. In spite of her own involvement in militant action in 1920, she tends to project an image of republican women as subsidiary to male activists, always devoted and admiring. Her heroines are independent and strong-minded working women, but in the republican context they accept without question the ideology and actions of the male combatants. Jacob gives an alternative view. She studies the same areas, writes on the same themes, believes in the same political cause, but where Smithson's approach is emotional hers is analytical and intellectual. Her heroines are, like herself, both republican and feminist, liberal and free-thinking. Even when accepting the traditional role of wife and mother they insist on their right to independent thought and action. Interestingly, though, their actual involvement in militant action is still limited – both authors are here providing a realistic reflection of their period.

The popular success of a writer depends, however, not only on subject matter and skill in writing but on finding the right audience for her/his work, and this Jacob failed to do. Smithson's novels reflect a simple, unquestioning belief in the absolute virtues of republicanism and Catholicism, expressed in the style and framework of the romantic novel at its simplest. She was read with delight by teenage girls, by their mothers and grandmothers, and even, it seems, by some men.[54] Jacob, on the other hand, was aiming at a more sophisticated public.

She obliged her readers to consider whether perhaps everything was not perfect even in a republican world. Encouraging her readers to question, rather than accept, the received beliefs of their time, she provided no easy answers. It was Smithson's perspective on republicanism, as on other social questions, which appealed to the general public. Sadly, pre-1960s Ireland was not ready for Jacob's writings, and she never had the success that she felt her work deserved.[55]

Chapter 7

'And behind him a wicked hag did stalk': from maiden to mother, Ireland as woman through the male psyche

Jayne Steel

Iconic maidens and mothers

> Pain, disaster, downfall, sorrow and loss!
> Our mild, bright, delicate, loving, fresh lipped girl
> with one of that black, horned, foreign, hate-crested crew
> and no remedy near till our lions return from the sea.[1]

> Lord thou art hard on mothers:
> We suffer in their coming and their going:
> And tho' I grudge them not, I weary, weary
> Of the long sorrow – And yet I have my joy:
> My sons were faithful, and they fought.[2]

Writing in *Women and Nation in Irish Literature and Society (1880–1935)*, C. L. Innes explores the many and varied ways in which 'as a nation … both in English and Irish writing and representation, Ireland [was] frequently allegorized as a woman'.[3] Moreover, claims Innes, these 'allegories [were] ones in which family or gender relationships [were] metaphors for political and economic relationships'.[4] Obviously, English, or British, and Irish iconographic images of Ireland as 'woman' served different political purposes. For instance, during the nineteenth century, English cartoons often 'depict[ed] Hibernia as a virginal maiden, threatened by Fenians and other Irish radicals and sorely in need of rescue by paternal John Bull',[5] whereas 'Irish portrayals of their country' tended to 'fall into two categories: those that depict Ireland as maiden, and those that depict[ed] her as mother'.[6] However, from 'Hibernia, Eire, Erin [and], Mother Ireland [to] the Poor Old Woman, the Shan Van Vocht, Cathleen ni Houlihan [and] the Dark Rosaleen', the main differences between nineteenth-century English and Irish portrayals of Ireland as woman concerned 'their perception of the nature of the [male] enemy and [male] would-be rescuers'.[7]

By the turn of the nineteenth century, the birth of the Irish Republican Army fed into an allegorical figure that, as mentioned, had long been important for the Irish psyche, especially the male Irish psyche. This figure was the 'personified mother'.[8] Here we recall a poem entitled 'The Mother' that was composed by the doomed Irish republican rebel Patrick Pearse while he was awaiting execution by the British for his involvement in the 1916 Easter Rising. Pearse's male ventriloquism of an Irish mother's voice summons an archetype, that being a 'good Mother Ireland' who, paradoxically, like the Virgin Mary nobly suffers the emotional trauma of the execution of her son in the name of a 'higher cause'. This said, it might be argued that the poem contains another archetype: the 'bad Mother Ireland'. Such a dualism can be traced back to the figure of the banshee and 'the figure of Fedhelm', the latter being 'a personification of sovereignty and prophetess of death'.[9] So, although the mother in the poem is 'weary, weary / Of the long sorrow', she has 'joy' because her 'sons ... fought'. Perhaps, then, Pearse's maternal ideal is an incarnation of two extremes: the good *redemptive* mother and the bad *fatal* mother. Linked to these ideas, the following investigates how, from maiden to mother, iconographic images of Irish nationalist women have been appropriated by modern British and Irish popular culture or, more specifically, British and Irish popular culture created by male authors and filmmakers who in turn attempt to supply a 'realistic' narrative of the Troubles (a euphemism for the ongoing political conflict within the north of Ireland). Central to my argument is the notion that, when it comes to portraying nationalist women as being the quintessence of Irishness, the British and Irish male unconscious have much in common. Further, I suggest how universal archetypes are often embedded within politically inspired iconography. The remainder of this section offers a methodological framework for a more in- depth discussion of Irish nationalist women portrayed within specific texts that deal with the Troubles. These texts include, for example, *Odd Man Out, The Psalm Killer* and *The Whore Mother.* From Irish maiden to Irish mother, from 'good' women to 'bad' women, and the blurring of this dichotomy, the last section to this chapter moves towards its conclusion with recourse to Lacanian psychoanalysis. Here I consider the various ways that male representations of Ireland as woman navigate a specific dilemma: the imagining of a desire that is ultimately maternal and demands devotion as well as self-sacrifice. Closely linked to questions about the male imagining of maternal desire are certain *repeated* images of the Irish nationalist female that are found in popular culture and are symptomatic of a more universal scapegoating for the Irish as well as the British male psyche and for the citizens of every 'Ireland', be they nationalist or loyalist.

During my research, I long debated the distinction between 'Britishness' and 'Englishness', or indeed 'north-of-Irishness' but, ultimately, found it impossible to maintain these types of boundaries, especially in relation to the North of Ireland where many individuals within the loyalist community consider themselves to be British as opposed to English or Irish. Moreover, following the suggestion made by the Runnymeade Trust's report on the Future of Multi-ethnic Britain (*The Parekh Report*) that Britain was a coded term for whiteness, it could be further argued, as exemplified by the loyalists, that whiteness is also coded as Protestant and centred on the Queen of England, English institutions and literature.[10] 'British' is a signifier, then, that binds together the Scottish, the Welsh and the loyalist Northern Irish in a subordinate relationship to the white Protestant Englishness of which they form an inferior copy. Although I am not suggesting that subjects from the North of Ireland, which, of course, include nationalists, consciously adopt Britishness, or vice versa, I am suggesting that, at both a conscious *and* unconscious level, national identities feed into one another, as do male identities in relation to women. Thus, underlying more glamorous yet deadly female images, such as the 'dangerous seductress' or femme fatale,[11] woman as Ireland has a long and, in some respects, 'universal' history which predates the more overtly political British or Irish nationalist iconography and relates to the structure of myth and witchcraft whereby 'witchcraft confronts us with ideas about women, with fears about women, with the place of women in society ... with women themselves [and] with systematic violence against women'.[12] Indeed, allegorical figures manifested by the Furies and the witch-whore named Acrasia, seen by recent critics of the Renaissance as being Spenser's allegory of the seductive charms of Irish women in *The Faerie Queen*, do of course form part of this history.[13]

When considering the reciprocal nature of British and Irish national identities, Jacques Lacan's 'neologism' concerning 'extimacy' is useful because 'extimacy ... neatly expresses the way in which psychoanalysis problematises the opposition between inside and outside, between container and contained [whereby] the Other is "something strange to me, although it is at the heart of me"'.[14] Here we can again recall Patrick Pearse who navigated a similar extimacy in terms of his own identity and parentage: his status as an Irish nationalist with an English father and Irish mother. However, when it comes to the appropriation of iconography by popular culture (vis-à-vis representations of Irish nationalist women), the Other is not merely the British for the Irish, or the Irish for the British, but, very often, the woman who is good *and* bad *and* always 'to blame'.

If Pearse supplies an iconographic yet fantastic, or 'false', representation of Irish nationalist women, then where, it could be asked, might we locate 'true' representations? Well, nowhere. It is, I argue, not possible to discredit one set of ostensibly 'false' representations and replace them with another set of ostensibly 'true' ones. On the contrary, it seems to me that *all* representations are to a greater or lesser extent 'fictive'. Representations of woman as Ireland within popular culture do not emerge as a unified whole from the individual psyche of a novelist or film-maker, but are instead selected, reworked then repeated from a range of pre-existing, archetypal *and* iconographic images. Selected, reworked and repeated thus, these images are used within popular film and fiction to both consciously and unconsciously express specific cultural fixations that fashion, nourish and articulate shared male anxieties about women. Like nationality qua extimacy, representations of woman as Ireland do not spring from a psychological vacuum but exist in tandem with other representations that evoke different meanings and different histories. For instance, Patrick McGee, an Irish republican ex-prisoner, has called recently on Irish writers, both male and female, to 'square up to their task of writing their own accounts of the Troubles in fiction'.[15] Claiming that 'what is needed is a realistic picture', McGee suggests that writing the unadorned truth in realist fictions will help to negate the negative stereotypes and replace them with real people.[16] While acknowledging the genuine desire for understanding that no doubt lies behind McGee's demand, I am more sceptical about the ability of literary realism to accurately reflect or transparently reveal reality. Indeed, literary realism has always relied on stereotypes, creating many new ones of its own. Further, precisely because of its claims on 'reality', *social* realism has become one of the most effective vehicles of ideology, the most persuasive popular means of constructing 'how it is' through drawing on the recognisability of certain characters, scenes and situations. The recognisability and plausibility of certain characters depends on their adherence to narrative conventions of plot and motive, and their similarity to characters in other fictions. Generally, realist fiction, or indeed film, does not change perceptions about reality; instead, the dependence on recognisability tends to entrench received ideas. Thus, irrespective of an author's or film-maker's political stance or desire to supply 'truth', there is no access to real Irish nationalist women in realist fiction and film.

All this said, there is a case for arguing that reader/spectator positioning affects the ways in which texts are received, and this positioning depends upon the complexity of desires, identifications and shifting allegiances that are the experience of most readers and audiences. While I am not dismissing this 'other voice', I maintain that, no matter how sophisticated the reader or audience, many popular novels and films depicting the Troubles depend upon and require some kind of stereotypes. And, ultimately, stereotypes, like universal archetypes, like iconographic figures, are pleasurable things – readers and audiences tend to like them because they are reassuring (good Irish women) or thrilling (bad Irish women) or both. Just because the audience or reader is often astute enough to realise that they are being confronted with a stereotype, and that 'novelists [are] using ... stereotypes [to] follow ... a common script', this does not mean that the stereotype's fictional or affective force is weakened.[17] In *The Sublime Object of Ideology* Slavoj Zizek reminds us how 'the cynical subject is quite aware of the distance between the ideological mask and the social reality, but he none the less insists upon the mask'.[18] For Zizek, 'cynical distance is just one way – one of many ways – to blind ourselves to the structuring power of ideological fantasy: even if we do not take things seriously, even if we keep an ironical distance, *we are still doing them*.[19] Thus, an intelligent and informed reader/spectator may 'know' that real Irish nationalist women are not either passively good or punitively bad 'but still' believe that they are passive and punitive.[20] The remainder of this chapter illustrates the above ideas with specific examples taken from British and Irish popular culture. Although, as I have argued, there is no access to real Irish nationalist women through these examples, they do repeat an archetypal and/or iconographic history that can be traced. And through charting certain aspects of their development, it should be possible to follow some of the shifts in perceptions of woman as Ireland as the current Troubles accelerated. Bearing in mind that the Provisional IRA (a major catalyst for the proliferation of images of Irish nationalist women) did not exist until the late 1960s, it might prove useful to briefly locate some iconic images appropriated and revised by popular culture that predate this period.

Demons of the cause and angels in the house

> He trusted her with important missions. Had she been a man, she would have been on the staff. But she was woman. He looked at her magnificent head and body, and the fact that she was a beautiful woman indicated one profound condition. She was pledged to her body: to her great beauty; to all the splendour of her hair, her exquisite countenance, her flesh in its woman's form; and the passions and impulses which that body dictated to her. And because of this condition, which he imagined was authentic, he never trusted her with the innermost secrets of the Organization, nor with missions of a particular kind. And never would.[21]

Taken from F. L. Green's novel, *Odd Man Out* (1945), the above quotation shows an IRA man musing upon the 'body' of an Irish nationalist woman, Agnes, who is, rather aptly, renamed Kathleen for the film version. I will return to both the novel and the film later but at this point it is worth noting one or two iconographic, not to mention patriarchal, origins that seem to have fed into Green's text. For instance, Louise Ryan has observed that 'war is a highly gendered experience which is both informed by and informs constructions of masculinity and femininity'.[22] Clearly, F. L. Green's Irish nationalist woman, who could 'never [be] trusted with the innermost secrets of the Organization', epitomises such 'constructions'. As an illustration of this idea, Ryan describes how the IRA commander Liam Lynch, during the War of Independence, refused to pursue a relationship with a young woman because he was committed to the cause of Ireland embodied in the iconic female figure of Roisin Dubh.[23] For Ryan, 'the fact that women were expected to take second place behind the cause of Irish freedom, symbolised by Roisin Dubh, suggests something of the gendered nature of the Republican campaign'.[24] Moreover, claims Ryan, the legend of Dubh highlights 'the celibate [male] devotion not to real women but to a mythical, virginal woman' or, perhaps, maiden.[25] A similarly gendered discourse is found within the poetry of W. B. Yeats who, as noted by Innes, advocated an ideal-isation of a 'desirable [Irish] female body' that did 'not speak about politics'.[26] Perhaps, then, Green's 1947 Irish female is a revival of a revival of the Irish nationalist icon named Deirdre, a figure who 'appeared as the central character in over thirty-five Irish plays' from 1859 to 1950.[27] As observed by Innes, although Deirdre 'has much in common with Cathleen ni Houlihan, and no doubt the two images reinforce one another' as fantasy women 'to be fought over', the figure of 'Deirdre is passive and sorrowing [and] emblematic of characters [that were] develope[d] … into embodiments of the dichotomy between masculine and feminine'.[28]

These points suggest how male representations of Irish nationalist women tap into misconceptions about women generally, relying on an archetypal, iconographical and 'patriarchal' framework that is common to most Western countries. 'It still shocks me', claims a female IRA volunteer, 'that I have two battles to fight – one against the Brits and secondly with the men of my own organisation'.[29] Dealing with these issues is Margaret Ward's comprehensive history of Irish nationalist women and Irish republicanism, *Unmanageable Revolutionaries*, the title of which is taken from a conversation between W. H. Van Voris and Eamon de Valera in which the latter suggested that women are at once the boldest and most unmanageable revolu-tionaries.[30] The tribute gives with one hand, only to take away with the other; female revolutionaries are credited with an excessive, undisci-plined bravery: they are *unmanageable*. Relying as it does on the use of the term 'man' to denote the universal subject, the term 'unmanageable' suggests that there is an un-man-like or inhuman quality about female revolutionaries. They are credited with something extra, an added boldness or bravery that is not subject to the standard of rationality or discipline that determines men, 'man', or male identity in general. As such, these women are invested with something that 'man' lacks: an excess of 'unmanageableness' – an excess of power. Like 'the warrior-queen Maeve' depicted by Yeats and Synge, these women 'act wilfully and imprudently'.[31]

The bold and unmanageable female is both the means and the goal of the revolution: the beauty of her unmanageable power is recognised as the power *to* manage. This is the power necessary to subject the citizens of a new state, a power that finds its iconic image and meaning in the martyrdom of the bold and unmanageable female revolutionary. Since the French Revolution, at least, 'Liberty' leads the people with blouse unbuttoned and breasts exposed, the very image of sexual desire (the maiden's breast) or bountiful social good (the mother's breast) to be had after the revolution. Unfortunately, though, for the women who survive, female 'unmanageability' justifies women's unequal status. Consequently, as Ward's book shows, when women were not unmanageable 'loose cannons', they had a secondary, auxiliary or domestic function in the republican movement.

Ward begins her study with The Ladies' Land League (1881–82) and details its development into Cumann na mBan, which commenced in 1914. Cumann na mBan was formed to encourage women 'to act as auxiliaries for the old Irish volunteers, the forerunners of the current IRA'.[32] With the advent of the current Troubles in 1968, women began to be recruited into the IRA itself and this, in turn, prompted the desire for representations of, in essence, more 'dangerous' fantasy figures. In British film, these figures are apparent within, say, *A Prayer for the Dying* (1987).[33] While making this film, British director Mike Hodges 'added' a 'deadly' yet desirable Irish nationalist woman, who shows no compunction about murdering a male comrade, to Irish screenwriter Martin Lynch's original script. And, in 1992, British director Philip Noyce supplied a repetition of Hodges' remorseless female with *Patriot Games*.[34] We can find traces of these femmes fatales within Irish iconography in the figures of Deirdre and Cathleen ni Houlihan. For instance, Innes claims that each of these figures summons 'the dual character of helpless woman and *femme fatale*, [a] witting and unwitting [instrument] of destruction'.[35]

However, it seems to me that as well as being highly selective in their appropriation of one aspect of this 'dual character', the femme fatale, Hodges and Noyce also repeated woman as Ireland in the role of universal archetype, the same archetype repeated by male constructs of Deirdre and Cathleen ni Houlihan – that being the lethal yet highly sexualised fantasy female of male desire. This might help to explain why, in 1993, an Irish screenwriter and director, Neil Jordan, gave us *The Crying Game* and a woman as Ireland called 'Jude' who is a psychotic, sexy and murderous member of the Provisional IRA.[36] Played by the British actress Miranda Richardson, Jude epitomises Zizek's notions about stereotypes and 'the structuring power of [male] fantasy'. After all, the film's Provisional IRA male recruits are shown as being more 'level-headed' and, in the case of a character named Fergus, more 'humane'. So, even though 'commonsense' dictates that Irish nationalist women are not really lethal, gun-toting, sex-bombs, within both British *and* Irish popular culture their ideological mask offers the cynical (male) subject a pleasurable thing.

Prior to the recruitment of Irish nationalist women into the Provisional IRA, fictional representations of them affirmed their auxiliary status to men. These representations appealed solely to the domestic and romantic stereotypes that characterised popular films like Carol Reed's *Odd Man Out*.[37] In this film the iconically named Kathleen is first seen in her domestic role as the good nurturing woman: the 'tea maker' for the male IRA activists. She then becomes a good desirable woman whose 'great beauty … exquisite counte-nance … and flesh in its woman's form' sparks the romantic interest for James Mason's IRA protagonist, Johnny.[38] This romance, and the fact that James Mason is British, plays the crucial function of human-ising an IRA activist for a British audience. As John Hill writes in his essay 'Images of Violence', this sort of moral technique is 'quite a typical characteristic of the British cinema'.[39] According to Hill, 'if violence is generally seen to be negative and destructive, it is also contrasted with emotions and actions which are positive and constructive'.[40] Moreover, claims Hill, 'for the British cinema, it is typically romantic love, the home and the family which fulfil this [more positive] function'.[41]

At the same time, however, romantic love can fail. This happens in *Odd Man Out* when the possibilities of romantic love apply a tragic gloss to Johnny's terrorist activities. Johnny has to pay a high price for his commitment to the republican cause. His activities thwart his relationship with Kathleen and destroy any hope he might have for a conventional family life. Here, Kathleen functions symbolically as the supreme good that terrorist activity is willing to sacrifice to attain its goals. Irish republicanism, and by association nationalism, is therefore exposed as being totally destructive of human value even, or especially, for the activist himself. Hence, *Odd Man Out* reveals how popular culture can appropriate and subvert the former ideological and Irish nationalist iconographic importance of Kathleen: like the figure of Deirdre, she must resonate with Cathleen ni Houlihan and become a metonymy for woman as Ireland so that Johnny's Irish nationalist actions can be seen as utterly self-negating.

Within *Odd Man Out*, Kathleen's symbolic function also serves a demand arising from British perceptions about post-war Irish republicanism. Analogous to an ideal image set in place for female identifications, this symbolic function is, in fact, *both* Deirdre *and* Cathleen ni Houlihan, virgin daughter and suffering mother, a twofold ideal resurrecting what Edna Longley terms 'Woman-Ireland-Muse'.[42] Modern popular culture preserves this ideal within images of southern rather than northern Irish women. The cult status awarded to *Riverdance* and Edna O'Brien's status as a woman who 'personifies all that is mystical and spiritual about the Celts' illustrates this tendency.[43]

But, it might be claimed, neither Green's nor Reed's 'Kathleen' is a 'real' mother and, therefore, although she might symbolise virgin daughter, she cannot symbolise Mother Ireland. I dispute this. After all, at a metaphoric level, her domestic and nurturing role with regard to her IRA 'sons' can surely be associated with 'mothering'. And, at the end of the novel, her symbolic role as 'Mother Church' as well as the 'Blessed Virgin Mary' creates a similar duality.[44] For instance, on the final page of *Odd Man Out,* she and Johnny are held at bay by the police. At this point, the badly injured Johnny 'hear[s] her voice softly uttering his name and waylaying the terse shouts from the police'.[45] 'He felt her arms about him', writes Green, 'encircling him warmly and supporting him'.[46] While Johnny senses 'the ecstasy of [her] possession' (note the religious as well as sexual connotation of the word 'ecstasy' here), she shoots him then herself.[47] The reader is informed that her deadly action arose from 'love' not malice.[48] Indeed, her quasi-divine status absolves Johnny of his paramilitary 'sins'. Thus the final line of the novel has the old priest saying how she 'redeemed' Johnny.[49] Her roles as the 'Blessed Virgin Mary' and 'Mother Church', or Irish mother and Irish maiden, tie in with Innes's observations that 'by the late nineteenth century, two female images had become potent, social, political and moral forces in Catholic Ireland – the images of Mother Ireland or Erin and the Mother of God, often linked through iconography to Mother Church'.[50] Further echoing this dualism, Ryan argues that 'nationalist iconography [has] simultaneously draw[n] on the emblematic young virgin or the motherly old woman' to stand for, respectively, 'the mother Mary [and] Mother Ireland'.[51] And, although such hallowed female images 'demanded the allegiance of men and women alike … it was for women that they provided models of behaviour and ideals of identity'.[52] With *Odd Man Out*, then, we have a blatant example of how Irish nationalist iconography can be hijacked and repackaged by British popular culture for British consumption and for patriarchy in general.

In tandem with more deadly and seductive representations of Irish nationalist women, such as those created by Hodges, Noyce and Jordan, British and Irish contemporary popular culture repeats the figure of the domestic auxiliary who, in turn, complements earlier Irish nationalist iconographic images of Mother Ireland. More recently, however, instead of being a romantic heroine, the domestic auxiliary now often endures the reality of the violence of the Troubles: Jordan's inclusion of Jude's violent death being a typical example. It is through her suffering body and cries of pain that the Troubles are now 'realised' in realist fiction. Once more, the origins of these images appropriated by popular culture seem to reside within Irish nationalist iconography. Indeed, Ryan has identified 'the interconnections between the iconography of rape and the actual incidents of violence, especially sexual violence, against women during the War of Independence'.[53] Ryan explains how this violence impacted on male identity whereby 'both armies of men' – that is, the British army and the IRA – 'were keen to assert their own chivalry and to depict the enemy as disorderly and unmanly'.[54] However, while acknowledging that violence against Irish women was also perpetrated by Irish men, especially punishments inflicted on women who fraternised with British soldiers, Ryan suggests that 'the symbolic "rape" of Ireland by Britain and the actual rape of Irish women by British soldiers formed part of a continuum which defined Irish woman as victim, British man as aggressor and Irish man as protector.'[55]

Although it might not be surprising that the legacy of sexual and physical violence against Irish women has been appropriated and 'rewritten' by popular culture, it is perhaps surprising that such a legacy has been appropriated by feminist fiction that seeks to challenge 'the normalisation of terror' within the domestic sphere in the north of Ireland where, according to Michelle E. Evans, 'though it is the second largest cause of killings … violence against the female has largely been overshadowed by sectarian violence'.[56] This situation is not particularly new, a fact made evident by Christina Loughran, whose 1985 report observed how 'in West Belfast … violence meted out by the security forces [could be] link[ed] to domestic violence'.[57] For Robin Morgan, 'everyone deplores the public violence in the history of Ireland [but] no one spends much time on the private violence'.[58] In her book *The Demon Lover*, Morgan cites as an illustration the case of 'the woman whose man poured a kettle of boiling water over her vagina just before she went into child-birth labour'.[59] While it is difficult to imagine anything more horrifying, or anything that could have been better chosen to shock and appal a reader, for other feminist writers the effectiveness of such examples tends to diminish with repetition. As Eve Patten writes:

> In addition to its dubious role in producing a collective identity, the effectiveness of confessional realism as part of a political lobby is debatable. The reality of (most) women's subjection is evident. Men smash bottles. Wives get hit. Relationships fail. Women get lonely and victimised and denied. Channelling this material into fiction may be considered an important aspect of a consciousness-raising incentive, but only up to a finite point at which it becomes reflexive and counter-productive.[60]

Patten suggests that the horrifying examples of male violence that repeatedly appear in feminist social realism eventually have the effect of conventionalising the reality of the suffering they are meant to expose and document. Thus, domestic brutality becomes, like woman as Ireland, yet another generic feature. Indeed, British author Chris Petit's novel *The Psalm Killer* (1997) describes the apparently common fate of the suffering Irish wife and mother.[61] This woman is the partner of a character named 'Big John' who, Petit narrates, 'poured a kettle of boiling water over her vagina, when she was pregnant, and afterwards just laughed and told her to stop making a fuss'.[62] While such repetitions certainly seem to bear out Patten's point, they also beg another question, it seems to me. What does it mean that female characters, especially Irish nationalist women, have to bear the burden of the 'reality' of the Troubles in such a sexually agonising way? As these anecdotes are repeated, and begin to function in a purely aesthetic manner, even social realism follows the trajectory of Gothic fiction. What further horrors will need to be related in order to provoke the requisite 'consciousness-raising' outrage?

To summarise so far, this section has charted some of the ways in which so-called realist film and fiction appropriate and revise universal archetypes together with British and Irish iconographic images of redemptive, fatally seductive, or suffering Irish nationalist women. The next section develops these ideas but draws upon Lacanian psychoanalysis to discuss more ambivalent representations of woman as Ireland, specifically Mother Ireland, found within Irish nationalist iconography as well as in British and Irish popular culture in the context of 'Troubles' novels. Such novels, often 'thrillers', have long been castigated by writers such as J. Bowyer Bell for ditching 'reality' in favour of a 'formula' designed to 'entertain rather than enlighten'.[63] As stated earlier, though, it is not my task to discredit one set of ostensibly 'true' representations (or realties) with a set that are ostensibly 'false'. Instead, I want to explore further why certain archetypal and iconographical images of woman as Ireland are appropriated and revised by British and Irish popular culture in a way that expresses specific cultural, inherently male, fixations.

The Irish mother of suffering and desire

At a literal and conscious level, or a metaphorical and unconscious level, many contemporary novels about the Troubles contain a Mother Ireland who is both marginal yet mainstream, extimate yet intimate, good yet bad, and frequently the abject maternal Other to male identity. Here, Mother Ireland offers male identity an inverted mirror image, a mercurial image that affects specific ideological viewpoints about women, especially Irish nationalist women. These viewpoints emerge through the imagining of a maternal Other that coincides with various failed attempts to establish an ideal, predominantly male, identity; an imagining that coincides with the Lacanian question: 'What does the (m)other want from me?' For our purposes, the question is, more crucially, 'What does the (m)other want from her Irish nationalist son(s)?'[64]

Linked to these issues, in a documentary film titled *Mother Ireland*, the late Mairead Farrell, a member of the Provisional IRA who was executed by the SAS in Gibraltar, supplies a feminist discourse that criticises Irish nationalist iconography of Irish women. 'Mother Ireland,' says Farrell, 'get off our back.'[65] The film's director, Anne Crilly, claims that '*Mother Ireland* explores the development and use of iconographic images which personify Ireland as woman in Irish culture and nationalism'.[66] For Pat Murphy, Mother Ireland is not a positive image. 'It's wrong,' insists Murphy, 'to call a country after a woman because [this creates] images of being penetrated or ploughed or won [by] male pioneers [and] the rape of a country [is then equated with the] rape of a woman.'[67] However, Rita O'Hara discusses an alternative image of Mother Ireland, as a 'woman who is clinging [and] sends her sons out to fight for her'.[68] This more destructive and vengeful Mother Ireland is prepared to sacrifice her sons for the 'Cause' and can be traced back to, for example, Yeats's play called *Cathleen ni Houlihan* where, according to Innes, 'Cathleen ni Houlihan celebrates death [and] summons men to die for an abstract notion of the four beautiful green fields and idealised concept of Ireland'.[69] Yeats's ambivalence towards Mother Ireland is endemic to British and Irish popular culture where there is an annexing of the Irish mother who is scapegoated on every side and the mother as Other who is always 'the one to blame'. Thus, for the male Irish republican paramilitaries within British author Campbell Armstrong's 1987 novel *Jig*, Mother Ireland signifies 'a darkly brooding mistress … the motherland', a woman who is 'an abstraction called the Cause' to whom the men are 'married' even though they are aware that 'freedom from the marriage lay … in the last divorce of death'.[70] Another British author, Alan Judd, portrays Mother Ireland as a gaggle of 'dirty … harridans' who spike British soldiers' 'tea [with] urine'.[71] And Mother Ireland fares no better when rewritten by Irish male authors. Thus, Eugene McCabe summons a Mother Ireland who is 'the bloody mid-wife of regeneration, a ruthless animal with dripping mouth and glassy merciless eyes';[72] while James Carrick describes her as 'an old whore … hungry for men'.[73] This type of female image is encoded even more terrifyingly within Irish author Sean Herron's novel *The Whore Mother*, where, paradoxically, an Irish nationalist and iconographic Mother Ireland is appropriated by Irish popular culture to become the 'whore mother' revenger, a primordial and perpetual force.[74]

Herron's protagonist and hero, Johnny McManus, falls foul of the Provisional IRA, escapes across the Irish border to the countryside where he encounters a sexual nightmare. This happens after he becomes dangerously sick, plunges into unconsciousness, then is rescued by an older woman called Kate Burke. At first, he mistakes Kate for his real mother. This is made clear when he regains consciousness and discovers himself alone in a strange bed from where he 'hears kitchen sounds' and imagines that he is 'a child in his own bed'.[75] He finds the bedclothes 'deep and warm and reassuring', and regresses to a state of infantile desire for the maternal figure: '"Mammy", he said … That was comforting too. His mother was close. He would call. He could hear. She would hear. She always heard'.[76]

For McManus, the desire of the maternal other is grotesquely played out when he becomes her helpless 'invalid … Child'.[77] His hallucinating of his real mother's voice is displaced by Kate's voice, words and unfathomable physicality.[78] 'How old was she?', wonders McManus, 'Forty? Forty-five? Fifty? It varied by the day'.[79] Yet, at an unconscious level, Kate *is* his real mother in terms of a figure of Oedipal desire. This becomes evident when McManus regresses into being 'a mother's boy' whose new 'mother cradle[s] his head and put[s] her bra-less nipple to his hungry mouth – Child, she called him'.[80]

At first, though, Kate is not a punitive Mother Ireland. We read that she 'gently … drew him and lay on her back, guiding his hand to her breasts [while] his senses birled in his head'.[81] 'I'm a country', she tells him, 'feel my hills'.[82] And McManus obeys, 'grasp[s] her breasts frantically, [feels] the hard nipples in his palm, [takes] them in his fingertips … , pull[s] his mouth from hers and suckle[s] the nipples like a feeding infant'.[83] But McManus is an 'insatiabl[e] … resentful son and jealous lover' to the woman who is a 'mother in the day, mistress at night'.[84] And the reader is left in no doubt as to her symbolic status when she tells McManus: 'the name they call me is Cathleen the Whore-Mother'.[85]

With Kate, Herron repeats a universal archetype, as opposed to an Irish nationalist icon, an archetype evoking a 'phallic' mother whose desire at both a literal and metaphorical level is rapacious, deadly and determines the fate of the male subject. This happens when McManus leaves Kate for 'Mother England' and a young woman called Brendine who is a 'happy little mother'.[86] Having once again eluded the Provisional IRA, he imagines freedom whereby he can 'leap from past to future, from land to land, from skull of bard and thigh of chief to daughter company to mother company, leap from foot to foot, from old woman to young woman'.[87] But, at a psychological level, he cannot escape the desire of Kate who has been deserted by her male 'child'.[88] 'We were born to self-destruction, child', says Kate.[89] Her words are an omen, a hint of her status as the apotheosis of the 'desire of the (Irish) mother'. Now, the good mother of desire mutates into the bad mother of desire and, for McManus, this inflicts a tormenting memory of 'consuming lust' that he tries to 'exorcise' through sex with Brendine.[90] 'She was not Kate', he thinks, 'these were not Kate's strong cunning thighs, Kate's hips not these little hips were for lustful, luxurious wallowing, this little belly was not Kate'.[91] In spite of his injunction to 'get out of my head, Kate. Let me go Kate', he cannot, or will not, escape the imagined desire of Whore–Mother– Ireland and the question: 'what does the mother want from me?'[92] Ultimately, Kate symbolises the determining matriarchal figure that presides over the novel's final and fatal event. Here, at the same moment that he is shot dead by a Provisional IRA assassin, he acknowledges Kate's absence as the presence of her inevitable vengeance when he screams: *Piteous Jesus Kate no no no not you Kate*.[93]

With this denouement, Herron shows McManus being punished for his treachery against Mother Ireland who is both Kate *and* the Irish republican cause. As a bad Irish son, he suffers maternal retribution, a retribution created by and, perhaps, displaced from, an Irish male author's imagining of Mother Ireland's unquenchable desire. This desire is, in turn, transferred to McManus's assassin whose hallucinations ensure that although McManus has been sacrificed for the cause, the desire of Mother Ireland remains alive and unabated. 'What does the [m]other want from me?' The assassin's recital of a prayer to the 'Motherland' implies that she wants, or he imagines she wants, further male sacrifice:

'O, Sacred Heart of Jasus!
We pray to Thee today,
To aid our sufferin' Motherland upon her bloodstained way.
For loyalty to serve her,
For strength to set her free,
O, Sacred Heart of Jasus!
We send our prayer to Thee![94]

Conclusion

In this essay, I have suggested how representations of woman as Ireland within British and Irish popular culture have appropriated and revised British and Irish iconography to repeat universal archetypes, such as the passive and virginal maiden, or the ferocious and sexualised mother, or a hybrid of these two figures. I have also suggested how popular culture reinforces and normalises notions about violence against women. Importantly, many of the male-authored contemporary texts discussed have been shown to reveal more about the male psyche than about 'real' Irish nationalist women. Manifested and repeated by both British and Irish male authors within so-called realist film and fiction, literal and metaphorical representations of woman as Ireland ensure that Irish nationalist women remain extimate and other to male identity. Further, as mentioned at the start of this chapter, I have argued that the pleasure produced by 'literary realism' is, paradoxically, often the 'fantasy' of the stereotype. When it comes to woman as Ireland, this fantasy psychologises, apoliticises, demonises, sentimentalises and eroticises the imaginary Irish nationalist woman who is sometimes good, sometimes bad, yet always the 'one to blame'. For those who still insist that readers can recognise and dismiss stereotypes, I want again to recall Zizek's ideas concerning 'cynicism as a form of ideology'. Hence, of course, we all 'know' that believing in metonymic constructs of Irish nationalist women is the same as 'following an illusion, but still [we] are doing it'. One reason we are still doing it is a continuing fascination both with woman as Ireland and with the Troubles, a fascination that in turn produces more and more stereotypes which all make claims to reality but are, inevitably, imaginary. At both a psychological and physical level, woman as Ireland is unattainable. Yet, precisely *because* she is unattainable, more and more, albeit illusory, representations of Irish nationalist women will continue to be repeated within popular culture.

Finally, the correspondences between British and Irish depictions of Irish nationalist women and their 'sons' imply that, irrespective of nationality or political affiliation, iconographic images have a tendency to become universalised into a series of quite bizarre female archetypes. These archetypes illustrate the way in which British and Irish male identities feed into one another at the level of a deep-rooted psychologising about woman as Ireland.

Chapter 8

'We had to be stronger': the political imprisonment of women in Northern Ireland, 1972–1999

Mary Corcoran

Although one in twenty prisoners who were detained for politically related offences in the course of the conflict in Northern Ireland were women,[1] the precise nature of the regimes in which they were confined, and the distinctively gendered dimensions of the punishment of women as political prisoners have only been infrequently addressed in the literature about the prison conflicts.[2] However, although the role of women republican prisoners attests to the prison campaign as a shared struggle, the nature of their experiences was as specific, localised and mediated through gender as were the experiences of the men. Similarly the forms of resistance to penal regulation and discipline that they developed prompt significant questions about the contexts in which they negotiated the considerable constraints on their ability to act politically and collectively in penal disciplinary structures which have customarily emphasised highly individuated forms of correction. This essay gives a brief historical outline of the development by female republican prisoners of a self-sustaining political structure while confined, despite many different administrative strategies to curtail them, between December 1972, when the first woman was interned, and February 1999, when the last female political prisoner was released on licence under the terms of the Good Friday Agreement of 1998. It traces the distinctive characteristics of the women's prison struggle, as they were borne out of their negotiation of, and resistance to, intersecting gendered and political modes of penal punishment. In exploring these sometimes contradictory and paradoxical positions, this account draws on the narratives of women who were imprisoned in Armagh Prison between 1972 and 1986, and between 1986 and 1995 in Mourne House, HMP (Her Majesty's Prison) Maghaberry.[3]

Gendered characteristics of political imprisonment in Northern Ireland, 1969–76

Throughout the Troubles prison policy and practice in Northern Ireland developed in three phases which reflected the prevailing counter-insurgency strategies: 'reactive containment' from 1969–76, 'criminalisation' from 1976–81 and 'normalisation', from the early 1980s until 2000. 'Reactive containment' was characterised by the use of internment, and extended emergency powers of arrest, interrogation and detention in pursuit of the official policy of 'defeating terrorism', in the context of Catholic and nationalist popular protest and the emergence of paramilitary violence.[4] The political mobilisation of women in civil disobedience campaigns brought many of them into direct confrontation with the security forces and the criminal justice system for the first time. While a minority of women were involved in direct combat roles in the IRA, 80 per cent of women imprisoned in the 1970s served short-term sentences for fine-defaulting in connection with rent and rate strikes, public order offences and offences connected with 'aiding and abetting terrorism' under the Emergency Powers Act, 1973, and related emergency legislation.[5] The prison population in general quadrupled during the operation of internment, but the number of women in prison rose disproportionately from 13 in 1969 to 162 in 1974, when the internment of women reached its peak.[6]

In the 1970s, the prison system for women was in serious disarray, 'faced with acute problems of accommodation, staffing, education and training and discipline', and was unprepared for the soaring intake of interned, remand and sentenced prisoners.[7] The sole institution for females, including juveniles, was Armagh Prison, which had retained a paternalistic and disciplinarian ethos that was not influenced by the prison reforms that had been developed in the rest of the United Kingdom.[8] As a consequence of the rapid rise in the prison population between 1971 and 1974, there were serious problems with overcrowding, and from the time a critical mass of politicised women prisoners entered Armagh there were confrontations between prisoners and the administration about the inadequate recreational and educational provision, the poor diet, insanitary conditions and inadequate medical and visiting facilities.

In 1972, politically affiliated prisoners gained a form of political status called 'special category status' following a republican cross-prison hunger strike in which the women prisoners participated. The new arrangement gave prisoners entitlement to political association, the right not to have to engage in prison work, segregation according to political affiliation, extra visits and parcels, and in the case of the men, the right not to wear the prison uniform.[9] The term 'special category status' was intentionally retained by the government to mean that the policy did not amount to the permanent legal recognition of the political status of prisoners, but was viewed as a relaxation of the regulations that would normally apply; it could be rescinded at the government's discretion.

In early 1974, women prisoners formalised their collective structure into the 'A' Company, Provisional IRA (Armagh), which was recognised by the prison administration as the organisation through which prisoners formally mediated with the authorities. An incoming prisoner could nominate to be held with her political peers and to be brought under the authority of her CO (commanding officer). All formal communication with external organisations, other republican prisoners, and the republican political and welfare structure was conducted through the CO, who had been selected by the leadership outside, and her officers, who were elected by the prisoners. Individual members consciously avoided all direct contact with ordinary discipline officers and welfare staff by electing their CO to negotiate directly with the governors on day-to-day matters. The general trend was to keep welfare and probation workers at a distance, as any dealings with state agencies suggested that such prisoners tacitly acknowledged the objectives of rehabilitation, with its implicit recognition of the legitimacy of the criminal justice system.[10] While using their services was not directly prohibited by the republican leadership, individual prisoners used them selectively to resolve problems with their families' welfare, including the welfare of their children, who had usually been taken into the care of relatives.[11] The principle of disengagement appears generally to have minimised the mundane conflicts that arise from daily interaction with prison staff and which contribute most significantly to the punishment of women in prison, as the rate of formal punishments for breaching prison rules was exceptionally low during this period.[12] This suggests that there were substantially fewer opportunities for staff to supervise prisoners, detect infractions or recruit informants, which are common forms of establishing control over individual prisoners, especially in women's prisons.[13] McKeown[14] has argued with respect to male republican prisoners and Crawford with respect to loyalists, that the insulation of prisoners from confrontations, and the self-discipline of political groups in managing their own structures, created the conditions for reducing staff–prisoner conflict.[15]

The climate of crisis and disorganisation in Armagh Prison during the 1970s enabled politically identified women prisoners to exercise opportunistic forms of resistance to the regime by incrementally pressurising the authorities for more facilities or for reduction in delays to incoming mail and visits. These demands were then increased to more significant concessions such as provision of education. During the period of special category status, the republicans established their own system of internal control and self-management on the lines of quasi-military routines that paralleled the larger prison regime:

> [B]y ten o' clock [in the morning] we had our own regime, between ourselves. Your cells … you had it ready and we inspected them ourselves. The CO would come down and go in and inspect it, make sure it was clean. The people who were in charge of cleaning the wings would be inspected. After that you did drill for about half an hour, and then directly after that you had all sorts going on. Maybe people were doing knitting, some were crocheting, and some were at crafts. You had your wash up routine, you'd take a rota on that, things like that. You'd get locked up for lunch, and then after that games. We had classes or a meeting or crafts or whatever. You literally planned your week. Or maybe you just wanted to read for an hour and a half. Then we had an association room. Basically, you got locked up again at about five. After six, you could go down and watch the news or whatever. There always seemed to be something. You had your time filled, literally. (Eilis: internee, Armagh)

Although 'A' Company was largely successful in preserving distances between prisoners and formal structures of authority, the practical gains of political status occurred in a much more uneven and tenuous form in the women's prisons. The introduction of facilities and resources such as access to educational and work programmes which prisoners defined as appropriate to their needs and status, came at a later stage and in a more incremental fashion than in male establishments, usually because the administration pleaded problems with economy of scale in resourcing the proportionally small women's population. Even during this period, when the separate status of political prisoners was ostensibly recognised by the administration, the boundaries between staff and prisoners were relatively susceptible to the interventions of discipline staff. Because the regulation of women in prison is conventionally exercised in individualised and interpersonal forms at the capillary levels of penal control, individual members of 'A' Company were susceptible to attempts to bypass their political structures.[16]

> You maybe had a screw coming in who was pretty decent. They'd have been nearly afraid, taking the stuff from your locker and going through it. Other ones would just come in and just turn the place over and put everything on the floor. Then we won a concession there too, insisting that they had to put everything back. When they came in they were mad that they had to do this. They weren't allowed to do that any more, turning your bed on the floor.
>
> (Anna: sentenced prisoner, Armagh)

The maintenance of discipline and good order in women's prisons is bound up with the common assumption that prisoners are more susceptible to personal interventions by female officers in 'setting personal example, gaining prisoners' trust and instilling personal loyalty … in theory at least, every effort was to be made to encourage moral reform by a process that combined an uneasy mix of coercion, encouragement and manipulation'.[17] In maintaining stringent group discipline and lines of communication through their elected officers, the prisoners subverted the personal authority of discipline officers from above, by bypassing rank-and-file staff and negotiating directly with prison governors, and from below, by selectively engaging with individual officers with the purpose of 'conditioning' them. Eilis claimed that discipline staff 'were either of the old school or they were raw recruits', and neither type could cope with assertive and politically conscious women prisoners: 'It was a learning process for the screws, for some of them, but not all of them.'

The history of prison conflict in the course of the Troubles demonstrates the extent to which organised and pre-emptive violence and disturbances were integrated into strategic phases of the prison campaign.[18] However, the use of organised and directive violence by women prisoners was much more tenuous because of the relatively small numbers of prisoners involved and their strategically peripheral position in both the prison system and the republican cross-prison structures. These factors made any organised form of confrontation more susceptible to being curtailed by the official use of force. On 5 March 1973, five women failed in their attempt to escape from Armagh Prison when they were apprehended on the prison wall and returned to punishment cells. A diversionary disturbance by the other prisoners was violently subdued by a joint army and police riot-control unit. On 16 January 1974, a number of prisoners took the governor and three members of staff hostage for three days, in solidarity with the republican men at Long Kesh, who had burned down one of their compounds as a protest against their conditions.[19] The occasional use by women prisoners of pre-emptive violence and disorder generated overwhelmingly retroactive consequences, such as collective punishment, injuries to prisoners and the introduction of more stringent security procedures. As a consequence, although major incidents of violent conflict did occur in Armagh Prison during the period of recognised political status between 1972 and 1976, and during the 'no wash' protest and hunger strike of 1980, and in Maghaberry Prison in 1992, these tended to be defensive physical reactions in the course of cell and body searches, or incidents in which specialised riot-control officers were deployed to enforce orders which had been refused. Two of the women involved in the failed escape described the consequences of engaging the administration with physical force:

> What they did was they just stuck the hose through the cell door and the force of the water, it just went all over. Not only that. At that stage you were able to get your fingers around the spyholes and we were just about able to hang onto the door. They batoned us; my fingers were up with swellings from my knuckles the whole way along. I was black and blue.   (Meg: internee, Armagh)

A couple of girls got out and they got up onto the stairs but they couldn't go anywhere because it had been blocked off with wood. So they actually had their protest, and they all got hosed. They did this to the whole wing. They were just going mad all over the place.

(Anna: sentenced prisoner, Armagh)

Well you always knew it [official violence] was a possibility, but it wasn't always foremost in your mind. I didn't think about it. Because if it had been then you couldn't have persisted, if you thought every waking minute 'I can't bear this, and I can't get out.'

(Meg: internee, Armagh)

The criminalisation policy, 1976–81

The removal of political status and conditions for incoming prisoners after 1 March 1976 followed the Gardiner review of the security agencies in Northern Ireland which recommended that paramilitary influences and structures should be dismantled in the prisons.[20] The criminalisation policy rescinded the status and conditions that had applied to politically affiliated prisoners since 1972. Furthermore, it reconstituted the administrative attitude towards political prisoners, which thereafter regarded them as 'terrorists' who had been engaged in criminality rather than prisoners of war, and as such the prison authorities were authorised to compel prisoners to serve their sentences under the ordinary, 'criminal' regime. The subsequent attempts to administer a 'normative' disciplinary regime precipitated the most intensified phase of conflict between republican prisoners and the prison administration. These years were marked by a significant increase in institutional violence and physical confrontation between staff and prisoners.

Following the removal of special category status, thirty-two women sentenced after March 1976 embarked on a campaign of non-cooperation with the regime by refusing to engage in what had now become compulsory prison work, withdrawing from educational programmes and refusing to conform to prison discipline.[21] During this period the prison authorities exercised the full panoply of disciplinary powers that had been temporarily held in abeyance during the operation of special category status. They initially responded by using the internal disciplinary system to adjudicate and punish prisoners who failed to conform to the normal regime as part of their protest, by removing discretionary 'privileges' such as letters, visits and association, imposing full cell confinement and taking days away from their remission, which in effect meant that prisoners who persisted with non-conforming served all of their sentence without reduction for 'good behaviour'. The number of punishments awarded for disciplinary offences in Armagh Prison rose twenty-threefold in the first year of the non-cooperation campaign, from 40 to 944 in 1977, and remained high throughout the following three years.[22]

The other front on which direct confrontation broke out in the prisons was with the intensified use of physical interventions and controls against the same group of sentenced prisoners on protest. Non-cooperating prisoners were moved to a segregated wing and, following a disturbance on 7 February 1980, were locked in their cells without access to toilets or other facilities. This led to the ten-month-long 'no wash' protest in which the prisoners were compelled to smear their excreta onto the ceilings and walls of their cells and disrupt the workings of the wing through a strategy of degradation, rather than comply with the new regime. After ten months in gruesome conditions and under complete lockdown, the women in Armagh stepped up their actions in December, when the then CO, Mairead Farrell, and two other prisoners, Mairead Nugent and Mary Doyle, joined the men who had been on republican cross-prison hunger strike since October for the reinstatement of the 'five demands': no prison work, their own clothing, freedom of association, educational and recreational facilities and visits and letters, and the restoration of remission which had been lost on protest. The women took their decision in the face of contrary advice from the IRA leadership outside the prison, having earlier coordinated their entry into the strike with the prisoners in the Maze to coincide with the weakened condition of the men, thereby increasing the pressure on the authorities. Even before the men had embarked on their hunger strike, Mairead Farrell had written in a smuggled 'comm' or communication to her counterpart, Bobby Sands:

> We had been making a general assessment of the no wash protest
> here to see if there is any way in which we could step up the protest

for status. We all believe that something else, some other form of action is needed to ram it home to the Brits. So discussion at present is heavy.[23]

This phase of the hunger strike was aborted on 18 December 1980, following republican recriminations that the Secretary of State, Humphrey Atkins, had reneged on the negotiated agreement that had prompted them to abandon their strike. A second hunger strike commenced on 1 March 1981, which involved the men in the Maze/H-Blocks only, leading to the death by starvation of ten prisoners, before it was halted on 3 October 1981, some of the demands having been achieved.

According to a prisoner on the 'no wash' protest during 1980, there were a number of reasons for the escalation of conflict in Armagh Prison over criminalisation. In 1979, three years into the campaign of non-cooperation with the prison regime, the women had decided to embark on further action because the impact of their strike was being absorbed by the prison authorities. On the other hand, the republican leadership, which was sensitive to charges that they were exploiting women prisoners by placing them on the penal front line, had strongly discouraged the women prisoners from upgrading any of their actions. This potentially left them at risk of remaining on the peripheries of the republican prisoners' structures, as well as making them the most vulnerable focus of administrative interventions to break the strike across the prisons. Therefore, the decision by women to escalate their actions entailed a multifaceted and complex tactical shift. Firstly, women prisoners wanted to open up another strategic front in the cross-prison protests, and to relieve the impasse that had occurred between themselves and the prison administration after three years of the 'non-cooperation' protest. Secondly, they wished to position their 'A' Company (IRA) as a distinctive group within the republican prisoner structure across the prisons and, in this context, to prompt the republican leadership to acknowledge their actions as legitimate and strategically worthwhile interventions in the overall prison campaign. Thirdly, their leadership wished to sustain the momentum of the protest, as some prisoners had elected to come off the 'no wash' strike and to conform to the prison regime. Finally, they took the risk of confronting the administration, notwithstanding the possibility that their protest would legitimise further punitive or even coercive measures.

It was a pushing and shoving sort of thing. We decided through discussion and everything else to try to escalate it. The Army Council outside wouldn't allow us. But we wanted to escalate it, because we thought we weren't doing enough to help the men up on the Blocks. We thought if we escalated it because we were women, we could be used as propaganda for the better. Like most things, you can say it's sexist or not, men are seen to be able to take it, the women aren't. This was the way we were thinking. We fought very hard to get it [clearance from the Army Council] and they wouldn't allow us to do anything. So we were very frustrated because we weren't allowed to escalate anything. At that time the men in the Crumlin remand were getting hammered.[24] So it was a case for us of [thinking], we're sitting here with no visits, no parcels or anything like that; we're losing our remission, but we're not doing anything else. It was as if the men were out there fighting for us and we weren't doing very much for ourselves.   (Áine: prisoner on the 'no wash' protest, Armagh)

The issue that precipitated the ten-month 'no wash' protest disturbance was the refusal by prisoners to attend their adjudications to hear what punishments they had received for refusing to conform to the criminal regime:

It was because the governor couldn't give way, and we wouldn't go up to see him. That's what I took out of it, because as far as he was concerned we were belittling him by making him come and see us, and he was going to prove differently, so he was! The main thing was his authority was confounded, and his idea of himself was offended, and he was determined to make an example of us, and that was that.
(Áine: prisoner on the 'no wash' protest, Armagh)

A notable aspect of the prison protests was the intensified struggle over the management of the bodies of the protesting prisoners, firstly through the withdrawal of resources as punishment, and later during the privations of the 'no wash' and hunger strikes, the prolongation of which did not constitute an infringement of the prisoners' rights as they were regarded by the administration as being voluntary and self-inflicted. During this time, the bodies of prisoners shifted to a central position in the struggle over power and legitimacy. The prisoners' bodies were not just terminal points of penal punishment;

rather prisoners actively deployed corporeal strategies of resistance. As Foucault reminds us, the body is a two-way conduit of power where 'power, after investing itself on the body, finds itself exposed to a counter attack in that same body'.[25]

> The first time I actually … I had to spread my own excreta on the wall, I cried because it was debasing. It was on the wall, and I was thinking 'Mother of God, what the hell am I doing?' It was like most things, you sort of pull yourself out … you're doing it because you've been put into it. You didn't ask to be put into that situation; you've been put into this situation, make the best of it.
>
> (Áine: prisoner on the 'no-wash' protest, Armagh)

The renewal of conflict in Armagh Prison, 1982–86

The period after the hunger strike of 1981 has been officially characterised as a transition to 'normalisation'[26] which was intended to establish 'further constructive progress' and enable the prison administration to 'put behind them the disruptions created by the hunger strikes'.[27] The term 'normalisation' refers to the new direction in penal thinking, founded on the recognition that the prison system could no longer be viewed as a mechanism that could 'defeat' political violence. This implied an abandonment of the criminalisation policy in favour of managing relations with the political groups. Despite the official language of negotiation and consensus, however, conflict in the prisons was renewed in the years immediately after the hunger strikes in response to proposed changes to security procedures which the prisoners considered to be an attempt to reintroduce the conditions of criminalisation by proxy. An integration policy – which the prisoners called 'enforced segregation' – was introduced in order to put into effect the new 'constructive regimes', which required the dispersal of their organisations and the integration of loyalist and republican political groups into the general prison population.[28] The second contentious question concerned the enhancement of the technical and operational security of the prisons and regimes, which was also viewed by prisoners as introducing restrictive procedures that in effect eroded the position gained by the hunger-strikes.[29] Moreover, despite the official claims that the prison regimes were being modernised and reshaped towards 'humane' and 'positive' goals, conflict increased even further in the women's prison.[30] In 1982 the normal procedural practice of strip-searching a prisoner on reception to Armagh Prison was extensively extended on a random and frequent basis 'in the interests of security and the safe custody of inmates', and as a response to the upgrading of security because of the segregation dispute.[31] The extensive use of strip-searching in Armagh between 1982 and 1985 provoked widespread political, feminist and civil libertarian criticisms about administrative mistreatment and violations.[32]

> After the 'no wash' ended, and the hunger strikes ended and you had the strip-searching and everything else, we were [back] on a 'no work' protest. We took a conscious decision to go into the system, because it was felt then that we weren't really making an impact outside. The men too were going into the system. But we were going in to look for segregation. At that stage we had segregation, but that was because we were on protest. We knew once the protest was going to be over that we weren't going to have that … I think they started panicking a wee bit in the 'Kesh, that they had to give some concessions to keep the men quiet, or whatever, whereas they did the opposite in Armagh – a stark contrast, you know. They started being actually more brutal, with the strip searching. I just seemed to be one of them people that flitted around listening, mostly, because they started on the remands then. They started the strip-searching on the remand prisoners.
>
> (Elizabeth: remand prisoner, Armagh/CO, Maghaberry)

Transfer to Mourne House, HMP Maghaberry

On 16 March 1986, Armagh Prison closed and the remaining female prison population of fifty-eight prisoners was transferred to Mourne House, HMP Maghaberry. Constructed at the cost of thirty million pounds, the Maghaberry prison complex comprised a purpose-built, maximum-security male prison for non-political prisoners, and political 'penitents' who had detached from their organisations in the Maze/H-Blocks; and Mourne House, a separate facility which was intended to house all of the female prison population, and politically-affiliated, 'ordinary' and juvenile offenders. The proposal to concentrate the whole female prisoner population in a single institution was criticised by prison welfare organisations, despite assurances from the Murray Commission on the modernisation of the prison estate that flexible security arrangements would be put in place to avoid exposing lower category and juvenile prisoners to a high-security environment.[33]

The objectives of normalisation were implemented through a series of prison reforms which offered 'constructive opportunities to those prisoners who wish to take something worthwhile out of their sentence' while enabling them 'to serve their sentences free from paramilitary influence.[34] However, the strong suspicion remained that 'positive regimes' were intended to enforce closer forms of governance over prisoners and to induce conformity through a combination of inducements and compulsion. Other underlying sources of contention persisted from the 1980s over security procedures, integration, the administration of parole and release licenses for life sentence prisoners, and the transfer of prisoners to Northern Ireland from British prisons.[35] Republican prisoners maintained the momentum of their campaign to oppose normalisation by diversifying their resistance strategies. Following a series of internal political and policy reviews within the republican movement in the late 1980s, largely prompted by prisoners themselves, they adopted a policy of 'pragmatic engagement' with the administration, which sought to negotiate with governors and administrators in so far as the prisoners' collective interests could be facilitated, while minimising the risks that outright confrontation would incur. In Maghaberry, as in the Maze, prisoners turned to the law and judicial review as a form of resisting the decision-making authority of administrators by challenging decisions made at formal disciplinary hearings, using the complaints procedures and pursuing legal actions in pursuit of parity of access with male prisoners to work and educational facilities. While the administration (rightly) recognised that this strategy was a continuation of a low-key but persistent assertion by prisoners of their political objectives, the effectiveness of this approach also reinforced the prevailing view among staff and governors that the political prisoners in general, and the women in particular, were engaging in vexatious and disruptive litigation. Moreover, the upgrading of security and surveillance systems in Maghaberry did not displace physical interventions such as strip-searches, and enhanced procedures for riot control. On 2 March 1992, the twenty-one political prisoners were subjected to an enforced mass strip-search, on the basis of an allegation that a prison officer had overheard a remark made by a child during a visit to the effect that a gun had been taken into the prison. The search was conducted by female prison officers assisted by male riot officers, after the prisoners had refused the governor's order to cooperate with the search:

> It was terrible because that started it, at about half nine or quarter to ten that morning and it went on until ten o'clock that night. And we had to listen each of us to each woman getting brutalised and beat and abused. They [women officers] literally came in, trailed the woman off the bars or whatever, took all her clothes. There were male screws outside with Alsatian dogs, and I could hear every single detail. Everyone was in riot gear, with visors, helmets, shades, gloves, black boiler suits, and it was all done in a military fashion, like eight fall in, right arm up the back, lock left, turn right, you know? It was all very strategic. That went on from ten in the morning 'til last thing at night and it was horrific. So what we did was, when they took our clothes off, we would say 'Right, you took them off, you can put them back on again'. So we made them put our clothes back on again and it was equally bad.
>
> (Kathleen: sentenced prisoner, Maghaberry)

With the 'return' to strip-searching, the prisoners:

> realised that there was going to be a sort of new policy here. And in a way you can see why, not that you can justify it, but the numbers of the women had risen to twenty-odd. You had a lot of women on the wing, and a lot of strong political women who would have had profiles, according to the RUC. And they saw that as a strengthening of our hand. It was embarrassing them because a group of women went into the jail who were actually dictating the terms. You had hundreds of men on the other end [of Maghaberry] who were conforming prisoners, who were going along with this notion that Maghaberry was the ideal jail. They had spent thirty and a half

million on the jail and security, and it was the model prison, and we were the disruptive element. And the politics of disruption just didn't suit the authorities at that stage so we were going to get punished for having our political structure. What better way to punish women than to humiliate them.

(Kathleen: sentenced prisoner, Maghaberry)

The closing years: prisons, politics and the peace process

The issues of prison conditions and status in the 1990s were dominated by the larger political dimensions of the search for a political settlement in Northern Ireland.[36] Following the intergovernmental 'Downing Street Declaration' in 1993 which formally initiated the process of negotiations that led to the Good Friday Agreement of 1998, the IRA declared a 'complete cessation of military operations' from 31 August 1994, followed six weeks later by a combined loyalist ceasefire. However, the political momentum was frequently mired by reversals and the possibility of collapsing, especially over the requirement for paramilitary organisations to disarm before political negotiations could take place, which led to the breakdown of the republican ceasefire in February 1996. The report of the international commission to set out an agreed framework for gradual decommissioning, the Mitchell Report, reopened the opportunities for graduated decommissioning to be linked to future incremental and conditional progress on prisoner releases. The IRA renewed its ceasefire in July 1997, but the modalities of phasing in a prisoner release programme in relation to decommissioning continued to be a major crux up to and beyond the Good Friday Agreement.

Events inside the prisons were equally significant. The prisoner bloc had emerged as a significant influence on republican political policy in the wake of the hunger strikes in 1981. While the prisoners' endorsement was necessary for continued political negotiation, there were internal differences between prisoners and the republican leadership over the ceasefires.[37] From 1995, as a direct response to the ceasefires, the government introduced a series of politically calibrated concessions, or 'confidence-building measures' that were intended to send forth positive political messages to the republican and loyalist communities. These included the reduction of the parole threshold from two-thirds to 50 per cent, which allowed prisoners to apply for release on licence after serving half their sentences, longer Christmas leave and the relaxation of eligibility for temporary releases, and further progress with the transfer of prisoners from British prisons.[38] However, in the eight months before the ratification of the Good Friday Agreement, the conditions for establishing a settlement over the prisoners appeared particularly distant. The Maze experienced a series of breaches of security, which included the discovery of an escape tunnel from the republican section of the prison, the successful escape of an IRA prisoner in December 1997, and the killing in the Maze of Billy Wright, commander of the Loyalist Volunteer Force, by republicans in the same month. These events prompted the critics of the political process to conclude that the prison administration had embarked on a mistakenly conciliatory approach in relaxing certain elements of prison security in the context of the political negotiations, such as withdrawing prison officers from the political wings to adjacent observation points. It was argued that the confidence-building measures introduced by the government in response to the republican and loyalist ceasefires amounted to a premature relinquishment of sufficient safeguards, as well as a forgoing of political leverage over republican and loyalist negotiators.[39] While some additional security safeguards were introduced at the behest of the Narey Report (1998) into the incidents at the Maze, any significant reversal of the new arrangements was unlikely to be tolerated by the prisoners and their organisations, and there was no widespread political will on the government's behalf to jeopardise the political process by rescinding them.[40]

Nevertheless, policy makers also recognised that confidence-building on the prison issue also required assuaging public and political anxieties about the apparently regressive levels of security, especially because the prisoner release scheme presented a serious electoral liability in the proposed referendum and Assembly elections for 1998. The first extensive release of prisoners under the terms of the Good Friday Agreement commenced in September 1998, with the first women released on 20 October. The unpalatable option of appearing to offer paramilitary prisoners an 'amnesty' was overcome by the technical device of increasing remission to two-thirds under the terms of the Northern Ireland (Sentences) Act 1998, enabling the majority of prisoners who had served one third of their sentence to apply for a release licence. The republican COs in Maghaberry and Maze prisons, Geraldine Ferrity and Padraic Wilson, were released temporarily to represent prisoners at the Sentences Review Commission. The last IRA woman political prisoner was released in February 1999.

Conclusion

The experiences of confined republican women prompt some productive insights into the influences that gendered and other forms of difference have on the direction of prison resistance. They suggest that prison resistance was sustained through specific, localised and situated strategies, and that these differences played a significant part in accounting for the tenacity and longevity of the broader republican campaign in the prisons. As feminist penologists have emphasised, gender provides a significant explanation for the distinctive ways in which penal punishment is conceptualised, organised and practised, which is as relevant to the construction of masculinity, punishment and resistance as it is to the relationships between femininity and struggle in the prison conflict. Gendered difference also provides an explanation for the structural and administrative influences that shaped the direction and forms of their experiences, as well as their struggle to move out of their initial peripheral position within the prison system, and within the republican prison structures.

On the other hand, women's active engagement in resistance reflects feminist concerns to move beyond conceptualising women prisoners in terms of a 'community of victims' who are always and already defined by subordination and victimisation.[41] Throughout each phase of the prison campaign, confined republican women necessarily negotiated and confronted the structural and discursive organisation of sexual difference in the prison system. Their experiences also resonate with the observations made in recent studies within penology that just as penal punishment is not evenly or universally applied, but rather is mediated through other structural influences such as ethnicity, gender, class and offence, it is often from these positions that women seek to resist penal power.[42] The brevity of this account does not permit an extensive critical discussion of the precise relationships between gendered and political punishment and the forms of resistance devised by women political prisoners. I have argued elsewhere that 'resistance' should not be viewed as an unproblematic or liberatory strategy.[43] Rather, the broader analysis proceeds from the Foucauldian paradigm wherein forces of power and resistance are in constant interplay. Since, as Foucault argues, 'power generates other forms of power', many of the contentions between prisoners and the administration did not arrive at a state of closure or resolution, but their outcomes created new types of struggle.[44] Similarly, the tensions and difficulties in accounting for women's experiences as mediated both by gender and political agency have only been briefly outlined. Nevertheless, the penal punishment of political women prisoners in Northern Ireland was characterised by often contradictory drives to regulate and discipline them as 'women' and as political prisoners. These contra- dictory pressures continued to shape their imprisonment even after the republican ceasefire and up to the release of the political prisoners:

> It's even harder being a woman. The men were always OK in the Blocks because there was a bigger number, over three hundred prisoners. So you got more power there. With Maghaberry, they saw it as the model prison. The official attitude was we can break them down and change them, because they weren't getting results and they weren't breaking the women. We had to be stronger because there was a smaller number of us. There was just constant fighting all of the time, and we just had to be stronger.
>
> (Hanna: sentenced prisoner, Maghaberry)

Chapter 9

Female combatants, paramilitary prisoners and the development of feminism in the republican movement

Rhiannon Talbot

This essay is concerned with the emergence of feminism in the republican movement. The focus is on women combatants in the movement and their development of a feminist consciousness as a result of their experiences both as combatants and as prisoners. It has been argued by republican feminists and others that '[a]s nationalist women and as feminists, we have very often given our support unconditionally to the overthrow of British colonialism in this country. We have often buried our demands for the sake of a common purpose – Brits out.'[1] However, when considering the participation of women as combatants, as the complexity of the relationship between women combatants and the development of feminism is revealed, this assumption of nationalist and feminist identities becomes more problematic This research attempts to highlight these complexities by reviewing the changes in the pattern of women's involvement and in the way they comprehend their experiences. It is explored in three thematic periods: the expansion of women's involvement in the Provisional IRA from 1969 to 1980; the prison protests and development of women's issues in the republican movement from 1976 to 1981; and women paramilitary prisoners and the growth of republican feminism from 1982 onwards. No conclusions are reached about the relationship between female combatants, paramilitary prisoners and the development of feminism. Instead, the research attempts to highlight three central questions concerning the ways in which female combatants and paramilitary prisoners may have contributed to the development of feminism in the republican movement.

Women combatants in Irish republican movements

Women, to varying degrees, have been involved in armed republicanism since such movements first organised. Their involvement in modern-day republicanism can be said to have begun with the formation, in 1914, of Cumann na mBan as an exclusively female republican organisation, pledged to work for Irish independence. Although very closely related to its male counterpart, the Irish Volunteers, it was at first an entirely separate organisation. Eventu-ally, though, Cumann na mBan became the women's branch of the Irish Republican Army.[2] While some women did participate as fighters in the Easter Rising, the majority of Cumann na mBan women participated in auxiliary roles such as caring for the wounded.[3] Many of the Cumann na mBan leaders held strongly feminist views and they stressed women's equality with the male Volunteers, but the fight for national self-determination was prioritised as the organisa-tion's goal over and above women's right to self-determination. The Cumann na mBan manifesto published on 5 October 1914 stated:

> We would point out to our members that it is their duty in all contro-versial matter to abide by the principles of nationality, which are the bedrock on which alone any vital national movement can safely be built. Since its inauguration Cumann na mBan has aimed at uniting those who, while differing on minor matters, were resolved that the integrity and honour of the Irish Nation were their first considera-tion, and we rely on our members to lift every difficult question out of the region of personalities and parties to the high ground of our country's welfare.[4]

In the Cumann na mBan constitution published in 1915, the national question was stated explicitly as being the organisation's primary concern:

> Cumann na mBan is an independent body of Irish women, pledged to work for the establishment of an Irish republic, by organising and

training the women of Ireland to take their places by the side of
those who are working and fighting for Ireland.[5]

From the time of Cumann na mBan's incorporation as the
women's branch of the IRA until the early 1970s, any woman who
wished to be a volunteer in the IRA joined Cumman na mBan.
However, as the social and political situation that existed in Britain
and Ireland at the end of the First World War and in the 1920s was
significantly different from the position that existed when the civil
rights movement emerged in Northern Ireland in the late 1960s, it is
unsurprising that the nature and extent of women's involvement as
combatants in the republican movement also changed.

The IRA re-formed from its almost defunct state in late 1969 and
early 1970. At this point in time, if women wished to join the IRA
they were directed to membership of Cumann na mBan.[6] From as
early as 1969–72, women were joining the republican paramilitaries
and there were even women internees.[7] In 1970 the IRA split into two
separate organisations: the Provisional IRA and the Official IRA. The
Provisional IRA is the organisation commonly referred to as the Irish
Republican Army. It was formed by a group of dissidents who
objected to the new policies of the original IRA leadership. The
dissenters felt the arguments about policy were a distraction from
their primary purpose of defending their communities and waging
war against the British Army.[8] Women were attracted to both organisations. The Official IRA appears to have given them opportunities as
combatants, and ex-members of the Official IRA have stated that
women were trained in all itsactivities.[9] This does not mean that all
women recruits to the Official IRA were happy about the roles they
played: 'There are an awful lot of women in the army who just sit back
and are the slaves of the men around them.'[10] After the split the newly
formed Provisional IRA retained a separate Cumann na mBan as its
woman's wing. Many women and girls became combatants through
joining Cumann na mBan. For example, Marion and Dolores Price,
who were found guilty of a series of car bombings for the
Provisionals in London in 1973, had initially joined Cumann na mBan
in 1970.[11] Bowyer Bell argues that Cumann na mBan acted as 'a feeder
for the IRA, first-level indoctrination units, and for some, especially in
the republic, simply a scouting opportunity'.[12]

After a disastrous atrocity in 1972 the Official IRA announced a permanent ceasefire and has since ceased to function as a paramilitary organisation.[13] This left the Provisional IRA as the single republican paramilitary organisation until 1976, when another split in the Officials led to the formation of a new organisation, the Irish National Liberation Army. This new rival to the Provisional IRA has never really attracted women volunteers. Perhaps its reputation for criminality and extreme brutality were dissuasive factors. The vast majority of women combatants have been members of the Provisional IRA.[14]

The expansion of women's involvement in the Provisional Irish Republican Army, 1969–80

The IRA re-emerged as a formidable force in the wake of the street violence and rioting associated with the civil rights movement. At this time the IRA's priority was to defend nationalist communities against attacks by loyalists. Women's rights as a disadvantaged group were not addressed as a distinct issue by any section of society until the development of the women's movement in Northern Ireland in the late 1970s.[15] When the IRA emerged as a force the majority of women in Northern Ireland lived in a traditional patriarchal social structure. It seems that through the decade women obtained greater admittance to Provisional IRA than they had initially experienced. There do not appear to be strong indicators that feminism or women's issues were of great importance to either the women volunteers or to the IRA.

In 1972 there were two women prisoners associated with paramilitary activities in Armagh Prison, a figure that rose to over one hundred between 1972 and 1976. The first female internee, Elizabeth McKee, arrived in January 1973.[16] She was one of twelve women interned there in that year.[17] Marion and Dolores Price were convicted on 8 March 1973 and imprisoned in England.[18] It would appear, however, that the majority of women volunteers were not fully deployed as combatants in the early stages of the conflict:

> In the early 1970s, the IRA embarked upon a military struggle to achieve the national liberation of Ireland and by this time gender divisions within the Republican Movement had long been established. Their [men's and women's] roles were determined by

tradition. Women's energies were channelled into Cumann na mBan, men's into Oglaigh na hEireann [IRA], and both into Sinn Féin. However, alongside these divisions women were increasingly coming to the fore in that struggle [for Irish liberation].[19]

As the decade progressed, women's involvement as combatants began to expand. The number of interned and imprisoned women, as indicators of their increasing presence, continued to rise throughout the 1970s. By 1976 over one hundred women were imprisoned for paramilitary offences.[20] Until 1976 all of these women were held under special category status, which was the State's recognition of their paramilitary affiliation. In 1978 thirty-seven of the women prisoners joined the protest against the withdrawal of special category status that would ultimately escalate into the dirty protests and hunger strikes.[21] By the mid 1970s the IRA was attracting a number of women recruits, who mostly joined the main organisation directly, rather than Cumann na mBan. These volunteers were not confined to supportive roles such as couriers or intelligence gatherers but were combatants. A woman who was active at this time said of her experiences, 'Today [1970s] women volunteers in the IRA are used just as the men are. They take part in armed encounters against the British soldiers. They are asked to plant bombs.'[22]

This gradual development of the position of women volunteers was reflected in a document discovered on Seamus Twomey, an ex-Chief of Staff of the IRA, in December 1977. The document, entitled 'Staff Report', was allegedly written by the IRA Army Council and outlined the sweeping changes that introduced the more secretive cell structure, the active service units. The report highlighted the increased importance of women members to the organisation: 'Women and girls have greater roles to play as military activists and as leaders in sections of civil administration in propaganda and publicity.'[23] This Staff Report revealed the IRA's military thinking and the fact that they had identified the strategic importance of women volunteers. For example, in the 1970s women began to plant bombs or transport them and other armaments as they were less likely to be stopped and searched by the security forces. Between 1977 and 1978, as recommended in the Staff Report, Cumann na mBan was 'dissolved with the best being incorporated in IRA cells structure and the rest going into Civil and Military administration'.[24] By this time

Cumann na mBan was mostly made up of older women, and the actions of the Army Council were partly in recognition of this fact. This report, however, only discusses the importance of women volunteers in terms of their potential contribution to the national question and does not include issues of specific concern to women. The decision to include women within the active service units was made partly in recognition of the reality on the ground, partly as a response to women's insistence on their inclusion, and partly from a desire by the IRA to attract more women.

Research on the internal republican process of transforming latent sympathy for the movement into membership of the IRA during the period between 1970 and 1972 reveals the importance of state repression.[25] There was, for example, a pattern of increased recruitment in the wake of acts of state violence such as Bloody Sunday in 1972.[26] Available information on what motivated women to join the IRA in the early years of the conflict suggests, as for men, that the national issue was women's priority, rather than forwarding a feminist agenda. In 1998 a woman ex-internee who was imprisoned for thirteen months in 1973 wrote of her feelings:

> I only know what faced us then – oppression, repression, Castlereagh, Palace Barracks, torture and injustice for the nationalist people. I don't know what degree of hope I felt back then ... Those who have suffered as we have suffered, and have resisted that injustice, understand the undeniable need for change in this society.[27]

Dr Paul McKeown, who was active during internment attempting to gain access to assess the health of the women internees said:

> They'll [the women] hold, that's certain. You see, the wholesale lifting of Catholic husbands, far from withering the cause has only set the women and wee ones on a blood-chilling course of defending what their men left behind – to the death.[28]

Significantly, perhaps, there have been almost no examples of early women combatants in the republican movement describing the reasons for their involvement as an attempt to advance their feminist ideals.

From this brief discussion it would appear that at the beginning of the 1970s, women recruits were encouraged to join Cumann na mBan, but by the mid 1970s this organisation had been disbanded and women were joining the IRA directly. The women had gained the right to greater participation. What is not clear is why this occurred. Perhaps, if the IRA were to continue recruiting women, as their Staff Report indicated that they wished to do, they had to accommodate the desire of women for full and equal participation. This important shift in the scale and range of participation by women combatants in the 1970s raises an important question. Was this development a reflection of a growing recognition of issues that were of concern to the mainstream women's movement by the women and the IRA, or was it simply a pragmatic admission that women were strategically important in furthering the aims of republicanism?

Prison protests and the development of women's issues in the republican movement, 1976–81

The prison protests were highly significant in the development of the political side of the republican movement. In particular, they encouraged the growth of Sinn Féin, the political wing of the movement. Internment and the lengthy prison sentences given to those convicted of attacks had given the IRA both time and opportunity to debate collectively the movement's political vision. The sheer number of prisoners and the growing political significance of their protest helped in this process. This was an opportunity that female prisoners also seized.

The prison protests began in the mid 1970s when the republican movement was dominated by its army, which controlled most of the political strategies and initiatives.[29] In 1976 the special category status given by the British government to paramilitary prisoners, which recognised the political motivation behind their crimes and was tantamount to an acknowledgment that they were prisoners of war, was withdrawn. The withdrawal of special category status was not only a refusal by the State to recognise the political nature of the prisoners' offences; it also resulted in the cessation of distinctive privileges for paramilitary prisoners. From 1976 paramilitary prisoners[30] were expected to participate in normal prison work, to wear prison uniform rather than their own clothes and to lose entitlement to fifty per cent remission of their sentences. Republican paramilitary prisoners of both sexes soon began protests against those changes in an attempt to have status reinstated. The male prisoners refused to work or wear the uniform and were forced to cover their nakedness with only the blanket from their cells, hence the 'blanket protest' was born.

The women also quickly began a protest, refusing to carry out prison work. They lost their privileges. As women prisoners wore their own clothes they did not have a 'blanket protest' like the men. However, in 1980 their protest escalated after a dispute with the authorities that saw the prisoners locked in their cells for a weekend, without access to any toilet facilities. As the contents of their chamber pots overflowed the women resorted to smearing their waste on the walls of their cells. The situation deteriorated further and very soon the women protesters were refusing to wash and, as a punishment for their refusal to carry out normal prison work, they were locked up in their cells, which did not have toilet facilities, for twenty-three hours a day. The contents of the chamber pots were again smeared on the walls. As a further punishment their bed frames were removed leaving them only mattresses on the floor. They rarely had clean clothes or were provided with sanitary items and their menstrual blood, like their excrement, was smeared on the walls. This protest has become known as the 'no wash' or 'dirty protest' and lasted until the hunger strike of 1981.

In 1980 two members of the organisation 'Women Against Imperialism', Liz MacCafferty and Margaretta D'Arcy, were imprisoned in Armagh following their participation in a protest outside the jail about the conditions the women were living in. These women were both strong feminists and they requested, in order to publicise conditions and to show solidarity with the prisoners, that their three-month sentences be spent on the wing in which the republican women on protest were imprisoned.[31] Whilst they were there the prisoners asked them to 'do some lectures on Women's Liberation'.[32] MacCafferty admitted that only a few women actually agreed with their feminist opinions,[33] yet the fact that the women asked for this lecture and the lively debate afterwards possibly indicates a developing interest in feminist issues on the part of the republican women prisoners. If this was true it would imply that during these prison protests the concerns of feminism had begun to gain prominence in the debates of the prisoners. MacCafferty declared that, from her experiences within

Armagh jail, she believed the war in Northern Ireland was itself the major block to women's emancipation because all other concerns were ultimately subservient to it.[34] Although the women were not unaware of the issues being debated in the wider women's movement, most of their contemporaneous statements seem to imply that they continued to prioritise their allegiance to the IRA and consequentially the main republican agenda: 'It is very difficult for those outside to understand … how the isolation of the prisoners on the protest reinforces their commitment to the IRA'.[35]

One could suggest, tentatively, that by this stage the republican women had gained the right to equal participation within the ranks of combatants and that feminist issues were of growing interest to them. Now, these prison protests were politicising them in ways they had not experienced before:

> Once the Republican Movement had decided to reject criminalisation, and once each prisoner on the protest had experienced for herself the ferocity with which the protest had been countered the very act of standing firm created its own unity and indeed formed out of these inexperienced and politically half-educated young women a totally new kind of republican.[36]

This unity, described by D'Arcy, echoes the experiences expressed by the ex-prisoner referred to above. What effect did this heightened commitment to republicanism have upon the women prisoners in terms of their sense of themselves as women and as republicans? During this period of the dirty protest, when the republican agenda was being refined and strengthened, did the women begin to analyse their experiences of the conflict in terms of both their gender and their politics?

Female paramilitary prisoners and the growth of republican feminism from 1982

The hunger strike was a watershed in the development of the republican movement, encouraging an engagement with the wider political arena and taking the movement into new ways of resisting the British State. Throughout, activism concerning the conditions of women paramilitary prisoners continued. While the women's dirty protest had ended in 1981 because of the focus on the hunger strikers, their protest around prison conditions was a prolonged campaign which included the wider republican movement and non-republican groups.

In November 1982 a new policy of strip-searching was introduced into all prisons, including the women's prison in Armagh.[37] Henceforth all women prisoners were to be strip-searched whenever they left the prison for court appearances, hospital visits and when they had visitors. This included the removal of all of their clothes and a visual search of their genitalia. Women could be searched whilst pregnant, lactating or menstruating and would have to remove their sanitary protection. There were also claims in republican literature that women were occasionally searched internally.[38] This was an issue of direct concern to both women and the republican movement.

Initially, however, there appears to have been little public debate or controversy on this issue. In the May/June 1984 edition of *Women's News*, a Belfast-based feminist publication, an article on page six of the paper lamented the 'lack of publicity both within and outside the Republican press on the current issue of strip searching'.[39] This quiet did not last. On 29 July 1984, former prisoners Linda Quigley and Mary Doyle, and the Sinn Féin Prisoners of War Department representative, Chrissie McAuley, addressed a meeting of the Sinn Féin Women's Department in Dublin. At this meeting those present decided to try to bring the practice to an end. They established the 'Stop the Strip Searches Campaign'. A publicity campaign was initiated and action groups in Dublin, Monaghan, Limerick, Cork, Waterford, West Clare, Shannon, Sligo, Louth, Armagh, South Down and Belfast were established. In 1984 alone rallies were organised in Crossmaglen in September, in Belfast in October and Armagh in November. The Sinn Féin Prisoner of War Department produced a pamphlet and the Derry Film and Video Collective produced a video. A writer from *Women's News* com-mented that the campaigns presented the practice as a humanitarian issue.[40] This largely humanitarian theme was echoed in a specialist issue on strip-searching by the London Armagh Group, the authors arguing that 'the imposition of anything so traumatic as the strip-searches, which are unnecessary, constitutes "inhumanity" …'[41] In an article on the validity of the British government's assertion that strip-searching was required for security reasons, the London Armagh Group concluded that:

the policy of strip-searching in Armagh has nothing to do with security. Strip-searching in Armagh jail is a policy of intimidation and harassment which is more than superficially linked with other methods currently being used to silence political opposition to the British presence in Ireland.[42]

Neither of these articles appears to suggest that a feminist perspective on strip-searching had yet entered the discourse of the republican movement. By the beginning of the 1990s, however, such a perspective had become evident in debates about the condition of women paramilitary prisoners. In a collection of unpublished testimonies about strip-searching (gathered and held by the Committee for the Administration of Justice), Mary McArdle gave evidence that 'As a woman I felt that my sexuality was being used as a powerful tool against me.' This feminist analysis by the women prisoners was not confined to the issue of strip-searching. In a 1993 article about women prisoners in Maghaberry, a new jail to which all women prisoners were transferred in 1986, it was argued that women were discriminated against in the provision of facilities because those offered to men were markedly better. Now it was asserted: 'Women prisoners believe that they are discriminated against for two reasons – because of their sex and their political beliefs.'[43] These prisoners did not restrict their feminist analysis to their experience as prisoners but articulated their feminism to include all the inequalities women endure: 'The women feel that … no woman should ever be expected to accept anything less than is offered a man in a similar position – regardless of whether that woman is inside or outside gaol.'[44]

Such analysis of republican women's experience of the conflict in both feminist and republican terms is now discernable in writings in the wider republican movement. In a 1988 publication Sinn Féin argued that nationalist women were doubly discriminated against – by society because of their sex and by the Royal Ulster Constabulary and the British army because of their politics.[45] In 1990 republican publications like *An Glór Gafa/The Captive Voice* (the publication by the republican prisoners) were discussing women's involvement in the republican movement in both republican and feminist terms: 'Republican women involved in the national liberation struggle are simultaneously challenging women's oppression in general and identifying how colonial rule has helped cultivate conservative anti-woman culture in Ireland both North and South.'[46] The women paramilitary prisoners linked these two themes more explicitly. In their eyes, their discrimination was not just an additional form of repression, but was exacerbated by discrimination on political grounds. There was an inextricable link between political discrimination at the hands of the British State and gender discrimination:

> Women world wide face various types of discrimination and find themselves in conflict with male power hierarchies, but these are aggravated for Irish women by the exploitation which takes place within the colonial Six-County State … Women in Ireland are forced into constant battle as members of Republican communities. The main source of our oppression is the British occupation and domination of our country. Until the British have been forced to withdraw, women will continue to bear the brunt of repressive policies and to fight oppression in all its forms.[47]

This brief description of issues highlighted by women prisoners from the period defined by the start of strip-searching to the phased release of women in the mid to late 1990s reveals the extent to which feminist discourse influenced the analysis of republican women. Not only were issues of concern to women more openly discussed by the women prisoners, but women's experience of the conflict was also being discussed in feminist terms in the wider republican press. This brings us to the final question: to what extent have the republican women prisoners and the campaigns surrounding their conditions of confinement encouraged the adoption of feminist views within the republican movement?

Conclusions

Republican feminism has become a distinct voice within the republican movement. This essay has tried to raise questions about how women combatants may have contributed to the development of that voice. My concern has been not to explain those developments but to problematise them in terms of three questions. Firstly, although women in the 1970s did gain a more equal participation as combatants in the Provisional IRA, was this because of a growing acceptance by republicans of issues that were of concern to the mainstream women's movement, or was it because women were strategically important? Secondly, did women during the period of the dirty protest begin to analyse their experiences of the conflict in terms of both their gender and their politics? Thirdly, have women's campaigns surrounding their conditions of confinement since 1982 helped to further feminism within the republican movement? Addressing these questions helps us to understand how secure the republican feminist voice might be within the republican movement as a whole. As a male paramilitary prisoner stated in 1990, merely wrapping a cloak of feminism around a movement does not make commitment to feminism secure if there is no change underneath the cloak:

> We may have taken up political positions in response to women's oppression. We may have plenty of the theory of feminist politics. But still, the question for us is to challenge our own sexism and the ideas and structures which give us privilege. At the end of the day, there is no point in putting a coat of paint called feminism over our thinking – we have to change that thinking.[48]

Chapter 10

Narratives of political activism from women in West Belfast

Claire Hackett

We lost a lot, but we learned a lot. You can't let those years be lost. They have to count somewhere. Maybe this history will be that reckoning.

Monica Culbert

Introduction

This essay describes the experiences of eight women activists from West Belfast who have contributed interviews to the Falls Community Council's Dúchas oral history archive. The Dúchas archive was set up in 2001 to record the history of the conflict in nationalist West Belfast from 1969 onwards. Although it is not specifically a women's history, more than half the interviews in the collection are by women, reflecting the organisation's commitment to representing the experience of women. The idea for the Dúchas archive took root at the start of the peace process in the mid 1990s when Falls Community Council began to discuss the significance of a community history for political transition. Falls Community Council itself was set up in 1974 to support community development and work for economic justice and social inclusion for the community in West Belfast. Underpinning the discussions, then, was the belief that the history of the conflict in

West Belfast was a history of a struggle for justice and that the recording of this history could in itself contribute to a process of change.

From the beginning oral transmission was considered to be the method that would be most appropriate for recording this history. In this, Falls Community Council was continuing a tradition in oral history of recording accounts of struggle and resistance such as labour movements, women's movements and civil rights movements. At the heart of the project for telling the history of the conflict in West Belfast was an understanding that this history would be one that would document power relationships. There was recognition that recording the history of a community meant acknowledging the differences within that community. This has indeed proved to be the case: the life histories reveal people's relationships within their own families and communities as well as to the State and State institutions. The oral history method facilitates this through the individual life histories, from which unfolds a complex and multilayered story. The histories therefore become a means to explore the conflict, not just recount it. A space is opened up to allow this exploration, which involves looking at the conflict within the community, not just between the community and the state. This is, of course, a risky enterprise for a community accustomed to self-reliance and solidarity for survival during the conflict. That it is being attempted is a measure of the commitment to the process of change.

Construction of narrative

The essay focuses on the range of ways in which women in nationalist West Belfast were politically active during the conflict in response to the British/Unionist military campaign in their communities. What emerges is an extraordinary history of resilience and resistance. An interactive process is implicit in the oral history method of constructing a narrative but it is a process that raises many issues about control and the relative power relations of contributor and interviewer.[1] This is a debate familiar to feminist researchers. The themes identified here were drawn from the content of the interviews. Although this content is the result of a collaborative discourse between interviewer and contributor I am aware that it is nonetheless my selection and interpretation that frames the narrative here presented. In the Dúchas archive the histories are not anonymous: contributors are made visible through their names and photographs as well as their recordings and transcripts of interview. The method that necessarily underpins this visibility is one aimed at establishing informed consent of the contributor to the process they are engaged in.[2] I have chosen to follow this through in the construction of this essay. The interviews of eight women form the content: Marie Moore, Clara Reilly, Kate Mc Gettigan, Jennifer McCann, Rosemary Lawlor, Monica Culbert, Mairead Gilmartin, and Eileen Loughran.[3] Mairead Gilmartin is also the senior researcher in Dúchas and carried out three of the interviews.

In writing this essay one of the issues I became most aware of was the power of activism in opening up public space for women. The outbreak of the conflict blurred the distinction between public and private domains. Feminist theory has articulated this division between public and private as a central concern for women, condensing the issue into the slogan 'the personal is political'. These concerns are played out in these narratives through women's connections to family and community in the context of State oppression. The family and community bonds are at once a source of strength and at times also restrictive and limiting. One of the strongest impressions from the narratives is the way women negotiated, subverted and challenged the restrictions while at the same time defending and building their communities.[4]

The lives of the women presented here reveal the development of activism throughout the conflict and the issues that emerged and were confronted. A very significant theme is the role of women in maintaining a social and community structure. The ways in which women directly opposed military occupation on the streets is outlined. The organised forms of activism developed by women to subvert and thwart military policies is described. Activism defined around imprisonment is a major theme. Activism on women's oppression developed around the issues of women prisoners and domestic violence. These were issues drawn directly from women's own experience and encompassed challenges to both State and male power and control. Isolation and hardship, friendship and comradeship are themes that emerge strongly. The public roles that in most cases women felt were thrust upon them are outlined. A constant theme is the juggling of roles and conflicting demands. Running through all the histories are stories of personal transformation of women's inner and outer lives.

Women's history

Nationalist women's activism is, of course, not a phenomenon of the recent conflict in Ireland. There is a long history of feminist struggle and its intersection with republican struggle in Ireland.[5] The re-emergence of the women's movement in Ireland during the 1970s was accompanied by a process, which continues, of recovering and analysing that history. Feminist scholars have spoken of the loss of that history and its rediscovery by each new generation of women activists. The very act of writing it has been conceptualised as feminist activism and is in fact frequently carried out by women scholars who are also activists. This means that the recovery and reclaiming of women's history is not just an academic exercise. There are different dimensions to this: the redefining and reinterpretation of hegemonic historical record, the importance of continuity of struggle, and the understanding of the historical significance of women's lives. In tracing that women's history, what is also being done is affirming the links between generations. Two of the women activists who speak in the following pages mention specifically the influence of their mothers. Marie Moore, now a Sinn Féin councillor, and Clara Reilly, a human rights campaigner, describe the influence of their mothers, who passed on to them ideas about the value of women's activity on behalf of the community:

> My mother's attitude was educate a woman, you educate a family, educate a man, you only educate one. She was very, what you would call, feministic then, for that time. Very much into promoting women and talking about women, to me, anyway …
>
> Marie Moore

> My mother was from the Lower Falls. She was more of a republican than my father. She used to thump the table and say, 'Don't let anybody down. You don't let anybody treat you as a second-class citizen.' The way she brought us up, we all grew up like that, having a vested interest in our community and in what happened to our neighbours … being there when people needed you.
>
> Clara Reilly

The activist lives of both women, now in their sixties, show the effect of that early influence. Implicit in their words is women's community activity.[6] Community solidarity was essential as the communities from which Marie Moore and Clara Reilly come were isolated from the structures of the State. Under the Stormont Government set up in 1921 with the partition of Ireland, Catholics, and particularly the Catholic working class, were excluded from government and marginalised in social and economic life.[7] In this context the need for solidarity was strong.

Emergence of activism

From the beginning of the conflict in 1969 women began to organise to provide support structures within their communities. In the summer of that year hundreds of Catholic homes and many businesses in Belfast had been burned and destroyed. Such large-scale attacks were not a new experience. Pogroms had taken place in previous generations under the Unionist regime.[8] In August 1969, however, in a departure from previous policy, the British government made a direct intervention with the deployment of the British army. The Catholic community's first reaction of welcome for the British troops had changed within a few months as it became clear that the army was there to support the status quo. In the meantime, the IRA had mobilised and begun an active campaign to destabilise the Stormont government as well as defending Catholic working-class areas in Belfast. These areas became ghettos, West Belfast the biggest of them, an area refugees fled to for the relative safety of a shared community. As the war continued these areas also became more and more isolated from civic and political structures of the State and were subjected to its repressive policies. It was in this context that women began to take on more public and politicised roles within their own communities.

Women came to the fore with the re-introduction of internment in August 1971. On 9 August 1971, 342 men were arrested in dawn swoops. This move was directed against the Catholic population and caused great alienation. Moreover, it failed as an attempt to crush the republican movement, as most of those interned were not actively involved in the IRA.[9] A number of civilians were killed in the operation, most of them from West Belfast, and the effect of internment

on that community was therefore particularly traumatic.[10] Marie
Moore recollects how women reacted:

> Then, when internment came in, I think women came to the fore,
> very much so. Most of the men from the area were arrested that
> morning. I remember them banging at my door and coming in. So the
> women were out on the street. We actually fought hand to hand with
> the paratroopers that morning in Clonard. We were struggling with
> their rifles and pulling them off them and we were getting beat. Then
> people drove in with buses and everything and parked them across
> the road. After that we couldn't even get deliveries into the area. The
> binmen wouldn't come in. The bread, or the vans and lorries would-
> n't come in to the shops then. We organised as women, to go out with
> shopkeepers and carry them in, the bread and stuff. We organised
> clean-up of the streets in which we got out with buckets of water and
> brushes and scrubbed the streets and kept them clean. We got lorries;
> people that had lorries came in and took the rubbish bins away and
> got them emptied and came back with them. We organised all of that
> from what you would have called behind the barricades, because that's
> when the barricades were very much at the forefront.

This account gives a vivid picture of women directly confronting
an armed British military. What is also depicted is the way in which
women organised civic services to maintain their communities. There
is a sense here of the gendered framework of the women's activism at
that time. The courage and defiance displayed by the women shows an
understanding and taking advantage of the military assumption that
they were not the combatants. Furthermore, in the organisation of
maintenance services behind the barricades can be seen the extension
of the domestic role of women into a more public sphere.

Collective support

In the early 1970s the relationship between the community and the
British army crystallised into a war situation. British army raids on
houses became a regular occurrence. Rosemary Lawlor's narrative
shows how much this became a way of life as she describes the strategies women developed to support each other:

You did whatever you had to do and then sometimes you would have been working and doing things and the next thing trouble started and you were away running. Somebody's house was getting wrecked and you would have went over and took the kids away just to make sure they were all right. Maybe the fellow was getting trailed out of the house. I'd say, 'Look I'll take the kids'. And they'd say, 'Will you?' I don't know if it would happen now but the people trusted you and everybody in the area was always there.

This is echoed by Kate McGettigan as she describes women coming out of their homes to go to the home where the raid was taking place. As well as being there to support the family being targeted it was an act of solidarity with them:

If somebody was lifted, everybody, they just seemed to go all out. It didn't matter who the fellow was, whether he was a relative or anything, everybody seemed to go out. It was really a community-based area. Everybody stuck together.

Clara Reilly sums up the feeling of collective support:

When you look back, it was the strength of the women that brought a little bit of sanity into it. Because we all supported one another, and we were all in the same boat. Most of people that lived in Turf Lodge and Ballymurphy were two and three generations of unemployed. So we didn't have much to share, but what we had, we shared with our neighbours. It was that sort of a community. I think it was because of all that trouble and trauma we went through in the end that made our communities the strong communities that they are today ...

Direct action

The resistance to the British army at the onset of internment became a form of organised direct action by women. Variously referred to as 'hen patrols' or 'bin-lid brigades', women in groups directly confronted the army patrols, which were called 'duck patrols'.[11] In this way the women alerted the community, and active republicans in particular, to the British army presence, thus thwarting military control in the community. Kate McGettigan recalls being part of the hen patrols:

> We went out on the duck patrols. You went all round the streets and you had a candle and your binlid, and you quack-quacked, as soon as you saw them coming along, you quack-quacked to let people know they were on the go. And followed them everywhere and we used to sing 'Old MacDonald had a Farm'. More often I was on those streets than I was in the house, I swear.

Her description conveys the visibility of women on the streets and the wit and humour that they brought to their direct action. Marie Moore describes the strategy behind the patrols and her pride in the women's activism:

> Then, what became known as the hen patrols – women who came out onto the streets when they heard the army and RUC coming in and rattled their binlids and blew their whistles to warn people who may be staying in houses, that there were raids going on. That was how they counteracted people being arrested, and local republicans being arrested. It was a very powerful thing to be done, because they got a lot of hassle and they got a lot of beatings. They walked round during the day when the patrols came in, blowing whistles, so that everybody in the area knew exactly where they were at any particular time of the day. They became the binlid brigade, but they were called the hen patrols before that. What I was proud to see was women coming very much to the forefront.

In the latter part of 1971 it became clear that this kind of activity was very dangerous, particularly for women actively involved in the republican movement. Two women, Dorothy Maguire and Maura Meehan, were shot dead by the British army as they were in their car sounding the horn to warn the neighbourhood about British army raids. Marie Moore reflects on this incident and others as a deliberate strategy to deter women's activism:

> Then, I was shot in Clonard. Maura Meehan and Dorothy Maguire were shot dead in the Lower Falls, out with loudhailers warning the

people that there were raids going on. Just a few weeks after that I was shot, and then Rita O'Hare was shot.[12] So there was a deliberate attempt by the British Army, if not the Government, to put women off the streets and to frighten them. Because naturally enough, women, with so many being in jail, they were the steadfast person within the house; they were the mother, the father, the breadwinner in some cases. And of course were naturally then frightened that they could be next and the family would be left without anyone. Psychologically, your children come first and your family comes first, and everything else that you see comes after that. I think that's in most women: make sure my family's all right and then I'll do what I have to do. I think that frightened quite a few women at that time, but still a lot of women came onto the streets and kept it up.

In this description we can see clearly the dilemma for women activists: the knowledge that there could be an enormous price to pay and that the consequences of their activism could affect their family. Women had come out onto the streets because of their families but the same motivation could also drive them back.

Family and activism

A recurring and consistent theme in all the women's narratives is the relationship between activism and family. The kinds of activism women engaged in changed and developed over the years of the conflict but this dilemma remained constant. Women had to juggle their roles, assess the risks of their activism. For some women their situation made this particularly hard. Monica Culbert, whose husband was serving a life sentence, articulates the responsibility she felt as the sole child-rearer: 'The fear I had, I always had the fear, was, if I die, what happens to them? It's a scary feeling.' Jennifer McCann, a political prisoner, describes the agonising situation of women prisoners who were also mothers:

But one of the most heart-breaking things that I ever witnessed was in Maghaberry one day. I can't remember whose child it was. But it was squealing for its mommy. The screw was trailing the mommy this way, and another screw was trailing the child the other way. I couldn't get over it. This child was only about three or four. We were all wrecked. Even women who didn't have children, when we went back to that wing we were just devastated.

She describes her own personal experience of that dilemma, after her release from jail when she had children of her own:

It wasn't until later years, until I had children myself. There was an incident happened in my own home. My daughter was one, and my other daughter was just born, she was only three weeks old, and the RUC attacked our house and came in through the windows and arrested me and my husband, and another fellow who was in the house, just a family friend who was up that day. We were all brought to Castlereagh. The only reason I got out of Castlereagh was because I was still haemorrhaging, from having the baby, so they weren't able to question me so they let me out again. My husband was charged, and the other fellow was charged, and when they were charged I was scared. I left my home and went down to Dundalk to live, because I thought they were going to come back for me, and charge me, and what's going to happen with the kids?

The kind of choices women face when they become mothers has been frequently discussed in feminist literature. For the women activists described here, living in a war situation, the choices were very stark and consequences could be very heavy. In some ways also, however, activism was seen as a necessity for a mother because it was regarded as a compelling choice to maintain and protect the family.[13] When Rosemary Lawlor speaks of the hardship of bringing up a family in a situation of war she also conveys her defiance of the military regime around her:

My mammy would have talked about how it was when she was growing up. In the mills when she worked in the mill. She talked about hard times yet she said to me one day, 'No, no, Rosemary, your generation had the hardest to rear children in'. I said, 'Mammy, I never lived in the hungry '30s. I never went barefoot. I never went to school hungry or anything, you did'. I find it very strange for her to say that to me, that my generation had a hard time rearing their children, but probably because she saw the war that was being waged against the children in the street and how it was trying to rear a family. It was an extremely extraordinary time to rear a family in. You were trying to keep normality and there wasn't any normality. The Brits wouldn't let … You looked outside the door and you said, 'That's not normal'. The day I accepted that as normal, I would have been defeated.

Rosemary here frames the bringing up of her family in a war situation as a political act. Looking back on that time Clara Reilly also recalls the strain of fulfilling all her responsibilities – as a mother and human rights activist:

That was the start of a long nightmare of documenting, trying to rear a family, trying to work part-time, being rapped up at all hours. Because you had to have an open house. People came at four, five, six in the morning to tell you that their son or husband or brother was arrested, and you had to bring them in.

But Clara also articulates another dimension to this in her description of her husband's role, something that Marie Moore speaks about also. Both women acknowledge the space for action that they had because their husbands were not directly involved but supported their activism:

My husband was a very quiet person. He wasn't a bit like me, he wouldn't get involved … but yet he had to be part of it, because when I was going off taking all these statements or speaking to reporters or going to London, or going to lobby or picket or whatever, he had to take over the role as housekeeper … to take charge of the children and so forth.

Clara Reilly

He was very supportive of me afterwards and was always there for the children, washed their clothes at night, put them on the clothes horse in front of the fire. Made sure they were at school, made sure they were in bed if I was out at meetings.

Marie Moore

This account reveals a different picture of male/female relationships than is usually portrayed, with men sharing responsibility for family and enabling the activism of their partners. It is interesting to note that Clara Reilly and Marie Moore were also the two women who spoke of the empowering influence of their mothers. Although their situation is not typical for women activists, they are also not unique in the community.

Prison activism

Prison shaped women's lives in many different ways – whether as prisoners, or as wives, relatives or supporters of prisoners. Much of women's activism was influenced by their relationship to imprisonment. Of the women who were imprisoned, most, as Jennifer McCann describes, were very young:

> It was in March 1980. I was arrested in Percy Street, in the lower Falls. It was a Friday evening. It was just three weeks after my twentieth birthday. I went to Armagh then, and I was on remand for about a year, and then I got sentenced. I got sentenced to twenty years. I did ten and a half, and got released in 1990. Your twenties were spent in jail. I was just after my twentieth birthday when I went in. But that was old compared to some of them. There were three that were in when they were just 17, and other ones 18, 19. That was the average age. I was a wee bit older than most, in those days.

By the mid 1980s, with more mothers amongst the prison population, it became prison policy that mothers could keep newborn babies with them until they reached one year. Jennifer describes the impact of this on the women:

> When I was still in jail, about 1986, when we started moving to Maghaberry, there were quite a lot of women came in who were single parents, and quite a lot of women with children. The first time we saw it was when Cathy Stanton came in ... she had the baby when she was out on bail and she brought the child in with her. And the child had to go home after twelve months, and Cathy was still there. That was heartbreaking. We got used to seeing Cathy and the child as well, having the child on the wing.

All of the women activists whose histories illustrate this essay were engaged in campaigning around imprisonment. Women were particularly active in the Relatives Action Committees (RACs), set up in 1976 to support the prisoners' campaign for political status.[14] Eileen Loughran's experience of struggle to maintain an ongoing active campaign is typical of most members:

> We were very active within the RACs, organising marches and demonstrations and on the go all the time. And I had two jobs. I worked during the day and I had a part-time job at night, in pubs or clubs. It was what you lived on. Because you couldn't live on the dole. And I was on my own, I had no support from my husband. So I had to do those jobs, and go to all the meetings as well. But the places I worked in were quite sympathetic …[15]

A vital part of the prison struggle was communication between prisoners and the outside movement. Marie Moore, who was in charge of Sinn Féin's Prisoner of War (POW) department, organised the communications between prisoners and the movement outside. Some of this was done by family members but Marie also co-ordinated a group of women to carry out this role.

> I had a team of girls, outside of families. Families were also very good, because when they started to take the visits they were smuggling in tobacco, and they took messages into the jails in the morning and then in the afternoon. These girls went in the morning, maybe took two visits in the morning, going to A Wing in H3 and going to B Wing in H3, and then in the afternoon going to C and D Wing in H4, and bringing communications from H3 into H4, and vice versa. And then bringing communications that were for the POW Department or the movement back into the centre at night. I could not say and I could not praise them enough, the work that they did, because if they hadn't the communications you would not have had the things that were done. You might not even have had an escape, the big escape, because communications were so important.

Smuggling messages in and out of the prison under the scrutiny of prison officers was difficult and it took skill to transfer and receive parcels from different parts of the body. It required women to reach beyond their feelings about personal boundaries. Monica Culbert, a prisoner's wife, looks back with something like amazement and also pride at what she did:

> And you brought an amazing amount of things in. When I look back on it I go, 'Jesus Christ, I couldn't do that in a month of Sundays.' And I think when people look at me now – you're old, you're very respectable, matronly looking – she couldn't have done that, she wouldn't have done that. And I've begun to think myself, did I ever do those things? But you did it, just because you had to.

Finding autonomy

Another way in which women were intimately involved with the prison regime was as wives and partners of prisoners. In many ways this was a more isolating experience for women. A sense of being defined in relation to another was a limiting factor. Monica Culbert describes the feeling of ambiguity and also the constraints of fulfilling the role of a loyal wife:

> After a death, there is grieving, but there is a closure, and you can move on. We never moved on. We were stuck static … you weren't single, you weren't married, and you weren't a widow. You were floating about there somewhere. You were somebody's wife, who was inside; you were somebody's mother, who you were looking after. You weren't anybody on your own. And dare you jump out of that role … you'd to watch where you go, and watch what you said, and watch who you were with, because people would talk.

The sense of being policed by the community and the sense of isolation that this imposed comes through in Mairead Gilmartin's account. It was a complex situation for women and there is a strong sense of the uncertain ground they occupied. Mairead describes the isolation and the reaction she received when she tried to ask for reassurance:

> Jail isolated me. It was very very rarely I ever talked to another prisoner's wife about inner feelings. You talk about the outer things,

like the amount of time, and how time passes, and telling people how time passes. Because time does pass, and you'll say, 'Well look, before I knew it he had ten years done.' And hoping that that makes them feel better. But you wouldn't go any deeper. You couldn't say, like, 'I feel really lonely.' I don't think it was a deliberate thing, that people had chosen not to support each other. I think it's like, it's nearly like a sign of weakness when you ask. I remember asking one of my husband's friends whenever he first got his life sentence, 'Do you think I'll be able to do this?' And I genuinely meant, 'do you think, knowing me as a person that I can get through?' And they were saying, 'Well what do you want, another man?' And that was not what I was thinking, I'm going 'No!' Because I'm just thinking, 'Do you know me as a person? Do you think I have the strength to –?' And they'd misconstrued the whole thing. Well I went, 'Oh, no, I'm not even going to ask that question ever again, because it's too … people don't understand what I'm talking about when I say that.'

This account conveys strongly the lack of support that was available to women whose partners were imprisoned. There was an inability to see them as individuals, to think of their situation as other than dependent upon the prisoner. Mairead and Monica's lives were enormously affected by the imprisonment of their partners, yet eventually both women found autonomy in their situation through being thrown on their own resources and finding from that the necessity for self-reliance and personal growth:

I really was so timid. Very shy. But that had to change, because I had to stand up, and I had to fight Michael's corner, with all these letters and all these things you did. And speak to people, force yourself out to do things like that. You become more independent. You can manage your own finances. Also, by doing other things, you forge a life for yourself where you're not dependent – you're afraid, almost, to be dependent on people. That comes from your partner being taken away. Now, I would go to Timbuktu on my own. I'm not saying I don't have fears, but I wouldn't be afraid to do things on my own. That's because you realised you had to. You couldn't always depend on people. You had good friends that you can depend on, or you could cry and know they'll not be upset by that, but …

Monica Culbert

Mairead also speaks about the independence that she achieved from her situation:

> I don't think if my husband hadn't gone to jail I would have done any of those things. I wouldn't have learned to drive, because he used to drive me everywhere. I didn't need to learn to drive. And I don't know if I would have gone to school. So, lots of stuff I did because I had to. And then I'm glad now that I did them. Because it just makes you a different person.

Both women chose also to stay in their marriages. From their interviews it is clear that they passed no judgement on women who did not make this choice. They saw it as a choice rather than an obligation. Mairead and Monica both took up activist roles around imprisonment and repression. In Mairead's description of activism and friendship what comes across is a breaking out of the isolation that the attempted policing by the community had imposed:

> I got involved in different community groups, and with different groups, and with republicans as well, because obviously I was still a republican. I used to lift the Green Cross and do things, whatever I could do, maybe sell papers, go to rallies always, go to meetings, go to functions. So I always did that that way, and a whole new network of friends developed up there, which was good, because for the most part the friends helped me through the life sentence, I have to say. Only for those friends, I probably wouldn't have gotten through.

The community Mairead speaks of here was still the same community that tried to police her, but she created her own network of friends for support. Monica also speaks of the importance of support from friendship. In her summing up she could be speaking for all the women activists:

> I regret those fifteen years. But I think I benefited in some way. I learned a lot, I learned to cope. You knew you were right. I'm not saying that there weren't times when I used to say, 'Why am I doing this? Why am I here?' And yes, you regret the separation. You regret the hurt and the pain. But there was so much that you got from it. The people you met. And the experiences. That bond we have, for

we went through it all, you know what people are feeling, and you can share that. I got a lot from it.

Links with feminism

When the prison struggle was at its height in the late 1970s and 1980s some women activists were also making links with the local and international women's movement and bringing that movement to their own struggle. This marked the beginning of a specifically feminist consciousness. A key organisation that articulated both feminist and republican politics was Women Against Imperialism (WAI). This group formed in 1978 from a series of splits in the organised women's movement.[16] At the same time women in the RACs were beginning to talk about their oppression as women and some of them joined Women Against Imperialism. WAI began to organise to challenge sexism and inequality within the republican movement and also to highlight the conditions of women prisoners in Armagh and their struggle for political status. They also began to recognise the issue of domestic violence and to talk about setting up a women's centre.

Eileen Loughran (who was active in the RAC and later joined WAI) describes becoming aware of one of the first major feminist campaigns against domestic violence. This happened in 1978, around the case of a young woman, Noreen Winchester from Belfast, who had been convicted for the murder of her father after enduring years of sexual abuse at his hands. The women's movement organised a successful appeal against her conviction and in the process galvanised public discussion about domestic violence and sexual abuse. Eileen recalled hearing about the case. Her account illustrates the relationship between republican women and the organised women's movement in the North:

> Then there was a young woman, Noreen Winchester who had murdered her father in Sandy Row. We had read about it in the papers and went down to the court and had a picket outside the court, a lot of us that were in the RACs and who were interested in the women's question, because we thought, imagine that woman living through all that abuse, and then they're going to bring her to court and jail her. The Northern Ireland Women's Rights were there

as well. We were all very polite to each other. Because on some issues
we could relate to each other. It was just the fact of republicanism
that they didn't want anything to do with, and they didn't recognise
our struggle. But on a basic thing they could. On women's issues.

The tension that Eileen implies between the different women's
groups continued throughout the conflict. It reflected the differing
attitudes and positions towards the British state, the republican
military campaign and the nature of women's oppression. Until the
late 1970s the situation of women republican prisoners had not been
viewed as an issue for feminist campaign. Within the republican
campaign for political status the focus was mainly on the situation of
male prisoners in the H-Blocks. In March 1979, Women Against
Imperialism decided to organise a picket of Armagh jail on
International Women's Day. Several women from WAI were arrested
at the protest and brought to court. Eileen Loughran describes the
action and the conscious identification of the issue as a feminist one:

> And then we decided it was time we raised the question of the
> women in Armagh. That we would go to Armagh and have a picket
> there. The hunger strike committee had tried to go to Armagh and
> they got stopped on the outskirts, they wouldn't let them in. But
> International Women's Day, or the women's movement going, they
> could get into Armagh, where the H-Block/Armagh Committee
> couldn't get in there. Because we were saying Armagh is a feminist
> issue they wouldn't stop those women. We were then brought to
> court. We got ourselves organised and we got a bus to take us down
> to court, and the court was packed. English women, French women,
> Scottish women, women from London, a whole load of places. Very
> few of them were from Belfast. The majority were from other places.
> We all wore black trousers and a black top, and we had the T-shirt
> made with the women's symbol on the front and the H on the back.

It is clear from Eileen's description that the international
movement of feminism could achieve what the local movement could
not. It was a demonstration of the power of internationalising the
struggle. The court case and subsequent imprisonment of some
protestors mobilised a wider feminist audience internationally.[17] The
following year the situation of the women political prisoners became

much starker as they were forced to embark on a 'no wash' protest. This year the protest was a great deal bigger and was the start of an annual international delegation of feminists to support the women prisoners.

> In 1980 when we went to Armagh there were eighteen buses. There were women from France, who were feminist, they recorded part of it too. There were people from Australia and New Zealand who went to the picket. And we had organised a big social in the Glen Community Centre in Lenadoon. I had never met loads of gay women before. There were women with double circles on their sweaters, and I was saying, 'Why do you have two circles?' And they said, 'Because we're gay women.' ... It was like a field day, in the Glen Community Centre.
>
> Eileen Loughran

The mobilising by nationalist women activists of international women's solidarity enabled local activists to publicise and gain support for the women political prisoners and in that process gain exposure to different politics, such as the encounter with lesbian feminists that Eileen describes. While women active in WAI and the RACs were campaigning on the State's abuse of women republican prisoners, they were also beginning to take action on violence from within the community they were defending. In some ways this was a more difficult battle. Eileen Loughran describes her growing awareness of domestic violence and the difficulty of breaking silence around this:

> And [I was] also meeting a lot of women within the RACs who were very active and into what was happening, and they would travel to England and do lots of things, and still they would go home and be beaten. Sometimes you'd be standing for a while, doing collections, and you'd have a bit of time, and sometimes they would say things to you. Or they didn't need to say anything, you just knew. And they didn't like to speak about it. It was not something you would like to talk about, really.

The space that was created to name and confront this issue came from women meeting through Women Against Imperialism. From these beginnings came the realisation that women needed autonomous space to address the issue of domestic violence:

> We were looking for a place to have a meeting. There was a place we found in the Bull Ring, which was an old Sinn Féin advice centre. It was a real dunderin' inn. It was full of mice and rats, I'm sure. But it was where we had, to go and be ourselves, and be women, and have all these different discussions. And then invite other women to come along, and organise socials and bring them along to speak at them. It was a whole learning process for us. For instance, we got in touch with Women's Aid, and we asked them if they would come along to our centre – we cleaned it up as best we could – and speak to us. We were a very small number, maybe six to eight people at that time. So we were saying, even from then, we would need to have a place for women to go to. We'd need to have it in West Belfast. We hadn't thought ahead to a women's centre at that time but we were thinking we need to have something, because these things are happening. And they are happening to women within the RACs. They would come in with black eyes, and bruises.
>
> Eileen Loughran

The action on identifying the specific oppression of women continued and led to the formation of the Falls Women's Centre. The international feminist links formed through the organisation of the Armagh protest were maintained:

> And through all this we were still trying to get a women's centre. We got support from women from across the water. They sent us books for our women's centre. They ran socials and sent us money. And we eventually got a women's centre opened, just past Dunville Park.
>
> Eileen Loughran

The Falls Women's Centre was formed in 1982. It was the second women's centre in Belfast and the first of a group of women's centres set up in working-class areas in the city.[18]

Political representation

Marie Moore's activism led her down the route of party political representation. A significant factor in her decision to become a councillor was the fact that her family obligations had become less pressing. She outlines this and is explicit about the dual oppression she faced as a woman and a republican entering City Hall:

> Then when I was asked to go as councillor I thought about it for a while. I had no young children so I was free. My husband had died. So I said, 'Yes, I will, I'll have the time to do it.' I didn't think it was going to take up as much time, but I went into it. I came into this City Hall, and I remember feeling, oh God, this is so male-oriented. It wasn't even the Brit orientation of it, it was the male orientation of it. Very few women had been involved as mayors, or anything like that. Looking round it all, working out it was all very male-oriented. Even the committees, everything was addressed as 'Chairman', this sort of thing. And I thought, my God, you're never going to make an impact on this place here.

However, Marie went on to become the first Sinn Féin deputy mayor in City Hall in 1999. She describes her awareness of being a role model for other women:

> When I was asked, I was really surprised, because I thought some of the male councillors would be running for it, but they had said they would like me to stand. I was honoured to stand as Sinn Féin. First of all because it was the first time Sinn Féin had ever held a position at that level within Belfast City Council and in some of the other councils up until then. It was also nice because I was a woman, and I thought that it would probably send a message out to women within the party, and women who were thinking of joining the party; and women who were involved in the community who hadn't just taken that extra step into politics would say, well, if Marie can do that I can do that; there is no reason why I can't move on. So I was pleased for that reason, that being a woman, I was there.

Marie suggests here a natural route from community activity to political representation. This is not, however, an unproblematic idea for women community activists.[19] A belief such as Marie's that there is a need for more women political representatives is a measure many feminists have used to assess gains for women. With the establishment of the new political institutions under the Good Friday Agreement there are now more avenues for political representation. The number of women political representatives nonetheless remains small.

Conclusion

As the epigraph indicates, this essay is more about where we have come from than where we are right now. The evidence, however, suggests that there is an ambiguity about the gains of the Good Friday Agreement and the attendant process for women. What happened during the war was that in many ways the usual boundaries between public and private space became blurred as families and communities in West Belfast were attacked and were thrown into the frontline. Paradoxically this gave women space to be active. Bringing up a family became a political act. The attack on families and communities drove women into action and enabled all women's actions to be defined as political. Activism developed over time, became more organised and also led to recognition and identification of power structures closer to home. History has shown that these public roles in times of war can be cut back when war has come to an end. There is some evidence now to suggest that the separation of public and private worlds has been reasserted. The narratives of activism presented here suggest that women can create autonomy in their lives through confronting power structures in a variety of ways and through creating networks of support and solidarity. The separation of public and private worlds inhibits this process and, ultimately, can only constrain and limit women's activism.

Chapter 11

The emergence of a gender consciousness: women and community work in West Belfast

Callie Persic

Introduction

In Northern Ireland, the rise in women's community activism is often associated with the outbreak of social and political upheaval that accompanied the Troubles. At this time women engaged in forms of activism, party-political and community-based, yet this did not fundamentally challenge their position, and their traditional roles remained largely unchanged. Since the first ceasefire in 1994[1] there has been a marked increase in community development in Northern Ireland. The changing social and political climate, coupled with the subsequent and substantial 'Peace and Reconciliation'[2] funding from Europe, enabled many groups, but especially women's groups, to develop throughout Northern Ireland.

In this essay I will examine how women renegotiate gendered power relations through their participation in community work, and will explore the formation of a grass-roots women's group that seeks to put forth a woman-centred community development agenda. For these women, the term 'feminist' creates difficulty and tension; however, they are aware of, and affected by, a feminist discourse and have addressed the question as to whether or not the group is a 'feminist' one. Through their involvement in community work

women have pushed the boundaries of 'political' activism and
challenged gender expectations and the role of women in the
community.

The political situation in Northern Ireland has long inhibited the
potential for women's social, political and economic development.
Although the degree to which people were affected by the violence
and unrest varied in different areas, it is generally accepted that
working-class areas suffered disproportionately. The following
material is derived from the experiences of working-class Catholic
women in Ballymurphy, a West Belfast housing estate.[3] As a result of
residential segregation that is common throughout Belfast,
Ballymurphy is considered a 'single identity' community[4] and is
characterised by close-knit family networks, dense living conditions,
multiple levels of deprivation and social exclusion. Importantly, there
is widespread experience of imprisonment among men and women
due to the political unrest and the area has suffered many deaths over
the course of the Troubles. The lives of residents have thus been
shaped on social, political, economic and personal levels as a result of
political violence.

Physically, Ballymurphy appears to the eye as a typical working-
class area, with post-war housing that blurs together in its uniformity.
However, a brief walk around the estate reveals a number of political
murals, commemorating significant political events as well as those
who lost their lives as a result of the Troubles. While local murals
seem to suggest a considerable amount of republican sentiment, it
would be naive to believe that all the residents hold the same political
views. What can be said is that the estate is very politicised and there
is a history of women's community activism there.[5]

Ballymurphy was inadvertently thrown into the upheaval associated
with the beginning of the Troubles. In August 1969 Catholic families
fled the Lower Falls to 'safe' areas as their homes were gutted by fire
as a result of attacks by loyalists and many families were temporarily
housed in Ballymurphy. This event had a tremendous effect on the
development of community solidarity. According to de Baróid,
Ballymurphy was transformed and a new sense of neighbourliness
was established with the need to work together, sustain a relief operation and maintain barricades to protect the community.[6] Since then,
the history of Ballymurphy has been inextricably connected to the
political situation in Northern Ireland. De Baróid comments that as a

result of the August violence, republicanism was firmly established in Ballymurphy. Men and women came forward and created the first IRA unit in the area in September 1969.[7] Owing to the image of resistance and its role in the conflict, Ballymurphy experienced heavy military surveillance and overt military presence during the Troubles. House raids, arrests and searches are common experiences for residents – indeed, it is reported that there is not a house in Ballymurphy that has not been raided.[8]

The information for this essay was gathered through extended conversations, participant observation and interviews. The narratives are taken from semi-structured interviews held at a time and venue that suited each woman.[9] Not all the women quoted are members of the women's group; some were kin, whilst others were friends. A range of perspectives is therefore presented, from women who are community activists as well as from non-activist women.[10] Although in a small community it is often difficult to ensure anonymity, all of the names and details of the women have been changed to protect their identity.

Internment was a significant marker in the lives of local women, altering and transforming their roles. Indeed, internment is often described as the catalyst for women's community activism, which led to women's increased involvement in the public sphere and eventually the political sphere. As the women cited in Claire Hackett's essay (pp. 145–66) acknowledge, internment forced women to enter and engage in political and social activism in an unprecedented way.

The political is personal: internment

With the arrival of internment in August 1971, the lives of women were transformed. Internment is of importance for working-class Catholic women because while it virtually paralysed the movement of men, it did not have the same effect for women.[11] Instead, internment had a massive influence on women due the high number of arrests of local men. Women were often at the fore of protests and pickets on behalf of husbands, fathers, sons and partners. In the aftermath of internment, women developed strategies in an effort to alert the community to the army's presence and established the famous 'hen patrols', which were a response to the army's night-time 'duck patrols'.[12]

Internment affected a larger and more diverse group of women than the civil rights movement that began a couple of years earlier. The ordinary woman, who may not have considered civil rights a personal issue, was suddenly thrown into the political arena. Edgerton reports that although women became politically aware, this did not necessarily change their views about their position in society. Women's political action at this time was understood as an extension of their domestic role.[13] This is widely acknowledged among women. In an extended discussion of their roles at that time, Teresa expressed her realisation that women's participation was on behalf of a whole community:

> Men were doing other things and women were just taking up the slack and doing something. And it wasn't seen to be doing nothing. Trying not to minimise this, you were actually protecting the estate and the street and the house you lived in – individually and in a group. Defending – you were protecting your way of life. Your way of life was turned upside down overnight and you had to start to learn the process on a daily basis of learning how to live in the circumstances you were living in.

Karen, another local woman, believes this is why, in terms of community development, Catholic women are more familiar with community work than Protestant women:

> I think women in nationalist areas would be far more sort of advanced than women in Loyalist areas are. Say when internment came out and I mean it was, I don't even know if there was any, loyalist interned, well there might have been like, but there were literally thousands of men, in Catholic areas interned, and that left women to do everything – you know what I mean? Which, they just got out and on with it. I think it would be now, women are starting to take more, sort of prominent role than they would have done years ago. Years ago it would have been women making the tea and all where it's not now.

In other words, Catholic women *had* to organise. Edgerton maintains that it was for the welfare of their men and communities,[14] while Aretxaga asserts that while this may have been the primary motivation, women's actions inverted dominant gender ideology.[15] In many respects, the everyday forms of resistance adopted by women[16] are difficult to define simply as resistance or subversion. Often, resistance strategies were not formally expressed, and were simply spontaneous. The role of women as protectors of the family and community established during internment provided a context in the years to follow in which women became likely candidates for future community activism. The women cited in Claire Hackett's essay (pp. 145–66) provide some evidence for this trend.

Women's community work

Women's continued participation in community work is a logical progression from this political activism. Women community workers built upon their historical roles, as there was increasing recognition of their previous contribution within the community. The 1994 ceasefire was a significant turning point because it brought increased resources, such as funding, and a willingness to address issues beyond constitutional politics. However, tensions arose within communities since there were changes in local power structures and the need to look at 'bread and butter' issues took on new prominence. Women working in the community did not always work towards a feminist or women's rights agenda, but understood their role as working for the betterment of the larger community. Importantly, women's participation in community activism does not necessarily mean it is connected to, or even informed by, feminist ideologies.[17] Women engage in community work for many reasons: maternal concerns, political and social interests, or the feeling that 'if we don't do it for ourselves, no one is going to do it for us'. Motivations vary among individuals, but a sense of giving back to the community and creating a better future for their children are frequently cited incentives. Liz, who participates in voluntary work, expresses her belief that gender roles are changing because women are taking the lead in community work as follows:

> I think the roles are changing because they see that if they don't go out and make a change nothing is going to change. I mean, they feel like they have to go out and make a change. All right, you have your politicians and all that, but they are sort of behind closed doors

negotiating this. When women are living in a community they are trying to make a community better for where they are living and better for their families and that is why they are out in the communities working.

Although more attention and research on women's participation during the Troubles is emerging, there is still a tendency to conceptualise women's work as 'supporting' and as the 'backbone', instead of fundamental to an understanding of the Troubles. Such simplistic depictions of women neglect the ways in which they are active political agents and indicate an androcentric view of women's contribution. In fact, this view is so widely held that it has become a cliché. I recall on one occasion a woman expressed her frustration and exclaimed, 'I don't want to hear about backbones!' In her view women were the 'meat' of the struggle. Working-class women were affected by their new experiences, which led to a questioning of bigger issues, including gender roles. Transformations occurred in various ways for women, ranging from power struggles in the home to the acquisition of transferable new skills among women, to protesting on issues.

Community work as empowerment

Community work carried out by women may not be informed by larger feminist issues, but has worked to empower women and, by extension, their community, by confronting the dominant culture of Northern Ireland. The term 'family feminists' has been used to describe activism among working-class women that is focused on practical, non-political, grass-roots issues.[18] However, both political and social issues motivated many of the women in Ballymurphy to participate in community work. It may appear as though women are family feminists, who work out of a maternal duty, but this does not lessen the impact of their work. Feminist understanding may partially have mobilised working-class women, but often they acted only out of concern to protect their way of life.

The clearest example of transformation and empowerment is witnessed in the continued and growing participation of women in community development. As the Troubles moved into a more party-political arena, women continued to work in the community, addressing a wide range of issues, not just 'women's issues'. Many women expressed awareness that community work was beginning to challenge male authority. As Bernie says:

> Women would have a lot of power in community work, I think, a lot of power. You don't see a lot of fellas going to meetings, maybe some, but it's mostly women attending meetings to fight for this and fight for that. It's mostly the wife and the kids that goes out and fights for things. If any meetings go on in an area you see a lot of women to men – probably the men are the chairperson of it, but that's about it.

Her view is interesting because, while she accepts that women have power within community work, she also recognises that they often do not take formal roles, such as that of 'chairperson'. However, this disparity is changing as women become more active in this work and push for increased involvement at a formal level – with the possibility that this might lead to power at party-political levels also.

It is clear that women's community participation encourages shifts in power, and by doing so challenges gender roles and expectations. Community work is a way to empower women, which often leads to increased personal development, such as further education or improved employment possibilities. Since gender ideology is conservative in Northern Ireland, community work is a means for women to begin challenging male-defined power and gender structures. Through community activism, women channel their energies and transcend traditional gender ideologies, thus creating a new space for themselves.

Negotiating gender ideology and the re-creation of motherhood

Through their political practices and new social experiences during the Troubles, women became aware of the 'political character of gender inequality' and multiple layers of oppression.[19] Their oppression as working-class Catholics was compounded by their gendered position within the community. To understand patriarchy is to understand the existence of power relations between men and women. Through their participation in community work, women challenged existing power structures and experienced empowerment on personal and communal levels. Many women attributed their personal growth to their participation in community work and, as a result of their activism, some returned to education after a long absence. Not only did this experience boost their confidence, it also taught them valuable skills needed to run a community organisation. Women learned how to write letters, fill in funding forms, arrange meetings and mobilise people – although, as we have seen, the difficulty in balancing family responsibilities and community work created tensions. Many women took a long-term view of the situation and linked community work to their domestic role. They felt that, as they become stronger, this confidence was passed on to their children, their families and their communities.

Naples has proposed the term 'activist mothering' as a way to understand how women account for their community activism.[20] In her view, 'the analysis of activist mothering provides a new conceptualisation of the interacting nature of labour, politics and mothering – three aspects of social life usually analysed separately'.[21] This argument is engaging as it draws attention to the ways in which women's life activities are inseparable. A local woman articulates this position: 'When you're out protesting against plastic bullets they say you're being political, but you're not, you're being a mummy.' The concept of activist mothering helps to explain the motivation for some women's community activism in Northern Ireland since it provides a way for women to affirm their positions as mothers in a world that offers contradictory messages relating to these roles. When asked why they become involved in community work, many women inevitably associate it with providing a better future for their children and see such involvement as an extension of their caring role. Historically, and in the present, their gender informed their community activism and provided the impetus for it. Abrahams points out that personal experience among women varies and community work may have more to do with 'giving back' to the community.[22] As Sheila, a local woman, explains, 'It's made me a lot stronger, a lot more confident. A lot more aware what's going on. I always wanted to go in and help the community in some way.' For Carol, a new mother, participation was directly connected with motherhood:

I'm not a child no more. I have a boy myself. So you would like a
community house or something like that for them to go to, so you
would. To get that built up and see the kids going into it – they're off
the streets and they're not going to bother anybody or bring harm to
your door, and then you know where they are like, they're safe.

A female community worker explains:

I think another thing is too, women had their children to worry
about, coming up in the troubles, so they were sort of there fighting
for their children's rights. I would say that pushed them a lot too,
wanting to make it better for them.

This attitude is also seen in Naples' work. 'The community workers
challenged traditional notions of gender and mothering in their work
and served as models for their children as well as others in their
community'.[23] Women in community development are often empowered by work that in turn challenges and negotiates gender ideologies.

Women are aware of changes in the community and in attitudes
towards women that have developed out of their protesting role.
Reflecting on the changes in traditional roles for women, Karen
commented, 'I'd say it's well broke out ... also in the community it
would be the majority of women who do the community work.'
Women see a strong connection between their initial protesting role
during the Troubles and their later community activism. As Bernie
recalls, before the Troubles women did not have a 'protesting role',
but now she believes that women need to move beyond protests and
engage in community work in their own right:

Women wouldn't have done that. A lot of changes came from that
too. I mean women says if you're calling on us to go out and protest
than we have a right to go out and do things men are doing; don't be
asking us to do one thing but not do another. If we're strong enough
and willing enough to do that then we are strong enough and willing
enough to do anything else that any man can do.

Through participation in community work women have recognised
that their involvement redefined traditional gender roles. As one
woman explained:

> When I was growing up there were always men on committees – not
> to say that women weren't doing anything; they were. But the men
> wanted to be seen to be on the committees and women always
> seemed to be doing menial work. It's changed now and women will
> go on committees.

Increasing political stability and funding opportunities have created
the conditions for communities to focus on grass-roots issues
neglected during the Troubles. In the section to follow I will examine
how a women's group emerged during this period and tapped into the
new vision of inclusive community development.

Grass-roots women's community activism

In Ballymurphy and the surrounding estates there is a strong community network and the local community resource centre often plays a
supportive role for emerging community groups. The resource centre
was well placed to help facilitate the early development of the
women's group since it provides support in many forms, such as
photocopying, phone/fax, and advice, or serves as a meeting place.
In January 1996 several public meetings were arranged in the centre
by local women to address what they perceived as problems within
the community. Motivating factors were concern over local power
struggles, both political and social, and the need to develop their own
agenda. These women advocated a rethinking of community development, to look at a wide range of issues, such as deprivation,
unemployment, education, health and women's development. As a
result of the public meetings a number of women came together and
formed a core group that met regularly, often in each other's homes,
discussing ways to address what they identified as needs in the
community. It is worth noting that this group of women was
composed of some of the more republican women in the area, many
of whom volunteered in the local Sinn Féin cumann or had participated in prison and street protests during the Troubles. However,
there was an uneasy relationship between republicanism, feminism
and the objectives of the women's group, since some women voiced
needs that moved beyond the traditional 'protesting' role of women,
yet did not identify with the goals of the feminism.

Initially, the focus was on women's development, but gradually the work broadened out to include general community development. As the women began to organise they drew upon recognised approaches to social activism that were used in the past, such as petitions and protests, to highlight their campaign. Through their everyday experiences of social exclusion and injustice, as well as previous political activism, they had developed the legitimacy and authority to take action. It was clear that many of the problems women faced were attributable to the political conflict and subsequent years of decay – isolation, loneliness, poverty, unemployment and poor health were common issues among the women. Everyday life issues compelled women to work for the improvement of their community and personal experience often gave them the incentive to address problems. Throughout the development of the group, women clearly expressed a growing consciousness of their position as women and the ways in which gender had limited their previous community activism. They expressed a desire to move beyond women's traditional activism to embrace a more dynamic view of community work, although this proved difficult to achieve.

How P/political is P/political?

At one point during the early development of the group, near the end of 1996, there was a series of house raids in the community. In the past, women had gathered outside the homes and banged bin lids.[24] This time, as the house raids continued, and perhaps fuelled by a new sense of duty and empowerment, the women began to organise loosely into relief committees. The group felt that the army was increasingly targeting women who were single parents, therefore the women's group had a part to play. In one instance the group received press coverage from two Belfast newspapers, situating them as following in the women's tradition as guardians of the community.

The group was called upon more frequently for every protest and picket. This proved to be a difficulty because, while they felt compelled to protest, they needed to maintain their own agenda. The group had mixed reactions and felt, as they continued to take a role in protests, that other community groups and residents were beginning to assume that was the role and purpose of the group. This also contributed to its image as 'political'. The women debated their participation in the protests. Many felt that the women of Northern Ireland were only called upon to take action in times of crisis or when political processes were strained. Moreover, women stated that they had been through this process before, working on relief committees, protests and pickets, but it was now time to address their own concerns. Liz phrased her misgivings in this way:

> I think women are second-class citizens to men here. They don't get appreciation shown to them. They don't get pats on the back when they are out protesting. The way men, it's always 'the men do this' and when you're talking about the IRA it's always a man – never a woman, you know what I mean?

These women clearly recognise that they have sacrificed and contributed a significant amount on behalf of the struggle. Now, all over Northern Ireland, women's groups were popping up and arguing for their own agenda. As Laura explained:

> People have seen too much of it, I mean people wonder, especially women – men, I'm not just ... but women are the ones who, I won't just say 'do all the dirty work', but I mean it would be like, pat him on the back, do you know what I mean? And it's not fair on the women because they go through all the hell and all the shite and it's not, it isn't fair like. That's why you might say 'Forget the big picture and let's focus on us.'

Milroy and Wismer highlight a key ambiguity associated with women's community work that I found in West Belfast, concerning the 'politicalness' of women's activism.[25] Women in Northern Ireland have low participation levels in party politics, or politics with a big 'P'. They tend to have influence within community activism, described as 'political' with a small 'p', which usually refers to 'bread and butter issues'. The difficulty in defining what is 'political' is linked to the difficulty in using male-defined criteria, which associates politics, power and the public realm.[26] Naples takes the need to reconceptualise what is 'political' as part of a general feminist project. Community workers in her study maintained an ideological separation between community work and politics, since one stressed the needs of, and the other was considered external to, the community.[27] The implications of all this for the women's group was a frequently debated subject because it is part of the P/political complexity of activism in Ballymurphy. As Chrissie explains, there is an acute awareness of politics in the area:

> Everything you pretty much do here is political. When you stand out in that street if you are going against something – I would look at it, I suppose, as normal – something that wasn't right. I mean if it is coming out of Northern Ireland and coming out of these areas it is always termed 'political', which is not necessarily the case.

Another difficulty for the group was that it planned to apply for funding and could not be associated with a political party. However, the uneasy relationship between the differing types of P/political activism never disappeared as some women participated in party-political work outside the group. It is difficult in a small community to fully separate 'Political' activism and community work since local residents often associate one's actions with party-political activity and previous community activism was largely focused on 'Political' concerns. Furthermore, the perceived composition of the group proved to be a difficulty for some members and limited the effectiveness of the group locally. The women's group gained visibility with their campaign, but it was also deemed 'too Political' for some members, who consequently left the group. The latter women felt that the group was not 'balanced' since the majority would have been perceived to be supporters of Sinn Féin. There was debate as to why the women left. Some thought it was because of personal differences and others felt it was due to the nature of the group's campaigns. However, women also had the difficulty and potential stigma of being associated with the 'Provo–lesbian–man-hating group', whilst other obstacles related to time commitment and familial responsibilities.

The renegotiation of feminism

Members of the women's group stress they are a 'women's group' and distance themselves from any claim of feminism. This is due in part to the problem of the term 'feminism' and the negative connotations surrounding it, but also because they do not feel themselves to be part of a larger feminist consciousness. Many of the stereotypes surrounding feminism are negative, relating to man-hating, lesbianism, anti-family ideas and a lack of what the women would call 'femininity'.[28] The reluctance of the women to associate themselves with 'feminism' is apparent and a cause of unease. The women in the group had to wrestle with the stigma of being labelled 'feminist' in a community that maintains a conservative gender ideology. Karen voices the difficulty many women face in relation to feminism:

> Most people associate it with these macho types, but my husband says I'm a feminist ... I don't know what the word is but I don't sort of – because that's what feminism – it comes across as, but I do believe women are equal and should be treated as equal ... It's just the word, but I don't know the alternative for it.

When asked if she would consider herself a feminist, Bridie spells out her difficulty with the term:

> Don't know what it means. I'm just a person. A people's person. I don't like ties and I don't like labels, because all your life people want to pigeonhole you. I don't want to be pigeonholed. I don't want to be called – been called a lesbian, a feminist, and a man-hater and all because of the women's group. Before that as well. If I'm out and about and I see an injustice I will do something about it – that's me, that's who I am. I've always been a people-oriented person.

While the projects and activities undertaken by the group were determined by their experiences as women within a particular community, in the process of participating in these activities the women found themselves renegotiating the limits of womanhood, femininity and the 'political'. As Liz states:

> Everyone has their own part to play, do you know what I mean? So it is the case that you carry on with that part; we're doing this part. We want to be recognised, ourselves, as women, trying to do things with the community.

Women are empowered through community work, which may raise awareness of gender roles and sexual inequality, but this does not entail a 'feminist' consciousness. Many women involved in community work embrace what seems to be a 'grass-roots' feminism, but when questioned further, fully reject associating their actions with a larger women's movement, which they view as unrelated to working-class problems. This is not simply a matter of semantics, but is related to larger theoretical and practical questions in feminism. Arguably, women in working-class republican areas have dealt with many negative labels and do not want another pejorative classification. Their rejection of the term 'feminist' is in line with their overall strategy of self-definition and (re)interpretation of gender roles.

'A woman's place is in the struggle'

One of the first public events held by the group indicates the way they negotiated the role of women in their community at the onset. In August 1997 the women's group prepared a photographic exhibit as part of the West Belfast Festival, titled 'A Woman's Place is in the Struggle'. It was held in the local club and was well attended by local men and women. This project was part of the negotiation of the politics of identity by the group, as they defined themselves as women in relation to their community. This was significant because the group subverted the traditional ideology – 'a woman's place is in the home' – and placed women directly in the public sphere and in a history of their own design. The expressed aim of the exhibit was to bring to the forefront the women who were always a part of the struggle, but remained invisible – the 'ordinary' woman. They wanted to honour women who visited the jails every week, banged bin lids, and offered support in countless ways, while never claiming the public spotlight. In the weeks leading up to the festival, the women made requests to the community for photographs of local women. Photographs poured in, and women went from house to house, collecting photos and looking through old photo albums. The result was unprecedented. It seemed as though the community was coming forward to acknowledge the work of their foremothers. As I watched the project emerge, it was clear that the group was demarcating their space and origins, as they expressed their understanding of a woman's place. It was not a simple matter of adding women into the history of Ballymurphy: the group constructed a woman-centred history that placed them as the current chapter in the struggle. Although it was repeatedly stated that the exhibit would not be 'too political', it was impossible to avoid it being so because the history of women's community participation *is* political. At the end, the group evaluated the success of the show, questioning if the exhibition had portrayed the 'ordinary' woman. Some felt it had reaffirmed a republican version of women's part in the struggle. Others felt it did capture the ordinary woman, but only in small ways. The dilemma is understandable, but was an important part in the process of self-definition. The exhibition claimed the space of women. It validated women's participation in the armed struggle, the community and the home, but it also played an important part in consciousness-raising among the women's group as they negotiated their position in relation to feminism and republicanism.

Conclusion

The women's group expresses a powerful voice that argues for recognition on their own terms. They work in conjunction with other community groups, but strive to retain their own perspective and empower local women, and by doing so, they challenge power relations and gender expectations. Empowerment is a redistribution of power, and women's community participation renegotiates power relations both in the community and in the home.

When the group originally came together there was an emphasis on addressing previously neglected issues in the community, such as education, health and domestic violence. However, as they developed, their direction expanded and the women became involved in the control and distribution of resources and began to argue for a role in the future direction of community development. By working in the community they came to understand the gendered nature of social structures, which also encouraged an exploration into women's issues. This is significant because women were not prepared simply to go back into the home once there was no longer a need for them to protect, protest and picket on behalf of their community. This points to larger questions for the future of women's role in community development. If the need to protect the community is reduced, then where do women fit in? All indications suggest that this is part of a process, questions arise as to the next stage. Furthermore, how will women redefine their position in light of increased opportunities and social changes? This issue will continue to evolve, but it is one that also concerns the role of women in the peace process and emerging Northern Ireland society.

The peace process opened up new opportunities for women's groups to develop. This is a long-term process, which must be recognised and accompanied by strategic approaches to ensure that women are integrated fully into society.[29] Furthermore, the recognition of the gendered nature of community activism has implications for strategic community development policy. The next challenge lies in the development of an inclusive vision of community activism that recognises and values the contribution of women.

Chapter 12

Times of transition: republican women, feminism and political representation

Margaret Ward

This essay will argue that Ireland has experienced two periods of democratic transition, in both of which gender has helped to shape the process of transition itself. In both periods of political and military resistance to the British presence in Ireland (in the first two and in the last three decades of the twentieth century), an independent women's movement articulated arguments for women's representation while a substantial group of republican women stated their own determination to ensure that women's voices would be heard.

In the years before the 1916 Rising competing discourses of citizenship circulated freely in Ireland, yet women were not fully regarded as citizens by either the British State, then in political control of the country, or by the vast majority of Irish men. Despite the vigorous campaign of the suffrage movement, the concept of citizenship remained heavily gendered. When, in 1913, nationalists formed the male-only Irish Volunteers to fight for Home Rule, recruits were reassured that they would be recognising themselves 'as citizens and as men'.[1] Women had national duties to perform in Cumann na mBan but they were not permitted to take part in the Volunteer movement. There was no indication that national independence would confer citizenship rights on Irish women because the Volunteers refused to make a commitment on the issue. Nevertheless, despite that unpromising situation, five short, tumultuous years later, women over thirty in Britain and Ireland had the vote and Ireland had the distinction of electing the first woman to parliament.

The second 'period of transition' emerged in the 1990s, as the North of Ireland began to consider the future after decades of armed conflict. Women had made a considerable contribution to the struggle for Irish self-determination, yet their long-term future within the decision-making structures of the republican movement was not assured. At the same time, feminists in the autonomous women's movement began to consider the opportunities for political representation offered by the changing situation. From those circumstances emerged the republican feminist organisation Clár na mBan and the cross-community Northern Ireland Women's Coalition.

Periods of transition

This evaluation of the political activity and democratic participation of women during the transition process is concerned primarily with a consideration of the extent to which feminism and nationalism worked together to challenge traditional male/female binaries determining political activity. Transition is a 'special moment', when the usual rules can be questioned, discarded or redefined. However, this can only be accomplished if there are sufficient numbers of activists.[2] Too often, the lessons learned from the experiences of others is that 'democratic transitions remain unfinished when citizens of both genders are taken into account'.[3] The dynamics that prompt a successful transition can be very different from those of consolidation when, once again, women find themselves excluded from the process.

Two important groups feature in this discussion: nationalist women who had proven their credentials in the military and political struggle against British rule, and feminist women unaligned to any party who welcomed the opportunity to challenge an all-male political structure. Republican women, during these two periods of transition, gained a prominence in political life unthinkable in previous decades. Constance Markievicz became Minister for Labour in the First Dáil Éireann while, fifty years later, Bairbre de Brún, as Minister for Health in the Northern Ireland Assembly, became the first Sinn Féin woman to occupy a seat in government since the short-lived tenure in office

of Markievicz. In addition, with the elections of June 2001, Michelle
Gildernew became the first Sinn Féin woman to be elected to
Westminster since that election of 1918 in which Constance
Markievcz had become the first woman (in either Ireland or Britain)
to be elected to Westminster (although she did not take her seat). For
non-aligned women, these transition periods have been equally fruitful. Several feminists were elected as independents to local
government in 1920, retaining office for a number of years. The
Women's Coalition currently attracts attention because of its rarity as
a party that has succeeded in having women elected on what is essentially a woman's platform.

War and citizenship

In the pre-1916 period, when women's campaign for the vote
challenged nationalist insistence that the Home Rule issue took priority, an uneasy relationship existed between republicanism and
feminism. While suffragist Hanna Sheehy Skeffington argued that
'[u]ntil the Parliamentarian and the Sinn Féin woman alike possess the
vote, the keystone of citizenship, she will count but little with either
party',[4] her republican feminist friend Rosamond Jacob responded,
'Political rights conferred on Irish women by a foreign government
would be a miserable substitute for the same rights won, even three
years later, from our own legislative assembly.'[5] Feminists and republicans agreed on the goal of full citizenship rights, yet disagreement on
political priorities always threatened to divide them. For many
feminists, women's entry into the political sphere was crucial to changing a patriarchal order that covered up child abuse and condoned
wife-beating, and that, in the years before 1914, was characterised by
an imperialist world view leading inexorably to war. Their belief that
participation would add a missing dimension to public life, contributing values of compromise, nurture and pacifism, fuelled their
insistence that women's citizenship could not be contingent on changes
to national boundaries.

    In contrast, many republican women were uneasy at the suggestion
that they might bring gender-specific values to the public sphere.
Their entry into the political world would enable them to add their
voice to that of their male comrades. It was a question of democratic

rights and there was no suggestion that they would be saying anything different from their comrades. Constance Markievicz's exhortation to 'dress suitably in short skirts and strong boots … and buy a revolver', and her hope that war would bring out the 'masculine side of women's souls' by 'shaking women out of old grooves' was shared by a significant number of activists.[6] Once the Irish Volunteers were formed and the possibility of armed conflict became a reality, a substantial number of women maintained that equality within the movement included the right to be militarily active on an equal footing with men. For them, essentialist claims for women's innate pacifist instincts were retrogressive.

How were these arguments played out in the fast-changing context of a war of independence, where women's status as political and military actors underwent significant transformation? The leaders of the 1916 Rising, through the pledges contained within the Republican Proclamation, had ensured that equality of citizenship would no longer be contentious. All true republicans had to accept that women had won the right to participate in the public sphere. They had fought with the men and shared the dangers of war. Their future rights as citizens of an Irish Republic were guaranteed. In the meantime, as nationalists regrouped in the aftermath of the Rising, republican women caucused together to ensure that the surviving leadership of the movement held fast to the promises made by their dead comrades. They formed an umbrella group, Cumann na d'Teachtaire (League of Women Delegates), to pressurise Sinn Féin into co-opting women onto the executive of the organisation. This took several months to achieve but the presence of well-known women in positions of seniority enabled the group to succeed in its goal of ensuring that the 1917 Sinn Féin Convention passed a motion affirming the equality of women and men within the organisation.[7]

With the Representation of the People Act of 1918, women over thirty in Britain and Ireland won the right to vote and to stand for election. Cumann na mBan, the organisation of republican women militants, sister organisation to the IRA (formerly the Irish Volunteers), even before parliament changed the law on voting had altered its constitution in recognition of this new mood. Members were instructed to 'participate in the public life of their locality and assert their rights as citizens to take part in the nominations of candidates for parliamentary and local elections'.[8] In choosing candidates for the 1918 elections Sinn Féin was ruthless, at least so far as the criterion for women was concerned. The only two chosen, Constance Markievicz and Winifred Carney, had both taken part in the Rising. As members of the Irish Citizen Army they had proven themselves the equals of men. They were not considered to be bringing a female quality to public life, but upholding the tradition of physical force republicanism, now firmly within the public arena. That the criterion for female candidates included transcendence of femaleness is substantiated when one considers other possible candidates. Kathleen Clarke, widow of 1916 leader Tom, found herself thwarted in her effort to be selected as candidate,[9] while Hanna Sheehy Skeffington was offered only the opportunity to stand in an unwinnable constituency.[10]

The republican leadership that took over from the executed men appeared less committed to equality in participation. The unimpressive groups of men sent by Sinn Féin to campaign for Markievicz indicate a lack of faith in her electoral prospects.[11] Meg Connery, a suffragist activist, considered the Markievicz candidacy to be no more than 'a sop thrown to the women of the country' by Sinn Féin.[12] The tone of Markievicz's electoral message to the readers of the *Irish Citizen* can possibly be explained by the fact that, sequestered in Holloway Jail, unaware of the behind-the-scenes controversies, she was optimistic that her electoral ward in Dublin would become a beacon of hope for the feminist cause: 'we could make St Patrick's a rallying ground for women and a splendid centre for constructive work for women'.[13] Her success owes much to the determination of suffragists and republican women from Cumann na mBan to ensure that one Irish woman at least would prove that women could be as effective as men in the political realm. It would have been difficult for suffragists to put forward their own candidates and, in the circumstances, probably counterproductive. While Rosamond Jacob expected Sheehy Skeffington, the three women in jail and some women in Dublin to be included on the list of candidates, she hoped suffragists 'won't try to run women as independent candidates ... That would be hopeless everywhere I should think, and would give the impression that they didn't care about the national issue.'[14] The election literature of the period saw many appeals made to that unknown factor – the female voter. The Sinn Féin appeal for women to vote for the party exhorted 'valiant women' to uphold the tradition of women playing a noble part in the fight for freedom, promising that they would in the future 'have a high place in the councils of a freed Gaelic nation'.[15]

In the aftermath of the elections, the women of Cumann na d'Teachtaire held a meeting to consider their position. They were overly self-recriminatory in their belief that they had missed a good opportunity to have more women elected.[16] Yet again, women put the blame on themselves, despite the fact that some of the leading figures in this group were women bereaved by the Rising and women who had recently emerged from prison. After the debacle of the Markievicz election campaign they decided to arrange speakers' classes, intending to urge that women be co-opted into the double seats created by some Sinn Féin members winning in more than one constituency. All this revealed a new determination to engage with the party hierarchy and with male domination of the party, capitalising upon the new spirit sweeping the country. There was some liaison with feminists – recognition that suffrage activists were much more experienced in the art of public speaking. But the War of Independence meant that the moment was lost. In 1919 women were back in jail with political machinery left in disarray as men went on the run.

By the end of the war circumstances had altered. The younger generation of women in Cumann na mBan were less interested in the vote than in playing an equal part with men in the IRA. They wanted to be a woman's army and to demonstrate their equality in this way. The political sphere was less attractive and, as the majority were under thirty years of age, it was fairly irrelevant as they were ineligible to vote or to stand for election. However, there were now six women members of the Second Dáil (Kathleen Clarke, Margaret Pearse, Kate O'Callaghan, Mary MacSwiney and Dr Ada English were elected alongside Markievicz), and, partly because it was so dangerous for men to stand, considerable numbers of women had been elected to local government office. Despite the terrors of war, opportunities for public participation had opened up for women. For example, their service in the republican courts that supplanted the British judicial system, because of a stipulation that a female justice be present if a woman was involved in the proceedings, appeared to promise greater influence in public life. This was to change after the Dáil, in January 1922, voted to accept the Treaty with Britain that was to bring an end to war, at a cost of a partitioned country and the maintenance of significant British influence within the Free State of the twenty-six counties. All six women in the Dáil voted against the Treaty.

Two months after the Treaty debate Kate O'Callaghan, one of the female deputies, introduced a bill to enfranchise women in their twenties, arguing that 'without their votes or their voice, nobody can say that the will of the whole people of Ireland will have been ascertained'.[17] Markievicz insisted that the demand for the vote was a spontaneous one, 'women everywhere throughout the country suddenly finding their position to be humiliating, and it was the fight that did it. They say they must have a say as to the Treaty, and that if they are good enough to take part in the fight, they are good enough to vote.'[18] From outside the Dáil, former suffragists organised delegations and pickets to claim citizenship rights for those young women whose efforts in the war had been so crucial. The motion was lost, largely out of fear that the introduction of a substantial proportion of younger voters would 'torpedo' the Treaty, although an undertaking was given by the Cumann na nGaedheal government that women would be enfranchised when the new state came into existence. Markievicz, Pearse, English and Clarke all lost their seats in the Treaty elections. A bitter civil war ensued, lasting until May 1923, when the republicans conceded defeat.

Although women over twenty-one were granted the right to vote in the 1922 Constitution, the ensuing decades were deeply conservative and many of the rights won by women during the republican struggle were swept away by governments determined to ensure that women's participation in public life would be short-lived. Restrictions on women undertaking jury service came in quickly, in sharp contrast to the days of republican courts.[19] In addition, a policy of abstention and non-cooperation with the Free State led to a marginalisation of republicans from the political process and the loss of many outspoken women from political life.

Second wave Irish feminism

The Irish Constitution of 1937, giving primacy to 'women's life within the home', provided the State with every justification for further exclusion of women. During the fifty years from 1922 to 1972, the average Dáil contained only four women, three per cent of deputies.[20] While women remained active on many other fronts, no woman politician followed Markievicz into cabinet office until the appointment of Màire Geoghegan-Quinn in 1979.[21] Not coincidentally, this period was characterised by the rise of 'second wave' feminism, an international movement that was embraced with enthusiasm by Irish women, who once again gave voice to their determination to challenge gender-based oppression.

In the North, the nationalist minority population existed in a state of reluctant acquiescence, discriminated against in political, social and economic life by a sectarian Unionist government with an inbuilt majority. Periodic skirmishes by the IRA were dealt with by the imposition of harsh law-and-order policies, including internment. All was to change in the 1970s as physical force republicanism emerged in response to the failure of Unionism to recognise the legitimacy of the demands of the civil rights movement. Northern feminists, hoping to develop their own 'second wave' movement, discovered that competing national identities and conflicting political priorities engendered similar disputes between republicanism and feminism as those of the pre-1916 era.

In an echo of the franchise debate, republican feminists argued that working for social and economic reforms in a context of an on-going national liberation struggle was tantamount to accepting British rule, and therefore campaigns to win divorce law reform or abortion rights could not be supported. The dominant slogan for republicans was, 'There can be no women's liberation until national liberation'. The other side of the debate concerned the situation of republican women prisoners. As the republican military campaign intensified, women became a vital part of the IRA. Feminists who did not support the republican campaign found it difficult to consider giving support to the campaign by women prisoners in Armagh jail who, in the early 1980s, suffered repeated strip-searching and the privations of a 'no wash' protest as a consequence of their determination to win political status. However, the difficulties of this period in feminist history are not part of a consideration of the opportunities thrown up in a process of transition.[22] Such topics are discussed elsewhere in this book, in essays by Corcoran, Talbot and Hackett. What is of concern here is the following decade and, in particular, the responses of republican women and feminist women outside of republicanism to the challenges thrown up by the emerging 'peace process'.

Eilish Rooney, analysing the differing discourses of Irish national-ism as a result of twenty-five years of conflict, sees women's issues as an integral part: 'It has been the discourse of resistance to British imperialism, of Catholic working-class struggle against oppression and injustice; of feminism and the politics of liberation.'[23] Yet despite the considerable contribution made by women to the republican movement (defined in its broadest terms to include community activism, and political and military engagement), as rumours of cease-fires and covert negotiations began to dominate political life from 1993, republican women who were outside of the organised political movement began to feel anxious that, despite their commitment and sacrifice, the process of exclusion that had been experienced so often in the past would occur once more.

Clár na mBan and Sinn Féin

In a striking parallel with Cumann na d'Teachtaire, a coalition of feminists had come together in 1992 concerned that 'women's voices have largely been absent from the formal discussion and debate'.[24] This coalition called itself Clár na mBan (Women's Agenda) and invited all women to join who shared the following aims:

• To secure the recognition and acknowledgement of women's role in shaping Ireland's future;
• To claim our right to our self-determination in the context of Irish national unity;
• To establish and maintain equality for women in all sections of Irish society;
• To encourage women to participate in the political process.[25]

In March 1994 a conference in Belfast attended by 150 women from throughout the country heard Oonagh Marron of the Falls Women's Centre encapsulate the historical dilemma of republican feminists in her opening address:

> As nationalist women and as feminists, we have very often given our
> support unconditionally to the overthrow of British colonialism in

this country. We have often buried our demands for the sake of the common purpose … The danger is that once again we are going to be asked to bury our demands, this time in the common purpose of achieving peace.[26]

Clár na mBan were determined to build the women's movement into an 'undeniable force' which would ensure that when politicians talked of peace they would mean by that 'peace with justice and when they talk about guarantees they mean a guarantee of equality for all the citizens of this country'. This left open the question of how responsive politicians in Northern Ireland would be to women's pressure, given the overwhelmingly male composition of all political parties, with the exception of Sinn Féin. As Clár na mBan represented the 'concerns and interests of women from the broad nationalist Catholic community',[27] Sinn Féin was undoubtedly the primary target. Claire Hackett, a leading figure in the group, was clear on the necessity for Clár's existence:

> Sinn Féin is still a male-dominated party and as such cannot always be trusted to make women's interests a priority. There is a need for a strong and independent republican feminist voice to bring our agenda to the fore … The feminist challenge to the whole republican movement must continue if we are to make real and radical changes to Irish society.[28]

In the heady atmosphere generated by the republican and loyalist ceasefires, republican feminists believed that all kinds of possibilities were opening up: 'There was a great excitement around, a feeling that change was possible in many different areas, that we could make things new, find new ways of doing things.'[29] Challenging Sinn Féin was regarded as part of the process of building new forms of political action. It was a challenge derived from a confidence that nationalists, no longer forced to give priority to the needs of war, were now strong enough to engage in internal analysis and constructive criticism. Marie Quiery, speaking at International Women's Day celebrations in March 1995, reiterated the point that women continued to see 'men negotiating with and for men'. She urged that the conflict of interest between women and men be addressed and not 'submerged to the greater glory of the movement as a whole'.[30]

Within Sinn Féin itself, determined efforts by feminists over past decades had resulted in the acceptance of progressive gender policies and a commitment to increasing the participation of women through a policy of reserving places for women on the party executive. In 1995 there were nine women on its twenty-four member executive.[31] When peace talks eventually began in 1997 the party also observed the principle of gender equity in deciding on the composition of its delegations: Lucilita Bhreatnach, Sinn Féin General Secretary, was the only woman at the table, apart from the two Women's Coalition members and Mo Mowlam, Secretary of State. However, this scrupulous adherence to principles of gender equity did not mean that Sinn Féin women were necessarily fully incorporated into all aspects of decision-making. There were reasons for feminists to feel uneasy with this public display of political correctness as observers wondered if some of those Sinn Féin delegates possessed a role other than note-taker:

> The women negotiators … stand out for their silence in the face of cameras while the three men [Gerry Adams, Martin McGuinness and Mitchel McLaughlin] all have significant media profiles. Little indication is given of whether feminism plays a part in shaping negotiation strategies or demands … media appearances and statements would suggest not.[32]

Forming a women's coalition

Outside of the republican community, many other women were wondering how they could have a voice in the future. Monica McWilliams and Kate Fearon, in an account of the formation of the Northern Ireland Women's Coalition (NIWC), have described the republican and loyalist ceasefires of 1994 as 'a catalyst for change', encouraging women from many different organisations to consider means of increasing their political involvement.[33] Women's community-based groups, which had played so crucial a role in maintaining some kind of fabric of society, as community and voluntary organisations filled the space left vacant by the absence of elected politicians, articulated their anxieties in a joint submission to the Dublin Forum for Peace and Reconciliation. In 1995 the European Women's

Platform in Northern Ireland and the National Women's Council in the Republic held a joint conference to express their concerns about the exclusion of women from discussions.[34] That level of mistrust of masculinist society, evidenced throughout women's organisations and experienced on both sides of the border, surpasses the anxieties of feminists in the early years of the last century. Contemporary women, well aware of past precedents, had the painful knowledge of past betrayals in their history to inform those fears.

Another conference, attended by a wide range of women from over two hundred organisations and with a wide variety of political views, was held in Draperstown in June 1995. On this occasion participants concluded that 'mechanisms for women to become involved in Constitutional talks are needed'.[35] While it was difficult to envisage what these might consist of, an opportunity emerged unexpectedly, early in 1996, when the Irish and British governments announced proposals for elections to choose delegates to forthcoming peace talks.

There was little faith in the likelihood of established parties ensuring that an equitable proportion of women would be selected as candidates for election. With hindsight, given the serious concerns women had been expressing over the previous months, the formation of a woman's party has the appearance of inevitability. However, in reality, as various accounts of the early days of the Women's Coalition have confirmed, there was no one moment when all recognised the opportunity that presented itself. What did happen was that a gradually growing groundswell of concern eventually crystallised into a conviction that women had to organise themselves for election. Proposals and ideas circulated around the community sector (while discussion documents sent by the women to political parties were ignored) until a meeting of over one hundred, held in the Ulster People's College on 17 April 1996, took a decision to stand for election. While 10,000 votes would be needed, this seemed entirely manageable when broken down into one hundred votes for one hundred women. A 'Northern Ireland Women's Coalition' was agreed, initially only for the duration of the talks process. At first, the Coalition was seen as a movement whose members could belong to other parties. Its core principles were agreed as inclusion, equality and human rights. All policies would be judged against these yardsticks. No position would be taken on the constitutional issue, partly because the Coalition was composed of so many disparate views and also because many felt that openness and flexibility were positive attributes that could contribute much to the process of negotiation.[36]

The Coalition contained within its ranks nationalists and Unionists, some who would describe themselves as 'republican but not Sinn Féin' and some who refused all labels. However, a significant number of republican feminists who had attended the initial meeting that gave birth to the Coalition voiced their dissent, refusing to support a party that stayed silent on the issue of the constitutional link with Britain. Their misgivings are expressed by the analysis of Eilish Rooney, couching the difficulties inherent in a women's coalition in the more neutral language of the sociologist:

> It is an obvious thing to say but still needs saying: 'women' are not a unified gender group, sharing essential qualities or experiences … Nationalist, republican, Catholic women and unionist, loyalist, Protestant women are situated differently in the social, economic and political hierarchies of the North … No serious engagement in political debate, and in the formation of tactical political alliances, can make fundamental political progress without these recognitions.[37]

For Rooney, 'The implications for feminism and coalition politics in a context of deep political division are enormous and complex.'[38] As the divisions are so entrenched, a truly inclusive feminism is improbable. This is a view shared by Claire Hackett: 'We can only create the basis for strong alliances by acknowledging the different identities of women rather than striving for a common ground that may only be an illusion.'[39]

In a letter to the Belfast feminist journal *Women's News*, republican feminists went public over the issue, making it clear that resolution of the national question rather than an immediate improvement in women's political participation remained their priority:

> The primary purpose of the 30 May election is purported to be to give a mandate to negotiating teams who will be negotiating a new constitutional arrangement. As citizens, we will be voting for the parties which we believe will best represent our views on this central issue. We do not believe that our interests as women in this society can be guaranteed by voting for women candidates simply because

they are women. The Women's Coalition are not agreed on a policy on future constitutional arrangements for this island. Its candidates hold both nationalist and unionist perspectives and other positions in between ... We believe that the Women's Coalition's inability to agree on fundamental issues of policy reflects the inherent weakness of the idea of a woman's political party. We recognise that many of the women involved in the Coalition are participating with the best of intentions, but we cannot give them our vote.[40]

Many of the signatories to this petition were members of Clár na mBan, some others were from Sinn Féin. Their rejection of the NIWC was based on fear that its presence on polling lists would prove a threat to Sinn Féin and hence damage the nationalist cause, because the list system (the variant of proportional representation being used for the elections) meant that voters were choosing parties rather than individual candidates. As it turned out, Sinn Féin received its highest ever votes (up to that point), indicating that there was little overlap in support. Ninety candidates would be elected using constituency lists and twenty from a regional list – these would be allocated to the ten parties gaining the largest numbers of votes regionally. The choice of system was a deliberate measure by the British government to encourage small loyalist parties to enter the political arena. This was the opportunity seized upon by the women – they knew they would not succeed in displacing established parties from the constituencies but reckoned that women had enough support across the province to win two seats from the regional list. They were right. The NIWC came ninth in the elections, was entitled to two seats on the Forum for Political Dialogue and able to send two delegates (Monica McWilliams, from a rural Catholic background, and Pearl Sagar, a working-class Protestant from Belfast) to the all-party talks.

Women and the peace process

Multi-party talks, which did not begin until 1996, had little impetus or relevance until the change of government following the May 1997 general election. Sinn Féin was excluded because the IRA ceasefire had broken down and the decommissioning issue meant that all discussion had ground to a standstill. Remaining true to their principles, NIWC members continued to argue for the inclusion of Sinn Féin and made a point of regular briefing meetings with the party: symbolic and practical affirmation of their commitment to a new way of making politics work.

The advent of a Labour government and, in particular, the presence of a new Northern Ireland Secretary, Mo Mowlam (the first woman to hold this post), rejuvenated proceedings. Her presence was crucial to the eventual outcome of the negotiations as she cajoled and persuaded reluctant politicians to consider and re-consider proposals from different viewpoints. Many accounts have also paid tribute to the constructive work of the NIWC, who were, apart from Mowlam, the only female politicians in the talks. Its delegates often acted as trusted arbiters between different factions. The Good Friday Agreement contains much that stems directly from the participation of those few women: recognition of the needs of the victims of the Troubles; the promise of a civic forum; and affirmation of the right of women to full and equal political participation:

> ... George Mitchell completed his last *tour de table*, and everyone responded ... Only one of those voices responding affirmatively was a woman's – the voice of the NIWC.[41]

Antagonism between republican feminists and the NIWC abated after it was realised that the principles of inclusion, equality and human rights that informed the working practice of the party were to the advantage of Sinn Féin. Although Clár na mBan did not succeed in regaining the political prominence it had achieved in the early months of the peace process, its presence within the heartlands of republicanism had some effect, particularly in the numbers of nationalist women elected to the Northern Ireland Assembly. Sinn Féin, with five women out of a total of eighteen Assembly members, emerged as the party with the largest number of female MLAs. In 1998, unlike the situation in 1918, women were not chosen because of traditional republican proclivities: some had participated in community women's activities before joining the party. Individual members of Clár na mBan have remained at the forefront of feminist struggle, particularly in challenging political parties to engage in dialogue with Irish lesbians and gays.

The NIWC succeeded in the election of two of its candidates,

Monica McWilliams and Jane Morrice, while also forcing rival political parties to stand female candidates in order to hold onto to their female voters. Although the figure of 13 per cent of the total female composition of the Assembly remains abysmally low for women's representation, it could be regarded as an encouraging beginning – but only if political parties do more to develop gender equity within their own ranks.[42] If women are not in positions of some seniority within their organisations they will hardly be selected as future candidates for election.

Moving towards an equal future?

Carol Coulter, discussing the relationship between feminism and republicanism, voices her conviction that criticism must extend beyond concentration upon a male-dominated leadership: 'The very nature of the republican movement, like all nationalist movements, requires a centralisation and homogenisation which is hostile to dissent.'[43] With this critique, gender becomes less of an issue because '[t]he women who break into this system are subsumed into it'.[44] It might be argued, however, that while women remain a small minority in any political organisation their ability to develop a vigorous and identifiable gender identity remains severely limited. Although not fully articulated by the Clár na mBan activists, the wish to break free from such centralisation and a desire to encourage grass-roots participation in political discussion had been an important motivation in their challenge to republicanism.

Recent developments within Sinn Féin would seem to indicate some backlash by a membership that has become less sympathetic to the leadership advocacy of greater participation by women. In 2000 the party's Ard Fheis (party conference) failed to elect any women to the Ard Chomhairle (central committee). In response, the party commissioned a working body to consider how this gender imbalance could be redressed. The result was a motion to the 2001 Ard Fheis, advocating reserved seats for women and providing for co-options to ensure that women held no less than 30 per cent of Ard Chomhairle positions. The ensuing debate indicated a profound commitment to women's equality on the part of many experienced activists – 'If Sinn Féin is to lead the way to national liberation, the party must reflect the gender balance of the society we live in' – while not all those opposed to quotas were hostile to improving women's participation. A number of delegates believed that the motion emanated from a perceived need by the leadership to appear politically correct by solving 'media image problems' and cautioned that positive discrimination 'would not address the difficulties faced by women within the party'.[45] This might be indicative of a wider problem in terms of internal gender relations, but why were no women elected to the Ard Chomhairle? Is there indeed a 'backlash' within Sinn Féin, a wariness of any imposition of a feminist agenda? There are some salient parallels with the situation within Sinn Féin in the period after the Easter Rising. Then, republican women fought hard within the organisation before they succeeded in winning election to the executive at the 1917 Ard Fheis. However, the evidence of individual branches indicated considerable cultural resistance to the selection of female representatives. A mere twelve women out of one thousand delegates succeeded in winning nomination as delegates and, because of this, women in the early years of nation-building did not come to prominence as political leaders. That dissonance between grass-roots and leadership would appear to remain.

If the experience of world war and nationalist uprising in the early years of the last century succeeded in transforming gender ideologies, it was a purely temporary transformation. Political control by Britain had been rejected through force of arms, institutions were collapsing, to be replaced by those more representative of the Irish people. During this time the opportunity to challenge existing norms and to insist on women's right to participate was recognised by a small group of women, both republican and feminist. The turmoil of that period can be characterised as an example of a society struggling to make a transition to new forms of participative democracy. Shortly afterwards, the counter-revolution that followed the formation of the Free State re-established traditional gender relations as an immediate priority and developed institutional arrangements that mirrored those they had initially fought to reject. Today, another period of transition exists in Northern Ireland. Again, the final outcome in terms of transformation of gender relations remains uncertain, contingent upon the maintenance of the impetus that led to the beginnings of the peace process.

Three nationalist (no Unionist) women sit on the Northern Ireland Executive: Carmel Hanna and Brid Rogers for the SDLP and Bairbre de Brún for Sinn Féin. For die-hard opponents of the peace process, feminism remains part of a 'pan-nationalist front'.[46] The need to confront and resolve the continued sectarian divisions existing in the North of Ireland has meant, and continues to mean, that gender equity sits far down the political agenda. At the same time, the continued presence of the NIWC serves to ensure that no political party can afford to ignore the potential threat to patriarchal practice posed by the existence of a woman's party at the heart of the political process. For many feminists, the opportunity remains to offer the potential to advance the interests of women in the interests of the whole community, to show how 'the process of peace-building can be done differently'.[47] The agreement signed by the political parties on Good Friday 1998 provides a template from which a society based on equality can be constructed, if the will is there. The challenge of moving towards building an inclusive society from a situation where sections of the community have been politically marginalised and deprived of economic and social resources are immense. For women, it is also a challenge to ensure that they do not return to the margins.

Endnotes

NOTES TO CHAPTER 1

1. G. Mosse, *Nationalism and Sexuality* (Madison, WI: University of Wisconsin Press, 1985), p. 17.
2. Ibid., p. 18.
3. K. Jayawardena, *Feminism and Nationalism in the Third World* (London: Zed Press, 1986); T. Mayer, *Gender Ironies of Nationalism* (London: Routledge, 2000); A. McClintock, *Imperial Leather: Race, Gender and Sexuality in Colonial Contexts* (New York: Routledge, 1995); A. Parker et al. (eds), *Nationalisms and Sexualities* (London: Routledge, 1992); R. Roach Pierson and N. Chaundry, *Nation, Colony and Empire* (Bloomington, IN: Indiana University Press, 1998); N. Yuval-Davis and F. Anthias, *Racialised Boundaries* (London: Routledge, 1993).
4. N. Yuval-Davis, *Gender and Nation* (London: Sage, 1997).
5. A. McClintock, 'No Longer in a Future Heaven: Race, Gender and Nationalism', in A. McClintock, A. Mufti and E. Shohat (eds), *Dangerous Liaisons: Gender, Nation and Post-Colonial Perspectives* (Minnesota, MN: Minnesota University Press, 1997).
6. McClintock, 'No Longer in a Future Heaven', p. 93.
7. Ibid., pp. 90–1.
8. A. Smyth, 'The Floozie in the Jacuzzi', *Feminist Studies*, 17, 1 (1991), pp. 7–28.
9. A. McClintock, 'Family Feuds: Gender, Nationalism and the Family', *Feminist Review*, 44 (1993), pp. 61–80.
10. See, for example, Jayawardena, *Feminism and Nationalism*.
11. D. Kandiyoti, 'Women, Ethnicity and Nationalism', in J. Hutchinson and A. Smith (eds), *Ethnicity* (Oxford: Oxford University Press, 1996), pp. 311–15.
12. Ibid., p. 15.
13. S. Thapar-Bjorkert and L. Ryan, 'Mother India/Mother Ireland: Comparative Gendered Dialogues of Colonialism and Nationalism in the early Twentieth Century', *Women's Studies International Forum*, 25 (2002), pp. 301–13.
14. L. Connolly, *The Irish Women's Movement from Revolution to Devolution* (London: Palgrave, 2002), p. 30.
15. L. West, 'Feminist Nationalist Social Movements', *Women's Studies International Forum*, 15 (1992), pp. 563–79.
16. Ardoyne Commemoration Project, *Ardoyne: the untold truth* (Belfast: Beyond the Pale Publications, 2002).

NOTES TO CHAPTER 2

1. Public Record Office (PRO), Calendar of State Papers, Ireland (CSPI), vol. 29, p.30, Letter from Lord Piers to the Lord Chancellor, 5 August 1569.

2. Carew Papers, vol. 1, pp. 490–1, Lambeth Palace Library, London (LP).

3. Carew Papers, vol. 2, p. 277, LP.

4. CSPI, vol. 30, 8 April 1570, p. 428, PRO.

5. CSPI, vol. 65, 11 February 1579, p. 86, PRO.

6. CSPI, vol. 3 (1574–85), p. 107, PRO.

7. In Ireland this was a group of people with a common surname or a common named ancestor.

8. C. Lennon, *Sixteenth-Century Ireland: The Incomplete Conquest* (Dublin: Gill and Macmillan, 1994), p. 58.

9. S. Brigden, *New Worlds, Lost Worlds: The Rule of the Tudors, 1485–1603* (London, Penguin, 2000), pp. 20–1.

10. Records of Henry Pyerce, recorder of Westmeath, MS 883/1, pp. 297–8, Trinity College Dublin (TCD).

11. Brigden, *New Worlds*, pp. 22–3.

12. Fynes Moryson makes this point numerous times in F. Moryson, *An itinerary of the present state of Ireland* (London, 1617), vol. 4, pp. 198–9, 237.

13. Carew Papers, vol. 1, pp. 60–1, LP.

14. See Lennon, *Sixteenth-Century Ireland*, p. 114.

15. See T. Barnard, *Cromwellian Ireland. English Government and Reform in Ireland, 1649–1660* (Oxford: Clarendon Press, 1975; repr. 2000), especially pp. xii–xv.

16. See P. Walsh (ed.), *Beatha Ruaidh Uí Dhomhnaill* (Dublin: Dublin Institute of Advanced Studies, 1948); K. Meyer (ed. and trans.), *Cath Finntraga: Anecdota Oxondiensa*, vols 1–4 (Oxford: Clarendon Press, 1885). Both contain texts, documents and extracts of manuscripts.

17. See A. Cosgrove, 'Marriage in Medieval Ireland', in A. Cosgrove (ed.), *Marriage in Ireland* (Dublin: College Press, 1985).

18. See Moryson, *Itinerary*, vol. 4, pp. 10–11.

19. See Cosgrove, *Marriage*, pp. 1–16; K. Simms, 'Women in Norman Ireland', in M. MacCurtain and D. O'Corrain (eds), *Women in Irish Society: The Historical Dimension* (Dublin: Arlen House, 1978), pp. 1–20.

20. K. Nicholls, 'Irishwomen and Property in the Sixteenth Century', in M. MacCurtain and M. O'Dowd (eds), *Women in Early Modern Ireland* (Edinburgh: Edinburgh University Press, 1991), pp. 17–31.

21. Ibid., p. 27.

22. See K. Nicholls, 'Some Documents on Irish Law and Custom in the Sixteenth Century', in *Analecta Hibernica*, vol. 25 (Dublin: Dublin Institute of Advanced Studies, 1970), pp. 102–30.

23. N. Patterson, 'Gaelic Law and the Tudor Conquest of Ireland: the social background of the sixteenth-century recensions of the pseudo-historical prologue to the Senchas mor', in *Irish Historical Studies*, 27, 7 (Dublin: Irish Historical Society, 1991), pp. 193–215.

24. M. Haderman, 'Irish Women and Irish Law', in *The Crane Bag*, 4, 1 (1980), pp. 55–9.

25. M. MacCurtain, 'Marriage in Tudor Ireland', in Cosgrove (ed.), *Marriage in Ireland*, pp. 51–6.

26. Ibid., p. 51.

27. M. O'Dowd, 'Women and the Irish Chancery Court in the late sixteenth and early seventeenth centuries', *Irish Historical Studies*, 31, 124 (Ireland, 1999), pp. 470–87.

28. J. Ohlmeyer, 'Introduction: A Failed Revolution?', in J. Ohlmeyer (ed.), *Ireland From Independence to Occupation 1641–1660* (Cambridge: Cambridge University Press, 1995), p. 1.

29. Ibid.
30. See Barnard, *Cromwellian Ireland*, pp. 4–5.
31. Ibid., p. 2.
32. See N. Canny, *Making Ireland British, 1580–1650* (Oxford: Oxford University Press, 2001), p. 275.
33. See R. Mitchison, 'Ireland and Scotland: The Seventeenth-Century Legacies Compared', in T. M. Devine and D. Dickson (eds), *Ireland and Scotland 1600–1850, Parallels and Contrasts in Economic and Social Developments* (Edinburgh: John Donald Press, 1983), p. 4.
34. See Barnard, *Cromwellian Ireland*, p. 2.
35. Ibid., p. 4.
36. See N. Canny, 'What really happened in 1641?', in Ohlmeyer (ed.), *Ireland From Independence to Occupation*, p. 27.
37. Deposition manuscripts are held in Trinity College Dublin.
38. See M. Bennett, *The Civil Wars Experienced: Britain and Ireland, 1638–1661* (London: Routledge Press, 2000); Canny, *Making Ireland British*.
39. See Bennett, *Civil Wars*, p. 67.
40. See Canny, *Making Ireland British*, p. 345.
41. Ibid., p. 548.
42. These manuscripts are held in the Public Record Office, London and Lambeth Palace Library, London.
43. N. Yuval-Davis, *Gender and Nation* (London: Sage Press, 1997; repr. 2000), p. 4.
44. These are contained in the Gilbert Library, Dublin (GLD).
45. Calendar of State Papers, Foreign series, vol. 2 (1557–77), 9 June 1577, p. 245, PRO.
46. CSPI, vol. 3 (1574–85), p. 173, PRO.
47. CSPI, vol. 15, 12 February 1581, pp. 424–5, PRO.
48. CSPI, vol. 17 (1588–92), p. 63, PRO.
49. CSPI, vol. 21 (1600–1), p. 282, PRO.
50. Deposition MS 813, ff. 3–6, TCD.
51. M. MacNeill, *Maire Rua, Lady of Leamaneh* (Clare: Ballinakella Press, 1990), p. 75.
52. J. Fergusen (ed.), *Ulster Journal of Archaeology, Ulster Roll of Gaol Delivery, 1613–1618*, 1st series, vol. 1 (Dublin: Irish Manuscripts Commission, 1953), pp. 260–70.
53. Gilbert MS, vol. 1, p. xlvii, GLD.
54. M. O'Dowd, 'Women and War in Ireland in the 1640s', in MacCurtain and O'Dowd, *Women in Early Modern Ireland*, pp. 91–112; B. Whelan, 'Women, Politics and Warfare in the Late Seventeenth Century', in B. Whelan (ed.), *The Last of the Great Wars* (Limerick: University of Limerick Press, 1995), pp. 139–60; P. M. Higgins, 'Women in the English Civil War' (MA dissertation, University of Manchester, 1965), especially pp. 44–8.
55. See Higgins, 'Women in the English Civil War', pp. 45–7.
56. Ibid., pp. 46–8.
57. Gilbert MS, vol. 42, p. 169, GLD.
58. Calendar of Marquis Ormonde MS, vol. 2, pp. 463–4, PRO.
59. See Canny, *Making Ireland British*, p. 510.
60. J. Casway, 'Rosa O'Dogherty: a Gaelic woman', in *Seanchas Armhacha*, vol. 10 (Dublin: Irish Manuscripts Commission, 1980), pp. 40–63.
61. Ibid., p. 54.
62. Ibid., p. 53.
63. Ibid., p. 55.

64. CSPI, vol. 207, 11 January 1600, p. 63.
65. CSPI, vol. 198, 27 October 1587, p. 131.
66. CSPI, vol. 1 (1509–73), p. 230.
67. See G. Kew (ed.), *The Irish Sections of Fynes Moryson's Unpublished Itinerary*, bk. 2, ch. 5 (Dublin: Irish Manuscripts Commission, 1998), pp. 36–8.
68. Moryson, *Itinerary*, vol. 4, pp. 198–9, 137.
69. William Camden, *Britain or a Chorographical Description of England, Scotland and Ireland* (London, 1610), p. 120.
70. CSPI, vol. 206 (1599–1600), p. 398.
71. See Deposition MSS 812, f. 45; 813, f. 360; and 818, f. 97, TCD.
72. See Fergusen, *Ulster Journal*, p. 266; MacNeill, *Maire Rua*, p. 75.
73. See S. L. Jansen, *Dangerous Talk and Strange Behaviour: Women and Popular Resistance to the Reforms of Henry VIII* (New York: St. Martin's Press, 1996).
74. J. Mikalachki, *The Legacy of Boadicea. Gender and Nation in Early Modern England* (London and New York: Routledge Press, 1998), p. 11.

NOTES TO CHAPTER 3

1. For a concise discussion of these terms and a summary of the debate see J. Donovan, *Feminist Theory: The Intellectual Traditions of American Feminism* (New York: Continuum, 1992).
2. M. Wollstonecraft, *A Vindication of the Rights of Woman with Strictures on Political and Moral Subjects* [1792] (New York: Garland, 1974).
3. C. Gilligan, *In a Different Voice: Psychological Theory and Women's Development* (Cambridge: Harvard University, 1982); N. Chodorow, *The Reproduction of Mothering: Psychoanalysis and the Sociology of Gender* (Berkeley, CA: University of California, 1978). For a discussion of nineteenth-century difference feminism, see K. Offen, 'Defining Feminism: A Comparative Historical Approach', *Signs*, 14, 1 (autumn 1988), pp. 119–57.
4. See for example D. Keogh and N. Furlong (eds), *The Women of 1798* (Dublin: Four Courts, 1998), and N. J. Curtin, 'Women and Eighteenth-Century Irish Republicanism,' in M. MacCurtain and M. O'Dowd (eds), *Women in Early Modern Ireland* (Dublin: Wolfhound, 1991).
5. I am indebted for this term to the women of Irish Feminist Information Publications in their book *Missing Pieces: Women in Irish History* (Dublin: Women's Community Press, 1983).
6. Quoted in L. Curtis, *The Cause of Ireland: From the United Irishmen to Partition* (Belfast: Beyond the Pale, 1994), p. 7.
7. D. Gahan, *The People's Rising: Wexford, 1798* (Dublin: Gill and Macmillan, 1995), p. 87.
8. J. Reidy, *The Influence of the Irish Woman on the National Movement* (Brooklyn, NY: Brooklyn Gaelic Society, 1906), p. 4.
9. J. H. Fowler, 'The Women of '98', in *Chapters in '98 History* (London: Joseph H. Fowler, 1938), unpaginated.
10. J. Holt, *Memoirs*, ed. T. Crofton Croker (London: Henry Colburn, 1838), pp. 49–53.
11. R. R. Madden, *United Irishmen, Their Lives and Times*, 8 vols (New York: Tandy, 1910), vol. 3, pp. 199–202.
12. Ibid., vol. 4.
13. Quoted in N. J. Curtin, *The United Irishmen: Popular Politics in Ulster and Dublin, 1791–1798* (Oxford: Clarendon Press, 1994), p. 177.

14. Bartlett cites several instances from testimony in the National Archives Rebellion Papers (620/ 3/ 23/ 4; 620/ 2/ 14/ 2; 620/ 6/ 63/ 9); T. Bartlett, 'Bearing Witness: Female Evidences in Courts Martial Convened to Suppress the 1798 Rebellion', in Keogh and Furlong, *The Women of 1798*, p. 70.
15. Curtin, 'Women and Eighteenth-Century Irish Republicanism', pp. 133–4.
16. S. McSkimin, *Annals of Ulster* (Belfast: Henderson, 1949), p. 58.
17. Quoted in Fowler, 'The Women of '98'.
18. M. McNeill, *The Life and Times of Mary Ann McCracken, 1770–1866: A Belfast Panorama* (Belfast: Blackstaff Press, 1988); J. Gray, 'Mary Anne McCracken: Belfast Revolutionary and Pioneer of Feminism', in Keogh and Furlong, *The Women of 1798*, pp. 47–63.
19. Gray, 'Mary Ann McCracken', p. 54.
20. C. Dickson, *Revolt in the North* (Dublin: Clonmore and Reynolds, 1960), p. 251.
21. T. Moylan (ed.), *The Age of Revolution in the Irish Song Tradition, 1776 to 1815* (Dublin: Lilliput, 2000), p. 66.
22. P. Kavanagh, *A Popular History of the Insurrection of 1798* (Dublin: Gill, 1884), p. 188.
23. T. Bartlett, '1798 in Perspective', paper presented at Boston College conference on *1798, The Great Rebellion: A Commemoration*, 28 March 1998.
24. L. Cullen, *Insurgent Wicklow, 1798* (Dublin: Clonmore and Reynolds, 1948), pp. 31–2.
25. Moylan, *Age of Revolution*, p. 65.
26. W. G. Lyttle, *Betsy Gray or, Hearts of Down* (Newcastle: Mourne Observer, 1968).
27. Kavanagh, *Popular History*, p. 137; Fowler, 'The Women of '98'.
28. Reidy, 'Influence of the Irish Woman', p. 4.
29. T. Cloney, *A Personal Narrative of those Transactions in the County of Wexford in which the author was engaged at the awful period of 1798* (Dublin: J. McMullen, 1832), pp. 41–2.
30. Reidy, *Influence of the Irish Woman*, cover illustration.
31. Ibid., p. 3.
32. Quoted by T. Crofton Croker, ed., in Holt, *Memoirs*, pp. 70–3.
33. Holt, *Memoirs*, p. 70.
34. Ibid., p. 176.
35. Ibid., p. 202.
36. R. O'Donnell, 'Bridget "Croppy Biddy" Dolan: Wicklow's Anti-Heroine of 1798', in Keogh and Furlong, *The Women of 1798*, p. 100; Holt, *Memoirs*, p. 202.
37. This term was coined by N. J. Curtin in her essay, 'Matilda Tone and Virtuous Republican Femininity', in Keogh and Furlong, *The Women of 1798*, p. 34.
38. Ibid.
39. P. Berresford Ellis, *A History of the Irish Working Class* (New York: George Braziller, 1972), p. 116.
40. M. H. Thuente, *The Harp Restrung: The United Irishmen and the Rise of Irish Literary Nationalism* (Syracuse, NY: Syracuse University, 1994), p. 220.
41. J. Cannavan, 'Romantic Revolutionary Irishwomen: Women, Young Ireland and 1848', in M. Kelleher and J. H. Murphy (eds), *Gender Perspectives in Nineteenth Century Ireland* (Dublin: Irish Academic Press, 1997), p. 213.
42. R. Patrick and H. Patrick, *Exiles Undaunted: The Irish Rebels Kevin and Eva O'Doherty* (Queensland: University of Queensland, 1989), p. 14.
43. Ibid., p. 12.
44. T. de Vere White, *The Parents of Oscar Wilde* (London: Hodder and Stoughton, 1967), p.18.
45. R. O'Conner, *Jenny Mitchel: Young Irelander* (Tucson, AZ: O'Conner Trust, 1985), pp. 91–2.

46. Revd P. Fitzgerald, *Personal Recollections of the Insurrection at Ballingarry in July, 1848* (Dublin: John F. Fowler, 1861), p. 14.
47. Quoted in R. Sloan, *William Smith O'Brien and the Young Ireland Rebellion of 1848* (Dublin: Four Courts, 2000), p. 275.
48. T. F. O'Sullivan, *The Young Irelanders* (Tralee: The Kerryman, 1944), p. 662.
49. O'Conner, *Jenny Mitchel*, p. 66.
50. *United Irishman*, 20 May 1848.
51. Quoted in O'Conner, *Jenny Mitchel*, p. 82.
52. Much of the material for this discussion can be found in my earlier article: J. Cannavan, 'Romantic Revolutionary Irishwomen', in Kelleher and Murphy, *Gender Perspectives*, pp. 212–20.
53. *Nation*, 30 January 1847.
54. Ibid., 25 March 1848.
55. O'Connor, *Jenny Mitchel*, p. 68.
56. McNeill, *Life and Times of Mary Ann McCracken*, pp. 138–9.
57. K. O'Neill, 'Friends and Unitedmen: Radicalism in an Irish Village', paper presented at Boston College conference on *1798, The Great Rebellion: A Commemoration*, 28 March 1998.
58. Gray, 'Mary Anne McCracken,' pp. 50–1.
59. Curtin, 'Women and Eighteenth-Century Irish Republicanism', p. 143.
60. A. K. Mellor, *Romanticism & Gender* (New York: Routledge, 1993), p. 210.
61. *Nation*, 12 June 1847.
62. Ibid., 11 March 1848.
63. White, *Parents of Oscar Wilde*, p. 104.
64. Ibid., p. 148.
65. M. Ward, 'Irish Women and Nationalism', *Irish Studies Review*, 17 (winter 1996/97), pp. 12–14.
66. Ibid., p. 8.
67. I have taken this term from S. Rowbotham, *Hidden from History: Rediscovering Women in History from the 17th Century to the Present* (New York: Vintage, 1976).

NOTES TO CHAPTER 4

1. T. Barry, *Guerrilla Days in Ireland* (Dublin: Anvil Press, 1997), p. 211.
2. S. Bose and and E. Ward, 'India's Cause is Ireland's Cause', in M. Holmes and D. Holmes (eds), *Ireland and India: Connections, Comparisons and Contrasts* (Dublin: Folens, 1997), p. 56.
3. R. English, *Ernie O'Malley* (Oxford: Oxford University Press, 1999), p. 48.
4. Ibid.
5. T. Barry, *Guerrilla Days in Ireland*; D. Breen, *My Fight For Irish Freedom* (Dublin: Anvil Press, 1997); F. O'Donoghue, *No Other Law* (Dublin: Anvil Press, 1986); E. O'Malley, *On Another Man's Wound* (Dublin: Anvil Press, 1994).
6. L. Conlon, *Cumann na mBan and the Women of Ireland* (Kilkenny: Kilkenny People, 1969).
7. M. Ward, *Unmanageable Revolutionaries* (London: Pluto Press, 1989), and *In Their Own Voice: Women and Irish Nationalism* (Dublin: Attic Press, 1995); S. McCoole, *Guns and Chiffon: Women Revolutionaries and Kilmainham Gaol* (Dublin: Stationery Office, 1997); L. Ryan, 'Splendidly Silent: Representing Irish Republican Women', in A. Gallagher, C. Lubelska and L. Ryan (eds), *Re-presenting the Past: Women and History* (London: Longman, 2001), pp.23–43.

8. Conlon, *Cumann na mBan*, p. 000.
9. Ward, *Unmanageable Revolutionaries*, p. 156.
10. Ibid., p. 163.
11. Ibid.
12. McCoole, *Guns and Chiffon*; M. Buckley, *The Jangle of the Keys* (Dublin, 1938).
13. Conlon, *Cumann na mBan*; L. Ryan, 'Drunken Tans: Representations of Sexual Violence in the Irish War of Independence', *Feminist Review*, 66 (autumn 2000), pp. 73–94.
14. K. Keyes McDonnell, *There is a Bridge at Bandon* (Cork: Mercier Press, 1972); K. Clarke, *Revolutionary Woman* (Dublin: O'Brien Press, 1991).
15. See Conlon, *Cumann na mBan*.
16. See Ryan, 'Drunken Tans'.
17. L. Ryan, 'Furies and Die-hards: Women and Irish Republicanism in the Early Twentieth Century', *Gender and History*, 11, 2, pp. 256–75.
18. Ibid.
19. See *Poblacht na hÉireann*, 21 October 1922.
20. C. Fallon, *Soul of Fire: Mary MacSwiney* (Cork: Mercier Press, 1986), p. 98.
21. *Irish Times*, 1 January 1923.
22. L. O'Dowd, 'Church, State and Women', in C. Curtin, P. Jackson and B. O'Connor (eds), *Gender in Irish Society* (Galway: Galway University Press, 1987), p. 10.
23. O'Malley, *On Another Man's Wound*, p. 290.
24. O'Donoghue, *No Other Law*, p. 107.
25. Ibid., p. 142.
26. Ibid., p. 117.
27. Conlon, *Cumann na mBan*, p. 238.
28. O'Donoghue, *No Other Law*, p. 277.
29. Breen, *My Fight for Irish Freedom*, p. 49.
30. Ibid., p. 96.
31. N. Yuval-Davis, *Gender and Nation* (London: Sage, 1997), p. 101.
32. See Ryan, 'Furies and Die-hards'.
33. E. O'Malley, *The Singing Flame* (Dublin: Anvil, 1992), p. 21.
34. M. Brennan, *The War in Clare* (Dublin: 1980), p. 99.
35. F. O'Donoghue, *No Other Law*, p. 107.
36. See Ryan 'Splendidly Silent'.
37. C. Enloe, *Does Khaki Become You?* (London: Pandora Press, 1983), p. 164.
38. Breen, *My Fight for Irish Freedom*, p. 177.
39. Ibid.
40. Ibid.
41. See, for example, Barry, *Guerrilla Days in Ireland*; Breen, *My Fight for Irish Freedom*.
42. O'Donoghue, *No Other Law*, p. 40.
43. Ibid.
44. Ibid.
45. M. Ryan, *The Real Chief: The Story of Liam Lynch* (Cork: Mercier Press, 1986), p. 26.
46. Ibid.
47. Ibid.
48. See Ryan, 'Drunken Tans'.
49. O'Malley, *On Another Man's Wound*, p. 176.
50. C. L. Innes, *Woman and Nation* (Hemel Hempstead: Harvester Wheatsheaf, 1993).
51. J. Augusteijn, *From Public Defiance to Guerrilla Warfare* (Dublin: Irish Academic Press, 1996), p. 143.

52 Ibid., pp. 143–4.

53. Ibid., p. 144.

54. Breen, *My Fight for Irish Freedom,* pp. 54 and 137.

55. Augusteijn, *From Public Defiance*, p. 144.

56. The *Irish Bulletin* was an underground republican newspaper that was produced under clandestine conditions throughout the War of Independence. It attempted to offer the republican version of the war and challenged the official British version of events.

57. Breen, *My Fight for Irish Freedom*, p. 47.

58. L. Deasy, *Brother Against Brother* (Cork: Mercier, 1998).

59. Ibid.

60. Ibid., p. 93.

61. Breen, *My Fight for Irish Freedom*, p. 145.

62. Ibid., p. 159.

63. Ibid., p. 38.

64. Ibid., p. 51.

65. O' Malley, *On Another Man's Wound*, p. 188.

66. Ibid., p. 189.

67. Deasy, *Brother against Brother*, p. 44.

68. H. Litton, *The Irish Civil War* (Dublin: Wolfhound Press, 1997).

69. G. Mosse, *Nationalism and Sexuality* (London: University of Wisconsin Press, 1989), pp. 17–18.

70. F. O' Connor, 'September Dawn', in *Guests of the Nation* (Dublin: Poolbeg, 1987), p. 65.

71 . F. O'Connor, 'Machine Gun Corps in Action', in *Guests of the Nation*, p. 85.

72. Ibid.

73. F. O'Connor, 'Laughter', in *Guests of the Nation*, p. 92.

74. Ibid.

75. Ibid., p. 92.

76. Ibid., p. 95.

77. J. Peteet, 'Icons and Militants: Mothering in the Danger Zone', in *Signs*, 23, 1, pp. 103–29.

78. Enloe, *Does Khaki Become You?*

79. Peteet, 'Icons and Militants', p. 105.

80. Ibid., p. 111.

81. Ryan, 'Furies and Die-hards'.

82. Ryan, 'Splendidly Silent'.

NOTES TO CHAPTER 5

1. W. B. Yeats, 'In Memory of Eva Gore-Booth and Con Markievicz', in R. J. Finneran (ed.), *W. B. Yeats, The Poems* (London: Macmillan, 1983), p. 233.

2. S. O'Casey, *Drums Under the Window* (London: Macmillan, 1950), p. 316.

3. A. Sebestyen (ed.), *Prison Letters of Constance Markievicz* (London: Virago, 1987), p. xxv.

4. S. O'Faolain, *Constance Markievicz or the Average Revolutionary* (London: Jonathan Cape, 1934), p. 295.

5. See E. Coxhead, *Daughters of Erin: Five Women of the Irish Renascence* (London: Secker & Warburg, 1965); J. Van Voris, *Constance de Markievicz: In the Cause of Ireland*

(Amherst, MA: University of Massachusetts Press, 1967); A. Marreco, *The Rebel Countess* (London: Weidenfeld & Nicholson, 1967); D. Norman, *Terrible Beauty* (Dublin: Poolbeg, 1987); and A. Haverty, *Constance Markievicz: An Independent Life* (London: Pandora, 1988) for feminist biographical reassessments. See L. Curtis, *The Cause of Ireland* (Belfast: Beyond the Pale, 1993); M. Ward, *Unmanageable Revolutionaries* (London: Pluto, 1983); R. Taillon, *The Women of 1916* (Belfast: Beyond the Pale, 1996) for historical treatments that have retrieved women – notably nationalist women – from the footnotes of revisionist history.

6. For a sampling of some of the most prominent feminist challenges to nationalism, see E. Boland, 'A Kind of Scar', in E. Boland et al. (eds), *A Dozen Lips* (Dublin: Attic, 1994), pp. 72–92; E. Longley, 'From Cathleen to Anorexia', in Boland et al., *A Dozen Lips*, pp. 162–87; A. Smyth, 'Paying our Disrespects to the Bloody States We're In: Women, Violence, Culture and the State', in J. Hoff and M. Coulter (eds.), *Irish Women's Voices, Past and Present: Journal of Women's History*, 6/7, 4/1 (1995), pp. 190–216. For some feminist defenses of nationalism, see C. Coulter, 'Ireland's Metropolitan Feminists and Colonial Women', *Éire-Ireland*, 35, 3–4 (2000–01), pp. 48–78; C. Coulter, 'Feminism and Nationalism in Ireland', in D. Miller (ed.), *Rethinking Northern Ireland: Culture, Ideology and Colonialism* (London: Longman, 1998), pp. 160–78; and M. Ward, 'National Liberation Movements and the Question of Women's Liberation: The Irish Experience', in C. Midgley (ed.), *Gender and Imperialism* (Manchester: Manchester University Press, 1998), pp. 104–22.

7. See D. J. Smith, 'The Countess and the Poets: Constance Gore-Booth Markievicz in the Work of Irish Writers', *Journal of Irish Literature*, 12, 1 (1983), p. 7.

8. See K. Steele, 'Constance Markievicz's Allegorical Garden: Femininity, Militancy, and the Irish Press, 1909–1915', *Women's Studies*, 29, 2 (2000), pp. 427–51, for an overview and re-reading of Markievicz's gardening columns and early career as a journalist.

9. For a complete list of Markievicz's journalism, see in Van Voris, *Constance de Markievicz*, pp. 361–3.

10. R. F. Foster, *Modern Ireland, 1600–1972* (New York: Penguin, 1988), p. 511.

11. Van Voris, *Constance Markievicz*, p. 335.

12. Haverty, *Constance Markievicz*, p. 287.

13. Quoted in O'Faolain, *Constance Markievicz*, p. 194.

14. See M. Clancy, 'Aspects of Women's Contribution to the Oireachtas Debates in the Irish Free State', in M. Luddy and C. Murphy (eds), *Women Surviving* (Dublin: Poolbeg, 1990), pp. 206–32; M. G. Valulius, 'Free Women in a Free Nation', in B. Farrell (ed.), *The Creation of the Dáil* (Dublin: Blackwater, 1994), pp. 75–90; and B. Gray and L. Ryan, 'The Politics of Irish Identity and the Interconnections between Feminism, Nationhood and Colonialism', in R. R. Pierson and N. Chaudhuri (eds), *Nation, Empire, Colony* (Bloomington, IN: Indiana University Press, 1998), pp. 121–38.

15. 'Women and the Treaty', *An Saorstát*, 18 March 1922, p. 5.

16. 'Easter Memories: 1916', *Nation*, 23 April 1927, p. 3.

17. Ibid.

18. 'Madame Markievicz Challenges O'Higgins', *Éire*, 7 July 1923, p. 2.

19. 'DeValera's Oath –The Truth', *Éire*, 21 April 1923, p. 4.

20. 'Tom Clarke and the First Day of the Republic', *Éire*, 26 May 1923, p. 3.

21. Clancy, 'Aspects of Women's Contribution', pp. 206–32.

22. Gray and Ryan, 'The Politics of Irish Identity', p. 127.

23. 'Citizenship', *Nation*, 13 August 1927, p. 2.

24. Ibid.
25. Ibid.
26. 'Tom Clarke and the First Day of the Republic', *Éire*, 26 May 1923, p. 3.
27. 'Going to Jail', *Éire*, 4 August 1923, p. 3.
28. 'Larkin, the Fianna and the King's Visit', *Éire*, 16 June 1923, p. 3.
29. 'James Connolly as I Knew Him', *Nation*, 27 March 1927, p. 7.
30. B. Novick, 'DORA, Suppression and Nationalist Propaganda in Ireland, 1914–1915', *New Hibernia Review*, 1, 4 (1997), pp. 41–57; J. Ellis, 'The Degenerate and the Martyr: Nationalist Propaganda and the Contestation of Irishness, 1914–1918', *Éire -Ireland*, 35, 4 (2000), pp. 7–33.
31. 'Stop Thief!', *Éire*, 17 February 1923, p. 4.
32. Ibid.; 'Interview', *Éire*, 13 October 1923, p. 4; 'An Open Letter to the Independent Labour Party', *Éire*, 28 April 1923, p. 4.
33. 'Liam Mellows – Pioneer', *An Phoblacht*, 28 May 1925, p. 1.
34. 'Wolfe Tone's Ideals of Democracy', *An Phoblacht*, 26 June 1925, p. 4.
35. Ibid.
36. See O'Faolain, *Constance Markievicz*, p. 297; Smith, 'The Countess and the Poets', p. 22.
37. Smith, 'The Countess and the Poets', p. 19.
38. For a rich account of how the Irish National Theatre facilitated women's political activism, see M. Trotter, 'Women's Work and the Irish Nationalist Actress: Inghinidhe na hÉireann', in *Ireland's National Theatres* (Syracuse, NY: Syracuse University Press, 2001), pp. 73–100.
39. Sebestyen, *Prison Letters*, p. 155.
40. Ibid., p. 306.
41. See E. Roper, introduction to Sebestyen, *Prison Letters*, p. 12; O'Faolain, *Constance Markievicz*, p. 306; B. K. Scott, introduction to 'Document: *The Invincible Mother*. A Play in One Act by Constance Markievicz', *Journal of Irish Literature*, 6, 2 (1977), p. 116; Van Voris, *Constance de Markievicz*, p. 229.
42. W. B. Yeats, *Cathleen ni Houlihan*, in W. B. Yeats, *Collected Plays* (London: Macmillan, 1956), p. 56.
43. *Blood Money*, National Library of Ireland MS 22, 636. Quoted by kind permission of the Council of Trustees of the National Library of Ireland.
44. See K. Steele, 'Editing Out Factionalism: The Political Consequences in Ireland's *Shan Van Vocht*', *Victorian Periodicals Review*, 35, 2 (2002), pp. 113–32.
45. *Broken Dreams*, National Library of Ireland (NLI) MS 24, 185. Quoted by kind permission of the Council of Trustees of the National Library of Ireland.
46. D. Kiberd, *Inventing Ireland* (Cambridge, MA: Harvard University Press, 1995), p. 221.
47. Van Voris, *Constance de Markievicz*, p. 339.
48. See Kiberd, *Inventing Ireland*, pp. 218–38.
49. Ibid., p. 226.
50. M. FitzGerald, introduction to M. Fitzgerald (ed.), *Selected Plays of Lady Gregory* (Gerrards Cross, Buckinghamshire: Colin Smythe, 1983), p. 16.
51. Ibid., p. 142.
52. '*Invincible Mother*', p. 120.
53. Ibid., p. 124.
54. Ibid., p. 127.
55. Ibid.
56. Scott, introduction to '*Invincible Mother*', p. 199.

57. Joseph McGarrity papers, NLI MS 17, 463. Quoted by kind permission of the Council of Trustees of the National Library of Ireland.
58. Sebestyen, *Prison Letters*, p. 238.
59. Ibid.

NOTES TO CHAPTER 6

1. Founded by Eoin MacNeill and Douglas Hyde in 1893 to revive the use of the Irish language and renew interest in Irish literature and traditions. It ran Irish classes, lectures, and sometimes ceilidhs. Its members tended to be anti-English, and attempted to support Irish home industries and reject English imports. See R. F. Foster, *Modern Ireland, 1600–1972* (London: Penguin Books, 1988), pp. 447–50.
2. It is interesting that Jacob's heroines are all agnostic, nationalist and convinced of the equality, if not superiority, of women.
3. 'That year the King and Queen of England visited Dublin, and as the Queen's name was Mary, the authorities decided to have all Marys of Ireland pay tribute through a collection of signatures to be presented to the royal couple. Inghinidhe na hÉireann circulated a repudiation of this to be signed by as many Irish Marys as possible.' D. Doyle, 'Rosamond Jacob', in M. Cullen and M. Luddy (eds), *Female Activists. Irish Women and Change 1900–1960* (Dublin: Woodfield Press, 2001), p. 172.
4. She was protesting against the refusal of John Redmond, leader of the Irish Parliamentary Party, to support women's suffrage in the Westminster Parliament. See Doyle, 'Rosamond Jacob', p. 174.
5. See M. Ward, *Unmanageable Revolutionaries: Women and Irish Nationalism* (London: Pluto Press, 1983; repr. 1995), pp. 125–6.
6. Co-founder and Secretary of the Irish Women's Franchise League, a committed feminist, suffragist and nationalist, and a close friend of Rosamond Jacob. See M. Ward, *Hanna Sheehy Skeffington: A Life* (Cork: Attic Press, 1997).
7. Set up in 1920 to organise the distribution of American aid for victims of the political situation. See Ward, *Hanna Sheehy Skeffington*, p. 239.
8. A. Smithson, *Myself – and Others* (Dublin: Talbot Press, 1944; repr. 1945), p. 56.
9. Ibid., p. 227.
10. Ibid., p. 229.
11. Ibid., p. 239.
12. Ibid., p. 259.
13. Smithson published twenty-one novels, all best sellers, between 1917 and 1946. They ran into many editions during her lifetime, and after. *The Walk of a Queen*, for example, was in its twelfth edition in 1951. The Mercier Press reprinted six titles between 1988 and 1990, including *Her Irish Heritage, The Walk of a Queen* and *The Marriage of Nurse Harding*.
14. Although the novels, *Callaghan* (1920) and *The Troubled House* (1938), and the biography, *The Rebel's Wife* (1957), were, on the whole, well reviewed, it is for *The Rise of the United Irishmen* (1937) that she is best remembered.
15. Novels in which the Easter Rising plays an important part include *Her Irish Heritage* (1917), *By Strange Paths* (1919), *The Walk of a Queen* (1922), *The Marriage of Nurse Harding* (1935) – which also gives a vivid fictionalised account of Smithson's participation in the Civil War – and *The Weldons of Tibradden* (1940). *The Light of Other Days* (1933) focuses on the activities of Sinn Féin in the country in the

period after 1918, and *By Shadowed Ways* (1942) on the activities of the Black and Tans.

16. Maud Gonne and Constance Markievicz, for instance, both felt the need to convert in order to feel truly part of the republican movement.
17. R. Jacob, *The Troubled House* (London: Harrap, 1937), p. 175.
18. A. Smithson, *Her Irish Heritage* (Dublin: Talbot Press, 1917). My references are to the Mercier Press edition (Cork and Dublin, 1988), p. 32.
19. Ibid., p. 77.
20. Ibid., p. 74.
21. Ibid., p. 77.
22. Frances Morrin's attempt to accost Redmond at a Volunteer review, for example, reflects Jacob's own tangling with Redmond supporters.
23. R. Jacob, *Callaghan* (Dublin: Martin Lester, 1920), p. 3.
24. Ibid., p. 69.
25. Ibid., p. 119.
26. Ibid.
27. Ibid., p. 192.
28. Smithson, *Her Irish Heritage*, p. 77.
29. Ibid., pp. 7–8.
30. Jacob, *Callaghan*, p. 165.
31. Smithson, *Her Irish Heritage*, p. 151.
32. Ibid., p. 168.
33. Ibid., p. 169.
34. Jacob, *Troubled House*, p 10.
35. '[On] 21 November 1920 … when the IRA killed eleven unarmed British Officers in Dublin on suspicion of their being intelligence operatives; later that day, Black and Tans fired into a football crowd, causing twelve deaths, many in the ensuing stampede.' Foster, *Modern Ireland*, p. 498. The Black and Tans were notoriously brutal British Auxiliaries to the Irish police force.
36. Jacob, *Troubled House*, p. 15. Terence MacSwiney was a Sinn Féin mayor of Cork, who, when arrested in 1920, went on hunger strike, and died seventy-four days later.
37. The football ground where the 'Black and Tan' massacre took place.
38. The original title of the novel was *A House Divided*, but the publishers discovered that this had already been used by Pearl Buck for one of her novels. See Rosamond Jacob Papers, MS 33, 115, National Library of Ireland, Dublin (NLI).
39. Jacob, *Troubled House*, p. 13.
40. Ibid., p. 67.
41. Ibid., p. 94. In Jacob's diary entry for 23 November 1920, she mentions her own reaction to the funeral procession, equally bloodthirsty, and presumably the source for Maggie Cullen's: 'Are there any more of your English dogs That [sic] you want to be slain?' Rosamond Jacob Papers, NLI MS 32, 582, vol. 38.
42. Jacob, *Troubled House*, p. 173.
43. There are other possible reasons. There is a strong feminist message in *The Troubled House*, as in *Callaghan*. A contrast to Maggie's conventional family life is provided by two female artists who live and work together, probably in a lesbian relationship. It is the character of 'Nix', in particular, which makes Maggie, and the reader, question traditional assumptions about the role of women. Nix is the self-centred 'new woman' that Maggie could never be, but whom, to a certain extent, she admires and envies.
44. A. Smithson, *The Walk of a Queen* (Dublin: Talbot Press, 1922; repr. 1951), p. 327.

45. In Charles Dickens's *A Tale of Two Cities* Sydney Carton saves the heroine's lover from the guillotine by taking his place. Another melodramatic element of plot in *The Troubled House,* where Liam unwittingly kills his father in an ambush, finds a parallel in Smithson's *The Marriage of Nurse Harding,* but in this case it is the father who kills his son.
46. Smithson, *Myself – and Others,* p. 258. This episode in Smithson's life forms an important part of *The Marriage of Nurse Harding.*
47. Smithson, *Walk of a Queen,* p. 6.
48. Ibid. p., 171.
49. Jacob, *Troubled House,* p. 205. For a discussion of the various and complex ways in which nationalist women have been portrayed in a range of literary texts and sources see Louise Ryan, 'Splendidly silent: representing Irish Republican women, 1919–23', in A. Gallagher, C. Lubelska and L. Ryan (eds), *Re-presenting the Past. Women and History* (London: Longman, 2001), pp. 23–43.
50. The similarities of plot and characters make one wonder whether there can have been a common source for these novels, but it seems unlikely to have been more than a common awareness of the literary possibilities of the already often melodramatic events of the period, combined with a background of familiarity with the classics of popular English literature.
51. Jacob, *The Rebel's Wife* (Tralee: Kerryman, 1957), p. 74.
52. Ibid., pp. 134–5.
53. See Rosamond Jacob Papers, NLI MS 32, 582, vol. 164.
54. In 1998 a group of former readers interviewed in Dublin talked of how, as teenagers, they had read her novels avidly, finding them 'daring', but 'moral', 'pure' and 'uplifting', 'very suitable for young people'. Nuala O'Faolain, in *Are You Somebody? The Life and Times of Nuala O'Faolain* (Dublin: New Island Books, 1996), talks of how in her convent school 'you had an afternoon to devour as much as you could of, say, Annie P. Smithson' [*sic*]. I was told recently by a friend of her frequent visits to the local library as a child to get 'the latest Annie M. P.Smithson' for her Presbyterian, Northern Irish grandmother. An elderly male reader encountered in a bookshop claimed to have awaited each new Smithson eagerly.
55. I have found nobody who could remember reading anything by Jacob other than her children's book, *The Raven's Glen.*

NOTES TO CHAPTER 7

1. Aogàn Ó Rathaille, untitled, in Thomas Kinsella (ed.), *The New Oxford Book of Irish Verse* (Oxford: Oxford University Press, 1986), pp. 195–6.
2. Patrick Pearse, 'The Mother', in Ruth Dudley Edwards, *Patrick Pearse: The Triumph of Failure* (London: Victor Gollancz, 1977), pp. 262–3.
3. C. L. Innes, *Woman and Nation in Irish Literature and Society (1880–1935)* (Athens, GA: University of Georgia Press, 1993), p. 10.
4. Ibid.
5. Ibid., p. 12.
6. Ibid., p. 15–16.
7. Ibid., pp. 2, 15.
8. Ibid., p. 58.
9. Ibid., p. 17.
10. Bhikhu Parekh, *The Parekh Report* (London: Profile Books, 2000).

11. See Jayne Steel, 'Vampira: Representations of the Irish Female Terrorist', *Irish Studies Review*, 6, 3 (December 1998), pp. 273–84.

12. Carol F. Karlsen, *The Devil in the Shape of a Woman* (New York: W. W. Norton, 1987), p. xii.

13. See Scott Wilson, *Cultural Materialism: Theory and Practice* (Oxford: Blackwell, 1995), pp. 67–72.

14. For Jacques Lacan, 'It is the mother who first occupies the position of the big Other for the child, because it is she who receives the child's primitive cries and retroactively sanctions them as a particular message …' At a more general level, 'the Other is also "the Other sex" … The Other sex is always WOMAN …' In the case of woman as Ireland , woman as Other is both unconscious and symbolic: 'it is only possible to speak of the Other *as a subject* in a secondary sense, in the sense that a subject may occupy this position and thereby "embody" the Other for another subject'. See Dylan Evans, *An Introductory Dictionary of Lacanian Psychoanalysis* (New York: Routledge, 1996), pp. 133, 58, 59. See also Jacques Lacan, *The Seminar. Book VII. The Ethics of Psychoanalysis (1959–60)*, trans. Denis Porter (London: Routledge, 1992), pp. 139, 71.

15. Patrick McGee, 'Do They Mean Us?', *Guardian*, 3 September 1997, p. 13.

16. Ibid.

17. Bill Rolston, 'Mothers, Whores and Villains: Images of Women in Novels of the Northern Ireland Conflict', *Race and Class*, 31, 1 (1989), p. 56.

18. Slavoj Zizek, *The Sublime Object of Ideology* (London: Verso, 1989), p. 29.

19. Ibid., p. 33.

20. Ibid., p. 18.

21. F. L. Green, *Odd Man Out* (North Hollywood, CA: Leisure Books, 1945; repr. 1971), p. 31.

22. Louise Ryan, 'Drunken Tans: Representations of Sex and Violence in the Anglo-Irish War (1919–21)', *Feminist Review*, 66 (autumn 2000), p. 73.

23. Ibid., p. 83.

24. Ibid.

25. Ibid.

26. Innes, *Woman and Nation*, pp. 76–7.

27. Ibid., p. 34.

28. Ibid.

29. Eileen Fairweather, Roisin McDonough and Melanie McFadyean, *Only the Rivers Run Free: Northern Ireland, The Women's War* (London: Pluto, 1984), p. 241.

30. Margaret Ward, *Unmanageable Revolutionaries* (London: Pluto, 1983), p. viii.

31. Innes, *Woman and Nation*, p. 34.

32. Fairweather, McDonough and McFadyean, *Only the Rivers Run Free*, p. 241.

33. *A Prayer for the Dying*, Dir. Mike Hodges. Samuel Goldwyn, 1987.

34. *Patriot Games*, Dir. Philip Noyce. UIP/Paramount, 1992.

35. Innes, *Woman and Nation*, p. 56.

36. *The Crying Game*, Dir. Neil Jordan. Palace/Channel 4 Films, 1993.

37. *Odd Man Out*, Dir. Carol Reed. Two Cities, 1947.

38. Green, *Odd Man Out*, p. 31.

39. John Hill, 'Images of Violence', in K. Rockett, L. Gibbons and J. Hill (eds), *Cinema and Ireland* (London: Croom Helm, 1987), p. 155.

40. Ibid.

41. Ibid.

42. Edna Longley, *From Cathleen to Anorexia: The Breakdown of Irelands* (Dublin: Attic, 1990), p. 15.

43. Terry O'Neill, *Daily Mail*, 15 January 1993, p. 21.
44. Innes, *Woman and Nation*, p. 35.
45. Green, *Odd Man Out*, pp. 250–1.
46. Ibid., p. 251.
47. Ibid.
48. Ibid.
49. Ibid.
50. Innes, *Woman and Nation*, p. 41.
51. Ryan, 'Drunken Tans', p. 76.
52. Innes, *Woman and Nation*, pp. 41–2.
53. Ryan, 'Drunken Tans', p. 76.
54. Ibid., p. 84.
55. Ibid., p. 92.
56. Michelle E. Evans, 'A Woman's Lot', *Fortnight*, May 1998, p. 14.
57. Christina Loughran, 'The Women's Movement in N. Ireland: Between Republicanism and Feminism', *Fortnight*, 27 May 1985, p. 4.
58. Robin Morgan, *The Demon Lover* (London: W. W. Norton, 1989), p. 315.
59. Ibid.
60. Eve Patten, 'Women and Fiction', *Krino*, 9 (1990), p. 7.
61. Chris Petit, *The Psalm Killer* (London: Macmillan, 1997).
62. Ibid., p. 253.
63. J. Bowyer Bell, 'The Troubles as Trash', *Hibernia*, 20 January 1978, p. 26.
64. See Jacques Lacan, 'Desire and the Interpretation of Desire in *Hamlet*', *Yale French Studies: Literature and Psychoanalysis*, 55, 66 (1977), pp. 262–3. Lacan's psychoanalytical concept termed '*che vuoi?*' poses a question which translates as 'what does the (m)other want from me?' or 'what does the (m)other desire from me?' According to Lacan, this question, or dilemma, over the desire of the mother often taunts the male psyche at an unconscious level.
65. *Mother Ireland*, Dir. Anne Crilly. Derry Film and Video, 1988.
66. Ibid.
67. Ibid.
68. Ibid.
69. Innes, *Woman and Nation*, p. 50.
70. Campbell Armstrong, *Jig* (London: Hodder and Stoughton, 1987), pp. 49, 442.
71. Alan Judd, *A Breed of Heroes* (London: Hodder and Stoughton, 1981), pp. 71, 191, 192, 194.
72. Eugene McCabe, *Victims* (London: Victor Gollancz, 1976), pp. 24, 22.
73. James Carrick, *With O'Leary in the Grave* (London: William Heinemann, 1971), pp. 76, 77.
74. Sean Herron, *The Whore Mother* (London: Cape, 1973).
75. Ibid., p. 150.
76. Ibid.
77. Ibid., pp. 160, 167, 162.
78. Ibid., p. 167.
79. Ibid., p. 162.
80. Ibid.
81. Ibid., p. 165.
82. Ibid.
83. Ibid.
84. Ibid., pp. 166, 207, 204.

85. Ibid., p. 222.
86. Ibid., pp. 260, 265.
87. Ibid., p. 271.
88. Ibid., p. 222.
89. Ibid., p. 251.
90. Ibid., p. 271.
91. Ibid.
92. Ibid.
93. Ibid., p. 274.
94. Ibid., p. 280.

NOTES TO CHAPTER 8

1. These figures include women who were interned as well as those sentenced.
2. See M. D'Arcy, *Tell Them Everything* (London: Pluto Press, 1981); also S. Buckley and P. Lonergan, 'Women and the Troubles', in Y. Alexander and A. O'Day (eds), *Terrorism in Ireland* (London: Croom Helm, 1984), pp. 75–87; E. Fairweather, R. McDonough and M. McFadyean, *Only the Rivers Run Free. Northern Ireland: The Women's War* (London: Pluto Press, 1984); and C. Loughran, 'Armagh and Feminist Strategy', in T. Lovell (ed.), *British Feminist Thought* (Oxford: Basil Blackwell, 1983), pp. 170–83.
3. Republican and loyalist former prisoners, prison staff and administrators, prison welfare personnel and republican and loyalist political prisoners' representatives were interviewed in 1997 and 1998. The quotations used here were taken from interviews with republican women prisoners who were interned or served sentences for politically related activities. In accordance with the ethical conventions for preserving the anonymity of respondents in penal ethnography, and because interviews were conducted while the conflict was still ongoing, all respondents were given aliases. The former prisoners have been given the names of women who were involved in labour, republican and feminist struggles in the late nineteenth and early twentieth centuries, many of whom had been interned or imprisoned for their political activities. Accordingly, the respondents whose narratives are included here were given the aliases Kathleen (Clarke), Nora (Connolly), Áine (Carney), Meg (Connery), Elizabeth (O' Farrell), Anna (Parnell), Eilis (Ni Riain) and Hanna (Sheehy-Skeffington). Their status and the establishments in which they were confined are also indicated.
4. B. Gormally and K. McEvoy, 'Politics and prison management: the Northern Ireland experience', in L. Noaks, M. Levi and M. Maguire (eds), *Contemporary Issues in Criminology* (Cardiff: University of Wales Press, 1995), pp. 276–313.
5. See Northern Ireland Prison Service, *Annual Reports,* for the years 1972–95 (Belfast, HMSO).
6. See Northern Ireland Prison Service, *Annual Report of the Prison Service for 1972–1976,* Cmnd, 40 (Belfast: HMSO, 1977).
7. Ibid., p. 5.
8. See P. Hillyard, 'Police and Penal Services', in J. Darby and A. Williamson (eds), *Violence and the Social Services in Northern Ireland* (London: Heinemann, 1978), pp. 117–39.
9. The requirement to wear the prison uniform was abolished for women in 1974 throughout the United Kingdom, although there was a compulsory uniform in

Armagh Prison prior to that date. The uniform was enforced in the Maze/H-Blocks after the introduction of the criminalisation policy; republican prisoners refused to wear it, preferring to cover themselves with a blanket. This was the beginning of the 'Blanket' strikes.

10. The prisoners also resisted the implications of engaging with the rehabilitative ethos of the welfare and probation agencies on the grounds that 'rehabilitation' assumes that an individual becomes reconciled to the consequences of their 'crime', and is willing to enter into an agreement to alter their behaviour. Rehabilitation, the politicals argued, reinforced the stigma of criminality, and obscured the political dimensions of their actions and conditions of confinement.

11. See C. Crawford, *Defenders or Criminals? Loyalist Prisoners and Criminalisation* (Belfast: Blackstaff Press, 1999), pp. 67–8.

12. See Northern Ireland Prison Service, *Annual Reports of the Prison Service* (Belfast: HMSO, 1972–80).

13. See A. Mandaraka-Sheppard, *The Dynamics of Aggression in Women's Prisons in England* (Aldershot: Gower, 1986).

14. L. McKeown, *Out of Time: Irish Republican Prisoners, Long Kesh, 1972–2000* (Belfast: Beyond the Pale Press, 2001), pp. 27–48.

15. See Crawford, *Defenders or Criminals?* pp. 27–52.

16. See M. Bosworth, *Engendering Resistance: Agency and Power in Women's Prisons* (Dartmouth: Ashgate, 1999); P. Carlen, *Women's Imprisonment: A Study in Social Control* (London: Routledge & Kegan Paul, 1983), and *Sledgehammer: Women's Imprisonment at the Millennium* (Basingstoke: Macmillan, 1998); and R. E. Dobash, R. P. Dobash and S. Gutteridge, *The Imprisonment of Women* (Oxford: Basil Blackwell, 1986).

17. See L. Zedner, 'Wayward Sisters: The Prison for Women', in N. Morris and D. J. Rothman (eds), *The Oxford History of the Prison* (Oxford: Oxford University Press, 1995), p. 309.

18. See B. Campbell, L. McKeown and F. O'Hagan, *Nor Meekly Serve My Time: The H-Block Struggle, 1976–1981* (Belfast: Beyond The Pale, 1994); also D. Beresford, *Ten Men Dead: The Story of the 1981 Hunger Strike* (London: Grafton, 1987); A. Feldman, *Formations of Violence: The Narrative of the Body and Political Terror in Northern Ireland* (Chicago, IL: University of Chicago Press, 1991); J. Stevenson, *'We Wrecked the Place': Contemplating an End to the Northern Irish Troubles* (New York: The Free Press, 1996); and K. McEvoy, *Paramilitary Imprisonment in Northern Ireland: Resistance, Management and Release* (Oxford: Oxford University Press, 2001).

19. I refer to Long Kesh when talking about the compounds in which the male prisoners were initially accommodated, and use the term the Maze (also known as the H-Block) to refer to the new prison, built on the same site, to which they were transferred after criminalisation. Prisoners retained the term Long Kesh.

20. See Lord Gardiner, *Report of a Committee to consider, in the context of civil liberties and human rights, measures to deal with terrorism in Northern Ireland* (London: HMSO, 1975).

21. Although there were also a number of republican prisoners on remand in Armagh Prison, the fact that they had not been tried meant that they would not have been eligible for special category status until convicted and sentenced. Similarly, the small number of prisoners who had been sentenced before March 1976 retained their status. Thus, only those prisoners who were sentenced after 28 February 1976, and who were denied political status, went on the protest.

22. See Northern Ireland Prison Service, *Annual Reports*, for the years 1979–81 (Belfast: HMSO).

23. Extract from smuggled communication 'to Liam Óg from CO Armagh Gaol',

written on a half-sheet of toilet paper in black biro, dated 27 September 1980.

24. Belfast Prison was situated on the Crumlin Road, Belfast. It held the male remand prisoners.

25. See M. Foucault, 'Questions on geography', in C. Gordon (ed.), *Power/Knowledge* (Hemel Hempstead: Harvester Wheatsheaf, 1980), p. 56.

26. In this context, it was anticipated that the provision of enhanced facilities and 'constructive regimes' could enable a working consensus to be developed between the administration and the political prisoner groups, both loyalist and republican.

27. See Northern Ireland Prison Service, *Annual Report of the Prison Service*, 1–2, 1982 (Belfast: HMSO).

28. See J. Hennessey, *Report of an Inquiry by HM Chief Inspector of Prisons into the Security Arrangements at HM Prison, Maze* (London: HMSO, 1984).

29. See Viscount Colville, *Report of an Inquiry into the Operational Policy in Belfast Prison for the Management of Paramilitary Prisoners from Opposing Factions* (London: HMSO, 1992).

30. See Northern Ireland Prison Service, *Annual Report of the Prison Service*, 1987/88: 4.

31. See House of Commons Debates, Written Answers, 21 July 1983, para. 204 (London: HMSO).

32. See National Council for Civil Liberties, *Strip Searching: An Inquiry into the strip searching of women remand prisoners at Armagh prison between 1982 and 1985* (London: NCCL, 1986), and Irish Information Partnership, *Strip-Searches at Her Majesty's Prison for Women, Armagh, Northern Ireland* (Gondregnies: Irish Information Partnership, 1985).

33. See Justice D. Murray, *Report to consider a proposal to acquire compulsorily under the above order certain land at Maghaberry County Antrim for the purpose of providing prison accommodation* (Belfast: HMSO, 1975), para. 57.1.

34. Northern Ireland Prison Service, *Annual Report of the Prison Service*, 1988: 4.

35. See B. Rolston and M. Tomlinson, '"The Challenge Within": Prisons and Propaganda in Northern Ireland', in M. Tomlinson, T. Varley and C. McCullagh (eds), *Whose Law and Order?* (Belfast: Sociological Association of Ireland, 1988), pp. 167–92.

36. This brief account of the broader political and strategic dimensions of prison politics in the years preceding the signing of the Good Friday Agreement can only reference the most salient developments. For an excellent analysis of the political debates within the prisons see McKeown, *Out of Time,* pp. 205–37, and McEvoy, *Paramilitary Imprisonment in Northern Ireland*, part three, for a richly detailed account of the political and administrative manoeuvres over the prisons issue during this period.

37. See McEvoy, *Paramilitary Imprisonment*, p. 321.

38. The remaining women IRA prisoners in British prisons, Ella O'Dwyer and Martina Anderson, were transferred from Durham Prison to Maghaberry in July 1994, under the new transfer arrangements.

39. See H. C. *Proceedings of the Standing Committee on Northern Ireland,* 29 January 1998 (London: HMSO).

40. See M. Narey, *Report of an Inquiry into the Escape of a Prisoner from HMP Maze on 10th December 1997 and the Shooting of a Prisoner on 27th December 1997* (London: HMSO, 2 April 1998).

41. See M. Bosworth, *Engendering Resistance: Agency and Power in Women's Prisons* (Dartmouth: Ashgate, 1999), pp. 120–4.

42. Ibid.

43. M. Corcoran, 'Talking about resistance: narratives of agency and transformation among female political prisoners, Northern Ireland, 1972–1995', paper presented to

the conference on Conditions of Domination and Modes of Resistance, 3rd Annual Conference of the British Section of the European Group for the Study of Deviance and Social Control, University of Lincolnshire and Humberside, 17–19 April 2001.

44. M. Foucault, *The History of Sexuality*, vol. 1 (Harmondsworth: Penguin, 1990), pp. 92–102.

NOTES TO CHAPTER 9

1. C. Connolly 'Ourselves Alone? Clár na mBan Conference Report', *Feminist Review*, 50 (summer 1995), p. 120.
2. M. Ward, *Unmanageable Revolutionaries: Women and Irish Nationalism* (London: Pluto Press, 1983; repr. 1995), p. 50.
3. Ibid., pp.107–14.
4. Cumann na mBan Manifesto, Dublin, 5 October 1914, National Library of Ireland.
5. Cumann na mBan Constitution, Dublin, 1915, National Library of Ireland.
6. J. Bowyer Bell, *The Irish Troubles; A Generation of Violence, 1967–1992* (Dublin: Gill & Macmillan, 1993), p. 163.
7. Northern Ireland Civil Rights Association, 'Information Sheet on Women Internees', pamphlet published in Belfast, 22 May 1973.
8. For more details of the split see Bowyer Bell, *Irish Troubles*, pp. 129–61.
9. See J. O'Neill (ed.), *Irish Women Speak* (Women for Irish Freedom: New York, 1973).
10. Ibid., p. 000.
11. M. Dillon, *25 Years of Terror: The IRA's war against the British* (London: Bantam Books, 1996), p. 164.
12. Bowyer Bell, *Irish Troubles*, p. 163.
13. T. P. Coogan, *The IRA* (London: HarperCollins, 1995), p. 458.
14. M. de-Pretis, 'To Take Arms in an Armed Patriarchy', paper presented at the Women and Law Conference on Strategic Thinking for the Millennium, University of Westminster, London, 23 June 2000.
15. For a detailed discussion of the development of the women's movement in Ireland see L. Connolly, 'The Women's Movement in Ireland, 1970–1995: A Social Movement Analysis', *Irish Journal of Feminist Studies*, 1, 1 (1996), pp. 1–17.
16 . R. Murray, *Hard Time; Armagh Gaol, 1971–1986* (Dublin: Mercier Press, 1998), p. 10.
17. Ibid., p. 33.
18. Coogan, *The IRA*, p. 270.
19. U. Gillespie, 'Women in Struggle, 1969–1994', in U. Gillespie, *Women in Struggle* (Sinn Féin Women's Department, autumn 1994).
20. Murray, *Hard Time*, p. 10.
21. Ibid., p. 59.
22. Arm the Spirit: 'IWD: Women in Irish National Liberation Struggle', http://burn.ucsd.edu/%7Earchive/ats-1/1996.Mar/0007.html, accessed 3 March 2000.
23. Coogan, *The IRA*, p. 467.
24. Ibid.
25. R. W. White, 'From Peaceful Protest to Guerrilla War: Micromobilization of the Provisional Irish Republican Army', *American Journal of Sociology*, 94, 6 (1989), pp. 1277–302.

26. During a peaceful civil rights march in Derry/Londonderry on 31 January 1972 the Parachute Regiment of the British Army shot dead thirteen unarmed civilians. The exact course of events leading up to the shootings is at time of publication the subject of a second public inquiry.

27. R. Walsh, 'Armagh Revisited', *An Glór Gafa/The Captive Voice* (summer 1998), p. 2.

28. Quoted in G. Sheehy, 'The Fighting Women of Ireland', *New York Magazine* (1972), from the Northern Ireland Office press-cutting files in the Linen Hall Library, Belfast.

29. See M. V. Page and M. L. R. Smith, 'War by other means: The problem of political control in Irish Republican strategy', *Armed Forces and Society*, 27, 1 (autumn 2000), p. 79.

30. I have used this term rather than 'combatants' because not all of the people jailed for paramilitary offences were frontline activists, although the vast majority of them were. People were also imprisoned for intelligence gathering, organising attacks, or securing finances or armaments. The term 'combatants' is therefore somewhat misleading as it implies a person who has been convicted of carrying out an attack.

31. They were arrested along with nine other women for picketing outside Armagh Prison and were fined. M. D'Arcy, *Tell Them Everything: A Sojourn in the Prison of Her Majesty Queen Elizabeth II at Ard Macha (Armagh)* (London: Pluto Press Ltd, 1981), pp. 35–9.

32. From a letter written by MacCafferty in Armagh Prison, 29 May 1980, published in *Scarlet Woman*, 11 (June 1980), p. 6.

33. Ibid.

34. N. McCafferty, *The Armagh Women* (Dublin: Co-op Books, 1981), p. 83.

35. D'Arcy, *Tell Them Everything*, p. 112.

36. Ibid. pp. 67–8.

37. Strip-searching is practised in all prisons in England, Wales and Northern Ireland. It is a contentious practice that has been alleged to be more widely used against women paramilitary prisoners than other women prisoners.

38. For example Pauline Quinn was allegedly forced to undergo internal searches of her vagina and anus on her return to prison after compassionate leave. 'Maghaberry strip search sexual assault', *An Glór Gafa/The Captive Voice* (summer 1991), p. 10.

39. 'Strip Searches in Armagh', *Women's News*, 3 (May/June 1984), p. 6.

40. C. Loughran, 'Security or Subjugation?', *Women's News*, 7 (December 1984), p. 5.

41. 'Strip Searches in Armagh Jail', *Women Behind the Wire*, 2, produced by the London Armagh Group (February 1984), p. 6.

42. Ibid., 'A Matter of Security?', p. 7.

43. 'Prison News', *An Glór Gafa/The Captive Voice* (spring 1993), p. 22.

44. Ibid.

45. 'Nationalist Women and the RUC', pamphlet issued by Sinn Féin Women's Department (Belfast, 1988).

46. Editorial, *An Glór Gafa/The Captive Voice* (summer 1990).

47. Women POWs (Maghaberry), 'Women and Struggle', *An Glór Gafa/The Captive Voice* (summer 1990), p. 2.

48. P. Whelan, 'Men & Male Power', *An Glór Gafa/The Captive Voice* (summer 1990), p. 12.

NOTES TO CHAPTER 10

1. See discussion on control and collaboration in oral history work with women in the introduction to S. B. Gluck and D. Patai (eds), *Women's Words: The Feminist Practice of Oral History* (London: Routledge, 1991).

2. The method of establishing informed consent involves giving all potential contributors a written information sheet prior to the interview. This outlines the destination of the interview and the possible ways it may be used. Contributors are informed that they can delete any section of their interview before they release it into the archive. They are also informed that Dúchas might remove sections to protect the archive from libel charges. This information is also discussed with the contributor prior to the interview. The full information sheet can be obtained from Falls Community Council.

3. For this article I selected the quotations I wanted to use and asked the permission of the authors to use their words. I also asked permission of one person who was named in a quotation. It needs to be acknowledged, however, that a great deal of the immediacy and complexity of each woman's oral history has been lost in this construction. The interviews can be accessed in their entirety through the Dúchas archive, which is publicly available via an interactive computer database in Falls Community Council.

4. This subject is discussed in more depth in 'The emergence of a gender consciousness: women and community work in West Belfast' by Callie Persic in this volume, pp. 167–83.

5. See, most notably, Margaret Ward's groundbreaking work, *Unmanageable Revolutionaries: Women and Irish Nationalism* (London: Pluto Press, 1983).

6. For fuller discussion see Persic, pp. 167–83.

7. See M. Farrell, *Northern Ireland: The Orange State* (London: Pluto Press, 1976), Chapter 4.

8. Ibid., Chapter 2.

9. Ibid., pp. 281–2.

10. See M. Sutton, *An index of deaths from the conflict in Ireland, 1969–1993* (Belfast: Beyond the Pale Publications, 1994).

11. See also Persic, pp. 167–83.

12. Dorothy Maguire and Maura Meehan were members of Cumann na mBan, the women's auxiliary of the IRA, which was later subsumed into the IRA in the restructuring of the organisation in the late 1970s. Rita O'Hare was imprisoned in 1971 and released later the same year. After she was shot in the incident described she went on the run to the Republic of Ireland where she won her case against extradition in 1978. She has held leading positions in Sinn Féin for many years.

13. See discussion of the concept of activist mothering by Persic, pp. 167–83.

14. See N. McCafferty, *The Armagh Women* (Dublin: Co-op Books, 1981), p. 84.

15. For further first-hand accounts of activism by the women in the Relatives Action Committees see McCafferty, *Armagh Women*, and E. Fairweather, R. McDonough and M. McFadyean, *Only The Rivers Run Free: Northern Ireland, The Women's War* (London: Pluto Press, 1984).

16. See K. Kelley, *The Longest War: Northern Ireland and the IRA* (London: Zed Press, 1982), p. 322.

17. See McCafferty, *Armagh Women*.

18. Although it remains under-resourced the Falls Women's Centre has developed and expanded since its formation and continues to work for women in West Belfast

through support services and campaigning. A number of years after the Centre was set up, a number of women's centres in other working-class areas were formed, drawing directly on its experience.

19. See discussion by Persic, pp. 167–83; also E. Rooney, 'Women in Party Politics and Local Groups: Findings from Belfast', in A. Byrne and M. Leonard (eds), *Women and Irish Society: A Sociological Reader* (Belfast: Beyond the Pale Publications, 1997).

NOTES TO CHAPTER 11

1. The 'first' ceasefire refers to the IRA cessation of violence in September 1994. This ceasefire ended in February 1996 with the bombing of Canary Wharf in London. The 'second' ceasefire was announced in July 1997 and continues to the present time of writing.

2. The Special Support Programme for Peace and Reconciliation funded women's organisations under the 4.1 measure. Community Action and Inclusion of Women Measure 4.1 supports 'community-based action, which can effectively build skills and capacity at community level (particularly of marginalised groups) and can show a clear contribution to peace-building' (Northern Ireland Voluntary Trust: 1998).

3. This is generally considered to be a republican/nationalist area, although like many labels in Northern Ireland this is misleading because there are a range of political positions on the republican/nationalist continuum. Electoral returns indicate support for Sinn Féin in the area.

4. In Northern Ireland 'single identity' refers to communities that are either Catholic or Protestant. Originally Ballymurphy was intended to be a (religiously) 'mixed' development, although this was never achieved. A closer estimate offered by P. Pistoi, 'Military Occupation of Ballymurphy, Belfast' (MA dissertation, University of Essex, 1975), although rough, indicates that at one time the area was between 15 and 35 per cent Protestant, although with the outbreak of the Troubles, many areas in Belfast were transformed into religiously homogeneous areas. However, despite residential segregation there are still a few Protestant people living in Ballymurphy.

5. Women were initially 'accidental activists' who became politically motivated through personal experiences of social injustice that was largely responsible for women's participation in, and organisation of, street protests, pickets and other forms of resistance. See M. McWilliams, 'Struggling for Peace and Justice: Reflections on Women's Activism in Northern Ireland', *Journal of Women's History*, 6/:4/7:1 (1995), pp.13–39.

6. C. de Baróid, *Ballymurphy and the Irish War* (Dublin: Aisling Publishers, 1989), p. 52.

7. Ibid.

8. Ibid.

9. Practically speaking, it was difficult to arrange interviews because something always seemed to come up for the women and the appointment would be cancelled at the last minute. On occasion the difficulties of finding the time and space to sit for even an hour proved complex, yet this reflects the demands women face on a daily basis. On many occasions an interview was postponed halfway through because of familial obligations or because of intrusion by children, family or partners. During several interviews I held a child on my lap or helped to prepare dinner or tea. At times, a personal interview wound up as a group interview, when friends called to the house for a visit.

10. The difficulties involved in giving voice to, or representing, the 'Other' has been at the forefront of anthropological and feminist debates. See, for example, S. Ardener, 'The Social Anthropology of Women and Feminist Anthropology', *Anthropology Today* 1, 5 (1985) pp. 24–6; R. Behar and D. Gordon (eds), *Women Writing Culture* (Berkeley, CA: University of California Press: 1995); R. Klein, 'How to do what we want to do: thoughts on feminist methodology', in G. Bowles and R. Klein (eds), *Theories of Women's Studies* (London: Routledge and Kegan Paul, 1983); A. Opie, 'Qualitative Research and Appropriation of the "Other" and Empowerment', *Feminist Review*, 40 (1992) pp. 52–69. I am aware of feminist debates regarding the interviewing of women, yet I felt compelled to use interviews as a way for women to relate their own experiences. I have integrated interviews with material collected through participant observation as a possible way to circumvent some of the problems raised by feminist researchers.

11. Women were visible and active in neighbourhoods as they banged bin lids as a warning system against army raids and escorted men home since an unaccompanied man was more likely to be 'lifted' by the army. See L. Edgerton, 'Public Protest, Domestic Acquiesence: Women in Northern Ireland', in R. Ridd and H. Callaway (eds), *Caught Up In Conflict* (London: Macmillan, 1986), p. 65.

12. De Baróid describes the women's strategy: 'Armed with whistles, football crackers, bells and rattling binlids and calling "Quack! Quack!", they would follow the invading troops from street to street', *Ballymurphy and the Irish War*, p. 110.

13. Edgerton, 'Public Protest', p. 69.

14. Ibid.

15. B. Aretxaga, *Shattering Silence* (New Jersey: Princeton University Press, 1997).

16. There are many examples of everyday forms of resistance among women in Ballymurphy, indeed, West Belfast. However, many strategies such as 'hen patrols', spontaneous pickets or standing beside men when they were searched on the street placed them in the frontline of violence (see Claire Hackett's essay in this volume).

17. M. Abbott and R. McDonough, 'Changing Women', in E. Deane (ed.), *Lost Horizons, New Horizons* (Belfast: Workers' Educational Association, 1989); E. Rooney and M. Woods, *Women, Community and Politics in Northern Ireland: A Belfast Study* (Ulster: University of Ulster, 1995).

18. The term 'family feminist' has been associated with the Women's Information Group, which is a cross-community organisation that addresses women's issues and holds monthly information days in alternating venues across the city. The Group is often considered to be 'non-political' and expressed a difference between their goals and those of 'feminists'. Joyce McCartan described feminists as 'men haters', which indicates the difficulty many women's groups have in associating themselves with feminism. See A. Mitchison, 'Ulster's Family Feminists', *New Society* (9 February 1988), p. 17.

19. Aretxaga, *Shattering Silence*, p. 78.

20. N. Naples, 'Activist Mothering: Cross-Generational Continuity in the Community Work of Women from Low-Income Urban Neighbourhoods', *Gender & Society*, 6, 3 (1992), pp. 441–63.

21. Ibid., p. 446.

22. N. Abrahams, 'Negotiating Power, Identity, Family and Community', *Gender & Society* 10, 6 (1996), pp. 768–96.

23. Naples, 'Activist Mothering', p. 454.

24. The *Irish News* (20 December 1996) described the scene as 'reminiscent of the seventies', and the *Andersontown News* (21 December 1996) reported how 'two

houses in Ballymurphy and the offices of the Ballymurphy Women's Support Group were damaged in the latest raids, which prompted angry street protests from local residents and community groups'.

25. B. Milroy and S. Wismer, 'Communities, Work and the Public/Private Sphere Models', *Gender, Place and Culture*, 1, 1 (1994), pp 71–90.

26. Ibid., p. 75.

27. N. Naples '"Just What Needed to be Done": The Political Practice of Women Community Workers in Low-Income Neighbourhoods', *Gender & Society*, 5, 4 (1991), p. 479.

28. R. Miller, R. Wilford and F. Donoghue, *Women and Political Participation in Northern Ireland* (Hants: Avebury,1996).

29. Specifically, the Good Friday Agreement/Belfast Agreement promises to promote 'social inclusion, including in particular community development and the advancement of women in public life'. Earlier in the document there is a pledge to safeguard 'the right of women to full and equal political participation', *The Belfast Agreement* (1998), pp. 19, 16.

NOTES TO CHAPTER 12

1. M. Ward, *Unmanageable Revolutionaries: Women and Irish Nationalism* (London: Pluto Press, 1983), p. 90.

2. Pamela Beth Radcliff, 'Imagining Female Citizenship in the "New Spain": Gendering the Democratic Transition, 1975–78', *Gender and History* 13, 3 (2001), pp. 498–523.

3. E. Friedman, *Unfinished transitions: women and the gendered development of democracy in Venezuela, 1936–1996* (Pennsylvania: Pennsylvania State University Press, 2000), p. 16.

4. M. Ward (ed.), *In Their Own Voice* (Dublin: Attic, 1995; repr. Cork University Press, 2000), p. 34.

5. Ibid., p. 43.

6. Ibid., pp. 46–7.

7. For further details, see M. Ward, 'The League of Women Delegates and Sinn Féin 1917', *History Ireland*, 4, 2 (1996), pp. 37–41.

8. Ward, *Voice*, p. 78.

9. H. Litton (ed.), *Revolutionary Woman: Kathleen Clarke* (Dublin: O'Brien Press, 1991), p. 164.

10. M. Ward, *Hanna Sheehy Skeffington, a life* (Cork: Cork University Press/Attic, 1997), pp. 225–9.

11. Ward, *Voice*, p. 83.

12. Ibid., p. 82.

13. Ibid., p. 81.

14. Ibid.

15. Ibid., pp. 78–9.

16. Ward, 'League', p. 41.

17. Ward, *Voice*, p. 119.

18. Ibid., p. 122.

19. M. Valiulis, 'Defining their role in the new state: Irishwomen's protest against the Juries Act of 1927', *Canadian Journal of Irish Studies*, 18, 1 (1992), pp. 43–60.

20. M. McNamara and P. Mooney (eds), *Women in Parliament, Ireland: 1918–2000*

(Dublin: Wolfhound Press, 2000), p. 16.

21. Ibid., pp. 109–11.

22. For Northern feminism, see C. Roulston, 'Women on the margins: the women's movement in Northern Ireland, 1973–1988', *Science and Society*, 53, 2 (1989), pp. 219–36; M. Ward, 'The women's movement in the north of Ireland: twenty years on', in Sean Hutton and Paul Stewart (eds), *Ireland's histories: aspects of state, society and ideology* (London: Routledge, 1991) pp. 149–63; M. McWilliams, 'Struggling for Peace and Justice: Reflections on Women's Activism in Northern Ireland', *Journal of Women's History*, 6, 4 (1995), pp. 13–39.

23. E. Rooney, 'Women in Political Conflict', *Race and Class*, 37, 1 (1995), pp. 51–6.

24. Clár na mBan, *A Women's Agenda for Peace*, conference report, Belfast, undated, p. 3.

25. Ibid.

26. Ibid., p. 9.

27. Ibid., p. 3.

28. C. Hackett, 'Self-determination: the Republican Feminist Agenda', *Feminist Review*, 50 (1995), pp. 111–16.

29. From conversation with Claire Hackett, January 2002.

30. *An Phoblacht/Republican News*, 9 March 1995.

31. R. Wilford, 'Women and Politics', in P. Mitchell and R. Wilford (eds), *Politics in Northern Ireland* (Colorado: Westview Press, 1999), p. 207.

32. C. Bell, 'Women, Equality and Political Participation', in J. Anderson and J. Goodman (eds), *Dis/Agreeing Ireland: contexts, obstacles, hopes* (London: Pluto Press: 1998), p. 223.

33. K. Fearon and M. McWilliams, 'Swimming Against the Mainstream: The Northern Ireland Women's Coalition', in C. Roulston and C. Davies (eds), *Gender, Democracy and Inclusion in Northern Ireland* (York: Palgrave, 2000), p. 118.

34. Ibid., p. 134, 1n.

35. Ibid., p. 118.

36. The NIWC had to register as a party because of local and Westminster election rules. For a full account of the formation of the NIWC, see K. Fearon, *Women's Work* (Belfast: Blackstaff, 1999). See too an early evaluation by Rosemary Sales, who concluded that their influence would 'remain marginal' unless 'women are involved with politics as it is traditionally defined'. In Anderson and Goodman, *Dis/Agreeing Ireland*, pp. 141–61. Another useful article, although not directly relevant to the argument of this essay, is Linda Connolly, 'Feminist Politics and the Peace Process', *Capital and Class*, 69 (1999), pp. 145–59.

37. Rooney, 'Women', p. 53.

38. Ibid., p. 54.

39. Hackett, 'Self-determination', p. 116.

40. *Women's News*, Belfast, June/July 1996. Women involved in this challenge included well-known activists like Oonagh Marron of the Falls Women's Centre and Clár na mBan; Claire Hackett; Marie Mulholland from the Women's Support Network; Tish Holland and Maura McCrory from Sinn Féin; Ruth Taillon of the West Belfast Economic Forum; and a number of local community activists in West Belfast.

41. Fearon, *Women's Work*, p. 121. For substantive consideration of the Good Friday Agreement (also known as the Belfast Agreement) see M. Cox, A. Guelke and F. Stephen (eds), *A farewell to arms? From 'long war' to long peace in Northern Ireland* (Manchester: Manchester University Press, 2000).

42. For more information on women and the Assembly, see M. Ward, *The Northern*

Ireland Assembly and women – assessing the gender deficit (Belfast: Democratic Dialogue, 2000); K. Cowell-Meyers, *Women Legislators in Northern Ireland: Gender and Politics in the New Legislative Assembly* (Queen's University of Belfast: Centre for the Advancement of Women in Politics, 2003).

43. C. Coulter, 'Feminism and Nationalism in Ireland', in D. Miller (ed.), *Rethinking Northern Ireland* (London: Longman, Adison Wesley, 1998), pp. 160–78.

44. Ibid.

45. *An Phoblacht/Republican News*, 4 October 2001.

46. Fearon, *Women's Work*, p. 61; referring to a remark made by Democratic Unionist Party member Iris Robinson, one of the most vociferous opponents of the NIWC.

47. Fearon and McWilliams, 'Swimming Against the Mainstream', p. 133.

Contributors

Jan Cannavan is an independent scholar in Boston, Massachusetts. She holds a BA in women's studies and an MA in European women's history. Her primary research interest is the intersection of gender, class and national identities, particularly as these are manifested in Irish history.

Marie Coleman is a Reader in modern Irish History in the School of History, Anthropology, Philosophy and Politics at Queen's University Belfast. She is the author of books including *County Longford and the Irish Revolution, 1910–1923* (2003), *The Irish sweep: A history of the Irish hospitals sweepstake, 1930–1987* (2009) and *The Irish revolution, 1916–1923* (2013), in addition to numerous articles and essays on various aspects of twentieth century Irish history. She is the joint editor of the journal *Irish Historical Studies*.

Mary Corcoran is Reader in Criminology at the University of Keele, England. She wrote *Out of Order: The political imprisonment of women in Northern Ireland, 1972–1996* (2006), which was a study of the prison resistance campaign by republican and loyalist women during the Troubles. Mary is currently working with academics and voluntary sector organisations in Ireland on projects relating to community activism and social/criminal justice.

Claire Hackett is the manager of Falls Community Council's digital oral history archive Dúchas which records personal experiences of the conflict. She has published articles about Dúchas and on the practice of oral history in post conflict transitions. She has worked with others to produce the document *Ethical Principles – Storytelling and Narrative Work*, HTR (2009). She co-ordinated the publication of a book of extracts from Dúchas archive oral history interviews called *Living Through The Conflict – Belfast Oral Histories* (2014). Claire has been involved in work to ensure that women's experiences of the conflict are recognised through the publication of a policy document on *Gender Principles for Dealing With The Past* (2015).

Andrea Knox is Senior Lecturer in early modern European history and women's history at Northumbria University. She has published on early modern female criminality and subversion, including rebel networks between Irish and Scottish women, female espionage and most recently Irish female migrants in early modern Spain. Recent book chapters include, 'Her Book-Lined Cell: Irish Nuns and the Development of Texts, Translation and Literacy in Late Medieval Spain', in 'Nuns' Literacies: The Kansas City Dialogue', Eds. V. Blanton et. al. (Turnhout, Belgium: Brepols Press, 2015) and 'Nuns on the periphery? Irish Dominican Nuns and assimilation in Lisbon', in *Catalonia and Portugal: The Iberian Peninsula from the Periphery*, eds. Flocel Sabate & Luis Adão da Fonseca (2015). She is completing a book entitled *Irish Women on the Move: Migration and Mission in Spain, 1499–1700*.

Sinead McCoole was Curatorial and Historical Advisor to the Ireland 2016 Centenary Programme and she is a member of the government's Expert Advisory Group on the Decade of Commemorations 2012–2022. She has curated an exhibition to commemorate the centenary of Irish women in politics and public life as a touring 'pop up women's museum'. Her books include *Hazel, A Life of Lady Lavery* (1996); *No Ordinary Women* (2003) and *Easter Widows* (2014).

Danae O'Regan obtained a BA in French and German at Dublin University and an MA in French classical theatre in Bristol University. She taught French and German for most of her working life. She then did an MA in Irish Studies at Bath Spa University and developed an interest in how Irish women writers reflect the attitudes of their women contemporaries towards situations and problems of their time. She published 'Anna and Fanny Parnell' in *History Ireland* (1999).

Callie Persic works in urban regeneration in Belfast City Council and has extensive experience in community activism and development with expertise in engagement, conflict transformation and women's issues. She is interested in the gendered impacts of urban design and ways to develop inclusive and diverse urban spaces. She has been involved in the creative transformation of urban spaces and through an initial guerrilla gardening project developed Peas Park, a community gardening space that has transformed blighted interface land into a playful, shared and welcoming green space. Originally from the USA, Callie has lived in Northern Ireland since 1995 and holds a PhD in Anthropology from Queen's University of Belfast.

Louise Ryan is Professor of Sociology at the University of Sheffield. Originally from Cork and a graduate of UCC, she has written extensively on topics such as migration, religion, gender and nationalism. Louise is the author of the influential paper 'Drunken Tans: Representations of Sex and Violence in the Anglo-Irish War (1919–21), *Feminist Review*, 2000. She has also written numerous books including *Winning the Vote for Women: the Irish Citizen newspaper and the suffrage movement in Ireland* (2018) and *Irish women and the Vote: Becoming Citizens* (co-edited with Margaret Ward, 2007/ 2018).

Jayne Steele was a member of staff of the Department of English and Creative Writing at Lancaster University. In addition to her academic publications she was a screenwriter who received several rewards, including the 2000 Kodak Showcase for New European talent and the Special Gold Jury Award for the 2001 WorldFest-Houston International Film Festival. She died in October 2015.

Karen Steele is associate vice provost and dean in the School of Interdisciplinary Studies at TCU. She is the author of *Women, Press, and Politics during the Irish Revival* (2007); co-editor, with Michael de Nie, of *Ireland and the New Journalism* (2014) and editor of *Maud Gonne's Irish Nationalist Writings* (2003).

Rhiannon Talbot is a former lecturer in law at the University of Newcastle upon Tyne. Her principal research interests have been focused on national and international legal responses to terrorism and women terrorists.

Margaret Ward is Honorary Senior Lecturer in History at Queen's University, Belfast and former Director of the Women's Resource and Development Agency in Belfast. Amongst her many publications are *Unmanageable Revolutionaries: women and Irish Nationalism* (1983), *Maud Gonne: a Life* (1989); (co-edited with Louise Ryan) *Irish Women and the Vote: Becoming Citizens* (2007/2018); editor of *Hanna Sheehy Skeffington: suffragette and Sinn Féiner, her memoirs and political writings* (2017); *Fearless Woman: Hanna Sheehy Skeffington, Feminism and the Irish Revolution* (2019).

Index

Index